Mastering Whole Family
Assessment in Social Work

Mastering Social Work Skills series

Edited by Jane Wonnacott

This series of accessible books focuses on the everyday key skills that social workers need in order to practise effectively and ensure the best possible outcomes for service users. Easy to read and practical, the books feature key learning points, practice examples based on real-life situations, and exercises for the reader to enhance their learning. The books in this series are essential reading for post-qualifying social work students and social work practitioners.

Jane Wonnacott is Director of In-Trac Training and Consultancy, UK.

other books in the series

Mastering Social Work Supervision

Jane Wonnacott
ISBN 978 1 84905 774 1
eISBN 978 0 85700 403 1

Mastering Approaches to Diversity in Social Work

Linda Gast and Anne Patmore
ISBN 978 1 84905 224 5
eISBN 978 0 85700 458 1

Mastering Social Work Values and Ethics

Farrukh Akhtar
ISBN 978 1 84905 274 0
eISBN 978 0 85700 594 6

of related interest

Making Sense of Child and Family Assessment
How to Interpret Children's Needs

Duncan Helm
Foreword by Brigid Daniel
ISBN 978 1 84310 923 5
eISBN 978 0 85700 298 3
Part of the Best Practice in Working with Children series

The Child's World
The Comprehensive Guide to Assessing Children in Need
2nd edition

Edited by Jan Horwath
ISBN 978 1 84310 568 8
eISBN 978 0 85700 183 2

MASTERING
Whole Family Assessment in Social Work

Balancing the Needs of Children, Adults and Their Families

Fiona Mainstone
Foreword by Jane Wonnacott

Jessica Kingsley *Publishers*
London and Philadelphia

Figures 1.1, 1.2, 1.4, 2.6, 2.7, 3.4, 4.2, 5.2, 5.3 and 6.2 are reproduced/
adapted from *The Family Model Handbook* © Dr Adrian Falkov, 2012
with permission of Pavilion Publishing and Media Ltd.

First published in 2014
by Jessica Kingsley Publishers
73 Collier Street
London N1 9BE, UK
and
400 Market Street, Suite 400
Philadelphia, PA 19106, USA

www.jkp.com

Library of Congress Cataloging in Publication Data
Mainstone, Fiona.
  Mastering whole family assessment in social work :
balancing the needs of children, adults and their
families / Fiona Mainstone ; foreword by Jane Wonnacott.
      pages cm
  Includes bibliographical references and index.
  ISBN 978-1-84905-240-5
  1. Family social work--Great Britain. 2. Family services-
-Great Britain. 3. Families--Great Britain. 4.
Dysfunctional families--Great Britain. 5. Family violence--Great Britain. I. Title.
  HV700.G7.M25 2014
  362.82'640941--dc23
                        2013043197

British Library Cataloguing in Publication Data
A CIP catalogue record for this book is available from the British Library

ISBN 978 1 84905 240 5
eISBN 978 0 85700 484 0

Printed and bound in Great Britain by Bell & Bain Ltd, Glasgow

CONTENTS

Foreword

When social workers have confidence in their own skills, purpose and identity, and in the system in place to back them up, they have a huge amount to offer. They collaborate effectively with other professionals and adapt to new roles and expectations. Most importantly, they forge constructive partnerships with people who find themselves vulnerable or at risk and make a sustained difference in their lives.

Report of the Social Work Task Force (2009, p.5)

This book is an important addition to this series. It tackles one of the thorny issues of contemporary social work: how can we work together as a social work profession in order to meet the needs of the whole family?

When social workers worked generically with mixed caseloads of children and adults there was a concern that practice skills were diluted and the specialist skills needed in specific areas of practice were lost. Since the separation of adults and children's services, social workers have been faced with the challenge of how to develop specialist social work skills with either adults or children and at the same time be able to keep the needs of the whole family in mind. Social workers sometimes report feeling de-skilled in areas of work with which they lack familiarity. Where both children and adults have apparently competing needs and social workers are working with colleagues from other services, changes to legislation, guidance and practice expectations may result in misunderstandings about each other's role which hinder the assessments being carried out.

This is an unusual book in that it is for social workers working with both children and adults. It addresses the criticism from too many serious case reviews that adults and children's services failed to work effectively together and as a result the needs of vulnerable family members were not addressed. This book aims to identify the challenges facing social workers in specific roles and explore on the fundamentals of a good assessment, giving the reader ideas and workable frameworks for practice. Like other books in this series there is a focus on the importance of reflective practice and the importance of relationships, both within and across organisational boundaries.

A comment on the title

The series has been entitled 'Mastering Social Work' as it aims to move beyond basic skills to those which may support the practitioner in more challenging circumstances. 'Mastering' is a process of developing expertise by applying learning and knowledge to practice. It is a continuous activity. Our aim and hope is that this series will assist social workers in this task by providing ideas and frameworks to support them in their day to day work.

Jane Wonnacott
Director of In-Trac and Consultancy, UK

ACKNOWLEDGEMENTS

Many people have been extraordinarily generous!

Several different systemic assessment models are referred to throughout this book. Bronfenbrenner's ecological approach, Boushel's framework for assessing the protective environment, Reder and Duncan's framework for risk assessment and Farnfield's ecological model of parenting all help us secure well-rounded, holistic, whole family assessments. Dr Falkov's Family Model provides an integrated approach that relates to supporting mentally ill parents and their children (see www. thefamilymodel.com). It is especially useful in the context of whole family assessment at the interface between adult and children's services, because it explicitly encourages critical reflection on the complex interactions between different aspects of each family's experience. The Family Model is reproduced and briefly explained in Chapter 1 and I am grateful to Dr Falkov for allowing me to refer to it under the terms of its licence. I firmly believe that its principles support holistic design and analysis in whole family assessment where adults face a wider range of complex life difficulties. Its emphasis on examining the dynamic between different dimensions of family experience inspires several exercises in this book.

Gill Berry, Jem Price, David Watson, Elaine Streeter, George Ware, Fiona Cole, Mike Pearce, Mary Wood and Brenda Robinson gave me much-appreciated ideas and encouragement in the early stages. Hundreds of social workers and practice managers that I met during the book's gestation contributed their experience and wisdom. Claire Blake, Rebekah Button, Amy Coombs and Claire Young gave particularly timely encouragement and reassurance. Sian Bennett, Fiona Lewis, Richard Agar, Julie Cherryman and Colin Newton all allowed me to pick their brains and use their ideas. Stella Keen stoically transformed rubbish doodles into elegant diagrams. Barry Luckock and Chris Taylor offered timely and indispensible critical friendship. Helen Bonnick, Lyn McLean, Gretchen Precey, Rachel Foggitt, Chris Sansom and my husband, Alan Prosser, supported me from beginning to end. I will always be grateful for their expertise, attention to detail, insights, inspiration, kindness and loyalty. The influence of Marie Wood, Ronnie Arden and the late Roy Porter is hidden between the lines.

PREFACE

This book sets out to help social workers understand how assessments undertaken in adult and children's services intersect, and to navigate the dilemmas of prioritising children's needs whilst supporting adults in their role as parents:

> The other day I was in a meeting where the medical director of a mental health trust said when discussing safeguarding issues: 'Children are not our business.' I shared a similar experience in a children's hospital where a medical director told me 'Parents are not our business.' Everyone at the meeting laughed about this complementary experience but everyone understood the implications of these juxtaposed statements: it means that organisationally the parent–child relationship is nobody's business.
>
> (Gopfert, McClellend and Wilson 2010)

The book is concerned with balancing the needs of parents and children with a view to helping families live together safely and well, while holding in mind that the welfare of children is always paramount in UK law. Wherever children's well-being is compromised their needs must take precedence over the rights of their parents.

Whether your primary responsibility is for children or adults, you need a working knowledge of assessment practice in both services. Assessment is the foundation of good social work: it enables the needs of each family member to be met and protects the most vulnerable from harm. Often, several different assessments have to be brought together before a holistic understanding can be reached. Sometimes, specialist assessments offer wholly new insights, or difficult, contradictory information. Individuals within families are sometimes subjected to multiple assessment processes. Social workers have to make sense of complex circumstances, so that the adult's difficulties and the impact of parenting on the adult are understood alongside assessment of family functioning, parenting capacity and children's needs.

Unfortunately, research and inspections consistently highlight the problem that social workers usually focus on the impact of the adult's difficulties *either* on their own personal needs, *or* on the children, but seldom on the whole family and how to enable parents to fulfil their responsibilities in adverse circumstances. Whichever service you work in, you have to make sense of how adults can be helped to live their lives in ways that keep the whole family safe. You also need to ensure that social work interventions do not add to the stresses on individuals and on the family as a whole.

In the UK, social workers complete a generic training that equips them to work across all services and across public, voluntary and private sector contexts. This approach to social work education echoes the holistic principle set out in the Seebohm Report (1968) that each social worker should engage with whole families to work with the full range of human problems. However, legislation promoting community care in the early 1990s initiated the separation of adult social care provision from children's services. Between 1999 and 2010, the emphasis on 'joining up' services led to adult social care forging closer links with the NHS. Services to adults are therefore generally organised around the particular difficulty they face. Typically, different teams hold responsibility for disabled adults, those with sensory or intellectual impairments, emotional/mental distress, problem drug/alcohol use, serious/chronic illness, and adults who are victims of domestic oppression. Meanwhile, many children and families services have been incorporated into large departments that include early years and youth services, education and schools. In English local government, but not in the other three UK jurisdictions, Lord Laming's first report (2003) in the wake of Victoria Climbié's death resulted in the separation of adult and children's directorates.

These initiatives were intended to increase inter-professional collaboration but have had the unintended consequence of weakening the links between social workers in children and adult services. As soon as they qualify, social workers scatter into these fragmented services. The availability of specialist post-qualifying professional development mostly reinforces early career choices and social workers may lose sight of current practice in other fields as they quickly acquire knowledge and expertise within their chosen specialism. The organisational dislocation of adult and children's services impedes collaboration with and learning from peers developing a different knowledge base and focus. Poor understanding about counterparts' roles and responsibilities, and diverse working cultures can create tensions both within and between adult and children's services. These tensions sometimes create problems of communication and co-ordination between practitioners from different fields of practice engaged with the same family.

The fabric of each person's everyday personal life is complex: as family members and friends we all fulfil multiple roles and responsibilities, and we often have to manage several of these at once. While services define us by one issue, we live our lives juggling many. People in contact with services have argued that social work specialisation causes problems, and needs to be revisited (Beresford 2007). Many adults have experiences that mean they belong in more than one 'service user' group. People with physical illnesses are also more likely to experience emotional/mental distress, and vice versa. These also often coincide with problem alcohol and/or drug use for a number of different reasons. Some people try to ameliorate distressing symptoms through self-medication; others may seek excitement and stimulation. Alcohol can trigger depression and anxiety. Failed solutions can become a problem so that some people get caught up in vicious cycles where, facing multiple challenges, they become particularly vulnerable to victimisation, violence and suicide (Weaver, Madden and Charles 2003). For people with emotional/mental distress who are also problem drug/alcohol users, dual diagnosis can give rise to prejudice and stigma, and act as a barrier to care from services that are ill-equipped to meet their needs (Banerjee, Clancy and Crome 2002; Franey and Quirk 1996).

Adults who face complex multiple life difficulties may have contact with several different services, or with none. An individual may experience overlapping problems, or problems may exist side by side in several family members. These families often find their problems addressed independently of each other by workers from various services. They may not be recognised as a family unit. For example, a parenting couple where one partner suffers from emotional/mental distress while the other misuses alcohol and there are concerns about their children's development could have three or more teams assessing, advising or supporting them. By contrast, adults on the autistic spectrum, perhaps struggling in their parenting role, may not meet criteria for help from either adult mental health or learning disability services.

Bureaucratic demands have come to compromise the professional role of social workers in children's services and have undermined their capacity to undertake the very practical assessment work that child protection demands (Ferguson 2011; Munro 2011b). In the UK, and indeed across the developed world, procedural approaches to improving child protection have led to expensive and defensive practice

(Turnell 2012). Anecdotal evidence suggests that similar processes are at work in adult services with the continued proliferation of technocratic strategies for rationing services. Together, business models and complex legal rules have combined to create mechanistic assessment procedures in both services. Lord Laming (2003) took issue with processes such as eligibility criteria when they effectively pre-empt professional social work assessment. 'Technical-rational' approaches to decision-making fail to take account of the complexity of family life, and undermine practitioners' ability to judge how to meet their needs.

Wherever, the term 'parent' is used in this book it should be understood as meaning any person acting as a father, mother or guardian, whether that caregiving role is fulfilled by a child's birth mother or father, step-parent, birth parent's partner, foster or adoptive parent, relative or family friend. Similarly, where it refers to 'children' this means any child or young person who has not yet reached their 18th birthday. Infants under 18 months old are referred to as babies; the phrase 'very young children' describes those who have not yet reached their sixth birthday; 'mid-childhood' refers to the years from six to twelve; and adolescence denotes children aged thirteen to eighteen.

This book draws upon a diverse, inter-disciplinary body of knowledge across which different terms describe similar ideas. The vocabulary used here follows guidance issued by the TUC UNISON (undated) and discussed by the Equality and Human Rights Commission (Sardar 2008).

Case studies based on real experiences in practice punctuate the text, sometimes to illustrate the theme under discussion and sometimes to raise questions for you to consider. Questions are intended to be thought-provoking. Sometimes they relate to your personal experience or invite you to hypothesise or consider various possibilities rather than eliciting definitive answers. You may need to look something up if you are unable to answer a question because of gaps in your own knowledge, for example of law or policy.

The book signposts the reader to sources of relevant information, ideas and research as well as to the many important debates conducted within challenging and complex fields of enquiry related to whole family assessment. Research literature is referenced throughout to illustrate specific issues. This book does not attempt to provide comprehensive overviews of the research evidence for the different areas of practice outlined: it would be impossible to do justice to the complexity of all the issues involved. Recommendations for further reading are made at the end of each chapter and these should guide you towards fields of research that you might choose to explore in more depth.

Since the mandate for assessment varies across the different UK jurisdictions, broad legal principles are usually discussed without reference to specific legislation.

Another key feature of the book is that it provides an overview of many different areas of specialist knowledge and practice relevant to whole family assessment, though it cannot replicate the extensive literature on assessment of the range of life difficulties that adults face, of parenting capacity, or of specific childhood problems. Nor can it engage in depth with the meaning of risk and its significance for those charged with protecting children and adults at risk of harm.

Several crucial issues such as inter-agency working and working with diversity are referred to but are not explored in depth. This book assumes that the reader is familiar with core social work theory and practice methods. Each reader is likely to notice that the areas of knowledge they deal with day-to-day are discussed very briefly. For example, workers in children's services may find the discussion of attachment theory in Chapter 6 very superficial, but for workers in adult services it should serve as a timely reminder about theory and research they may not routinely use in their everyday practice. Similarly, there is a great deal more to be said about assessment of mental capacity: the outline in Chapter 4 is intended to alert workers in children's services that they need to anticipate its significance for family assessment, and be aware that this is an ever-present issue for many workers in adult services. Readers should find pointers throughout the book to aspects of relevant social work specialisms that they do not routinely need to examine closely in their current role.

This book is intended as a practical resource to help social workers harness the knowledge and expertise they have developed in their respective fields of practice, stand back to look at the larger picture, examine how its component parts fit together and think collaboratively about the whole family's needs. It does not focus on the technical-rational aspects of social work that are dealt with through law, policy and procedures. It draws on a range of sources of knowledge including inquiries into untoward serious injury or deaths of both adults and children (known as serious case reviews in England and Wales, significant case reviews in Scotland, or case management reviews in Northern Ireland). Some suggest that these tragedies are not representative of day-to-day social work practice, but the premise of this book is that these analyses provide invaluable insights into how we can help families live well and safely (Brandon *et al.* 2012; Vincent 2004). The book aims to bring together what social workers across different settings need to know, and what they need to do, with tools and frameworks to help them to make sense of the interface between adult problems, family relationships and functioning, and children's well-being.

Above all, social workers need to think together holistically, embrace complexity, harness emotional intelligence, understand the impact of assessment work (on themselves, colleagues and families), build relationships and use a range of different approaches so that they can work collaboratively with each other and with families where adult life difficulties impact on parenting (Brandon *et al.* 2009; Ferguson 2011; Howe 2005):

> Dealing with the variety of need is better achieved by social workers understanding the underlying principles of good practice and developing the expertise to apply them…they may use procedures to get started as novices but need to move beyond this to achieve mastery. Social workers in a culture where procedural compliance is expected, and deviation is met with blame, are discouraged from building up that expertise.
>
> (Munro 2011a, p.62)

CHAPTER 1

Assessment at the Interface Between Adult and Children's Services

Key messages

- Most parents who face life difficulties put their children's needs first and raise them well.

- Most adults who face life difficulties need additional support to fulfil their role as parents.

- Most children who need help live in families facing multiple disadvantages.

- When parents harm their children it is usually because they are overwhelmed by their own difficulties.

Twenty-first century social work

At the turn of this century social work was summed up as:

> Paid professional activity that aims to assist people in overcoming serious difficulties in their lives by providing care, protection or counselling or through social support, advocacy and community work.

> (Smale, Tuson and Stratham 2001)

Points to consider

- Does this description match the responsibilities you fulfil in your current role?

- When you first embarked on your career in social work what did you hope and intend to achieve?

- What did you imagine your working day might be like?

- Is what you are doing now what you hoped for when you started out in social work?

The future of social work remains somewhat uncertain. Social work responsibilities are likely to shift further into the voluntary and business sector, and, as ever, changes to patterns of service delivery have to be understood in the context of wider social and political change (Parton 1996). Responsibilities for adults and children in need and for family support have already shifted towards health professions and low-level interventions to the private or voluntary sectors so that unqualified staff or volunteers now fulfil support roles formerly undertaken by social workers. However, holistic assessments of need and risk are still social work's uncontested core business. Recent years have seen a rapid increase in referrals about adults who may be at risk of harm. Child protection referrals have increased throughout the past 50 years across all the Western democracies. In many settings, qualified and experienced social workers are now expected to focus on risk assessment.

Assessment at the interface

Assessment is all about action:

> ...a perceptual/analytical process of selecting, categorising, organising and synthesising data...with the main purpose being to develop an informed impression leading to action.

> (Butler and Roberts 2004, p.208)

> ...a process by which professionals acquire and process information, communicate about it, and determine what action to take...a process of understanding...its purpose is to guide action.

> (Reder, Duncan and Lucey 1993, p.83)

There are many dimensions to assessment at the interface between adult and children's services. Every parent feels stretched, and sometimes overwhelmed, by the responsibility of bringing up children. Workers in adult services with responsibility for parents facing life difficulties have to take into account the demands of parenting and consider the impact of family life on the adult. Sometimes parents are themselves the victims of abuse and exploitation. Adults who need additional support sometimes need help to equip themselves for the physical demands and the psychological stresses of these challenges. Workers in adult services have a crucial role in differentiating between adults' personal needs and their needs as parents and ensuring that colleagues in children's services understand these. If you work in adult services you also need to be able to recognise children's needs, consider what action is required on their behalf and take responsibility for communicating any concerns about their safety (HM Government 2013, p.11, para. 3). This may seem too obvious to be worth re-stating here, but sadly, reviews of child deaths consistently note how children who suffered harm came from families already known to adult services (Brandon *et al.* 2008).

Children's social workers assess a remarkable spectrum of concerns about safety and well-being. Consider, for example, the experience of a two-year-old left alone, a ten-year-old boy encouraged to access internet pornography, an adolescent girl punished with a beating, a baby shaken by her exhausted parent, and an eight-year-old monitoring her mother's medication. All these differ fundamentally from each other and assessment is therefore not just a question of determining severity or dangerousness (Cooper, Hetherington and Katz 2003). Each family presents a unique constellation of strengths and vulnerabilities and requires assessment designed and carried out in a way that fits with its unique experience. If you work in children's services, you, too, have a responsibility to consider how an adult's difficulties might be exacerbated if they are not able to meet their own expectations of themselves as a parent. All child assessments should include evidence from all the professionals involved with their families and take account of family history and significant events (Laming 2009).

If you work in children's services, the challenge is to understand the parents' difficulties and how these impact on their behaviour in the family, while taking care not to lose focus on the child. When children experience harm it is usually because of the behaviour of the adults who care for them. We cannot afford to narrow our thinking down:

> Social workers seemed reluctant to offer help to people with poor mental health, those using alcohol and drugs and those experiencing domestic abuse. The family members said that they had heard time and again 'We are here for your children, not for you.'

> (Children's Commissioner 2010, p.21)

Reviews of child deaths and children's own accounts combine to provide poignant evidence of how readily workers in adult and children's services alike can be overwhelmed by parents' vulnerability, or troubled adults' demands, leaving children's needs overlooked (Ofsted 2011; Royal College of Psychiatrists 2004). The evidence base for what works in the field of mental health provides a strong ethical imperative for collaborative working using whole family approaches (Colmer 2010; Falkov 2012).

Whole family assessment

This book is concerned with how parents' well-being, children's experiences and family relationships all impact on each other. *Crossing Bridges* (Falkov *et al.* 1998) introduced a developmental and systems perspective to assist in assessing families where a parent experiences emotional/mental distress. Falkov has subsequently revised and refined the model (see Figure 1.1) to provide a conceptual framework to support family-focused assessment and practice (Falkov 2012).

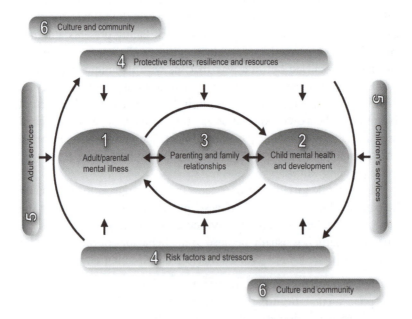

Figure 1.1 The family model. An integrated approach to supporting mentally ill parents and their children. Reproduced here with the permission of Dr Adrian Falkov (2012)

Falkov's model aims to help you understand the processes that underlie and influence how:

- adult/parental mental illness can affect children's mental health and development (1→2)

- adult/parental mental illness can affect parenting and family relationships (1→3)

- parenting and family relationships can influence adult/parental mental illness (3→1)

- children's mental health and development needs can influence adult/parental mental illness (2→1)

- protective factors, resilience and resources available to the family can contribute positively to family life (4→1&2&3)

- risk factors and stressors can impact negatively on family life (4→1&2&3)

- adult and children's services impact on family life (5→1&2&3&4)

- the family system is affected by cultural and community influences (6Þ1&2&3&4).

EXERCISE

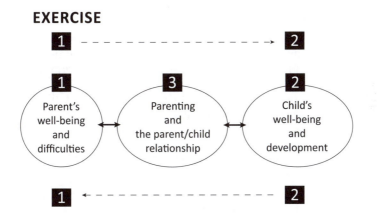

Figure 1.2 Mapping influences in your family of origin (adapted from Falkov 1998)

Use this tool to map your experience in your family of origin.

- How did your parents' well-being and difficulties impact on your well-being and development? (1 → 2)

- How did your well-being and development impact on your parents' well-being and difficulties? (2→1)

- How did your parents' well-being and difficulties impact on their parenting and family relationships? (1→3)

- How did parenting and family relationships impact on your parent's well-being and difficulties? (3→1)

- How did your health, well-being and development impact on parenting and family relationships? (2→3)

- How did parenting and family relationships impact on your well-being and development? (3→2)

Have you participated in assessments where one of these dimensions of the family's experience was not addressed?

Principles and themes

Several statements apply to the experience of all kinds of families:

- Adult life difficulties do not inevitably compromise parenting or cause harm to children (Kumar 1997; Olsen and Tyers 2004). Indeed, most parents manage their problems, fulfil their responsibilities well and enable their children to grow up into happy and healthy adults (Blewitt et al. 2011; Weir 2004).

- Research helpfully highlights common patterns of distress in families where there are parental problems but rarely establishes exact cause and effect.

- Taking into account societal factors such as stigma or poverty sometimes brings practitioners into conflict with those more comfortable with thinking about problems in terms of individual deficit and family dysfunction.

- Whole family assessment should differentiate between the adult's personal needs, the help that will enable them to be the best parent possible, the developmental needs of their children and support that will benefit children fulfilling care roles. There are implications for children's health, development and sometimes safety if the parent's needs are not met.

- Most research on parenting has focused primarily on mothers and tells us little about fathers' experience and contribution in families.

- The data we have about parents accessing health services is flawed because the NHS often fails to identify the fact that 'patients' may have a role as parents. This results in their own, and their children's, needs remaining invisible (Blewitt *et al.* 2011).

- Many parents and children fear and avoid social services, and may seem reluctant or hostile when subjected to assessment.

Points to consider

- What challenges do you face when you undertake assessments in families with children?

The mandate

Case study

Jim has Type 2 diabetes and a very long-term problem with alcohol. He uses a wheelchair because his right leg was amputated two years ago. Jim has been without a permanent home for eight years, prefers to sleep on the street, and has firmly refused offers of accommodation in the past. In early winter he developed a chest infection and is still unwell. Matt, a student social worker on placement with a street homeless charity, talks with Jim at 4 pm on the coldest night of the year. Matt knows that Jim has already refused to see a doctor and that he was assessed at the police station last week by social workers and a psychiatrist. They concluded that Jim's decision-making, though idiosyncratic, was not impaired, and that he did not suffer from mental illness. Matt can hear Jim struggle for breath, notes signs of a soaring temperature and offers to take Jim to hospital. Jim tells Matt to mind his own business.

On the same snowy afternoon, Melissa, a duty social worker in children's services assessment team, is asked by the police to collect Samuel (11) and Jake (9) and place them in foster care. Jake has a moderate learning disability and hearing difficulties. Their father, Jason, has a long history of emotional/mental distress and hospital admissions at times when his thinking becomes psychotic. Jason is arrested after he enters Samuel's school playground to 'punish' a girl for bullying. Jason's psychiatrist has assessed him at the police station and compulsory admission to hospital for treatment has been arranged. Jason vociferously refuses to make any plans for Samuel and Jake to be looked after overnight. Aware that the police have contacted social services, Jason asks to see and speak with his sons. When they are brought to him, he gives them instructions to stay at the police station, not to talk to social workers, and to run away or do whatever they need to do but on no account to go to a foster home.

- What are the fundamental issues that Matt and Melissa have to consider?
- How are these two cases different from each other?
- What interventions does the law require?
- What interventions does the law allow?

The legal mandate for social work sets out the duties and powers of local authorities and other public bodies. These responsibilities do not usually attach to the individual social worker (with the significant exception that, after formal training, approved mental health practitioners are held personally responsible for their decisions about compulsory treatment and assessment of psychiatric patients).

Understanding the legal mandate enables social workers to know what they *can* do but only the naïve would imagine that it tells social workers what they *must* do in complex and uncertain situations, and it certainly cannot be relied on to identify the *right* thing to do. There will have been many situations when your assessments have thrown up legal and ethical questions that did not have obvious answers – not least because most legislation promotes general principles such as self-determination, while some parts of the law embody and enforce judgements about how individuals should behave and the choices they should make:

> Resolution…requires assessment skills informed by values, knowledge, practice wisdom and the perspectives of experts by experience, and a delicate balance between law and ethics in a framework of professional accountability.

> (Braye and Preston-Shoot 2010, p.5)

Our legal mandate assumes that adults have capacity, are entitled to self-determination and hence are entitled to take risks. Since we all have the right to choose to make unwise decisions, the starting point for investigations of whether an adult is at risk of harm is whether they have mental capacity (see Chapter 4 for further discussion of mental capacity). Social workers often struggle to reconcile these principles with a more paternalistic sense of responsibility. Indeed, the phrase 'vulnerable adult' (DoH 2000a) is highly controversial even though it has come into common use in England and Wales. Anyone contacting social services to share worries about a child or adult at risk of harm will be questioned extensively with a view to establishing whether their concerns reach local thresholds for enquiries to be made or can be 'signposted' elsewhere.

Points to consider

- What are your expectations when you refer a family to another service?

- What are the threshold criteria for accepting a referral to your service?

- Does your service always meet the expectations of practitioners from other services?

- Is there a dissonance between the public's perception of your service and how it is delivered?

- Have you ever considered 'whistle-blowing' about levels of service provision for a family you work with?

EXERCISE

Think back over your assessments and identify examples of times when you have faced dilemmas about:

- raising concerns about an individual's safety

- care versus control

- welfare versus justice

- the individual's needs versus society's needs

- the individual's right to self-determination versus safety

- needs-led versus resource-led planning.

Despite significant developments in human rights legislation the welfare system in the UK is largely structured around duties placed on public authorities to provide services rather than around the rights of groups who might need services. UK law very rarely enshrines individual entitlement. This means that:

- Statutory children and adult services operate with high thresholds for intervention because need routinely outstrips resources (ADCS 2012; Brawn *et al.* 2013; Munro 2011b).

- Services focus on individual care needs rather than support to enable people to achieve independence.

- In many social work roles assessment is construed as identifying 'needs' to be met by other services and 'risks' that have to be managed.

Consequently, some children and parents simply do not receive the support that they need (Braye and Preston-Shoot 2010).

Case study

Dominic is on call on New Year's Eve. Transport Police have arrested Jasmine after a member of the public restrained her from jumping in front of a high-speed train while holding her six-week-old daughter Ava. They take her to a local psychiatric ward before either Dominic or a psychiatrist has the opportunity to attend and assess her in police custody. By the time Dominic arrives on the ward, both mother and daughter are asleep in a side room. Dominic gently wakes Jasmine who says she doesn't know why she suddenly decided to take her life, but that she wants to stay on the psychiatric ward to make sure she and the baby are safe. Jasmine is clear, however, that if there is any question of her being separated from Ava she will leave immediately. Aware that the hospital has no mother and baby facility, Dominic seeks to transfer them to a specialist unit but the hospital administrator refuses to agree this. Without a suitable placement, Jasmine would have to be admitted to hospital compulsorily and an application made to magistrates for an emergency protection order to remove Ava from her care.

- What are the questions for assessment?
- What does the law require Dominic to do?

- What does the law enable Dominic to do?

- What do you think Dominic should do?

The media regularly portray social work practice either as neglectful or as draconian. Whereas the first charge may sometimes be true (Brandon *et al.* 2012), there is evidence that local authorities do not bring care proceedings without good reason (Masson *et al.* 2008), and that existing measures (e.g. Mental Health Tribunals) are robust enough to ensure that legal interventions to protect adults at risk of harm are justified.

Oppression

Points to consider

There will have been occasions in your life when you have witnessed injustice. You probably thought to yourself 'this is not right!' and asked yourself 'what can I do?'

- Did you follow your conscience?

- Look at your reasons for whether you did, or did not, act on your moral impulse. Consider psychological, cultural, social and strategic reasons and think about the different levels at which these influenced your decision.

- Compare your actions with those of your colleagues. How satisfied are you with how you responded to the injustice?

(Adapted from teaching material by Isaac Prilleltensky, University of Miami)

Why is oppression relevant to social work assessment of families where parents face life difficulties? Simply because these families are more likely than others to be disadvantaged by stigma, harassment, poor housing, poor education, unemployment and poverty. The challenges and demands they meet are exacerbated by material adversity.

Jack and Gill (2010) summarise research that shows children are most likely to experience poverty if:

1. They live in households headed by a lone parent, especially if this parent is a young mother, when the children are young, and where

there are three or more children (Bradshaw 2002; Bradshaw *et al.* 2006; DWP 2005).

2. They live in households where there are no adults in paid work (DWP 2005).

3. They belong to black and/or minority ethnic families, particularly those of Bangladeshi, Pakistani and Black-African origin (Craig 2005; Marsh and Perry 2003; Platt 2007).

4. They belong to asylum-seeking or refugee families (Oxfam and Refugee Council 2002; Scottish Refugee Council 2006).

5. They live in a family that includes a disabled adult or a disabled child (Northway 2005; Strickland and Olsen 2005).

In families where two or more of these five different risk factors co-exist there is a build-up of stressors and the impact of disadvantage on children and their parents accumulates. Children who live in chronic poverty experience more risks than other children and the risk factors have a more negative impact on them (Barnes *et al.* 2010). The Cabinet Office (2005) identified indicators of risk as:

- no parent in work

- living in poor accommodation

- no parent with qualifications

- mother experiences emotional/mental distress

- one or both parents have a limiting illness, disability or impairment

- low income.

The international definition of social work offers a politicised, campaigning interpretation of the social work role:

> The social work profession promotes social change, problem-solving in human relationships and the empowerment and liberation of people to enhance well-being. Utilising theories of human behaviour and social systems, social work intervenes at the points where people interact with their environments. Principles of human rights and social justice are fundamental to social work.
>
> (IASSW and the IFSW 2005, p.1)

Radical social workers in the 1970s often quoted the phrase coined by African-American civil rights activist in 1968: 'you're either part of the solution or you're part of the problem.' However, in the UK, social work has gradually adopted assessment practices that focus on individual and family pathology and distract attention from the impact of oppression. A more individualised, essentially psychological rather than sociological definition of its function has evolved. According to the British Association of Social Workers (BASW), social work is:

> ...a profession that is centred around people – from babies through to older people. The profession works to protect vulnerable people, enhance relationships and help families to stay together where possible and enable people to live fulfilled lives as independently as possible.

(BASW 2012)

Research evidence indicates that community-based interventions to enhance social support networks can reduce harm and improve the futures of children and their families. The inclusion of wider family and environmental factors are included in the National Assessment Framework, but these factors are not always emphasised in social work assessments (DoH *et al.* 2000; DoH 2013; Jack and Gill 2003; Utting 1995). An alternative model designed by Boushel (1994) places the child's safety at the centre of an ecosystem. It aims to encourage workers to adopt an anti-oppressive stance and consider cultural issues by asking them to focus on four key assessment issues:

1. the value and status accorded to the child's mother, and other key carers

2. the extent to which the child is valued and feels valued

3. whether or not the child can make use of society's protective mechanisms and how well they are included in society

4. the formal and informal protective resources available to the child.

Each issue is examined in relation to the immediate family, the extended family, community and state (Figure 1.3).

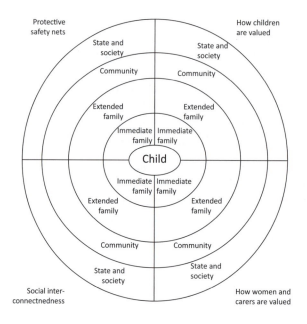

Figure 1.3 Boushel's framework (1994) for assessing the protective environment (cited by Calder and Hackett 2003, p.191)

Case study

Charles, aged 7, is the eldest boy in a Zimbabwean family with three children. They live in a predominantly white area. In his class 'Golden Time' Charles talks with his teacher about 'the evil eye' and visits from spirit relatives. The teacher has always been aware that Charles' family are practising Christians and travel some distance to attend church. She asks the social worker based in the school, 'Do you think this is anything to worry about?'

The teacher and social worker have many issues to consider. What has actually happened? Is the child upset? Has the child experienced harm? Is the family's sense of the spirit world a culturally specific way of making sense of the material world? Do Charles' parents suffer from a delusional psychiatric illness? Does this talk of spirits have the same meaning as it would if a white British child came in talking about ghosts and haunting?

- Who might help the worker answer these questions?

- How can the worker negotiate the issues of cultural sensitivity?

- How should the worker navigate the pitfalls of cultural relativism?

Analysis of the dynamic between the child, the parent and their environmental context is often overwhelmed by a primary focus on reviewing the psychological profile of the parents for evidence of risk (Jack 2006). Unless assessment addresses families' cultural and community context it risks ignoring their experience of issues, such as homelessness or racism, that can have a crucial impact on individuals and on relationships. Families are more likely to engage fully as participants in assessment when they feel confident that the impact of oppression and disadvantage is appreciated by the worker (Graham and Bruce 2006, cited by Lefevre 2010). People are a product and reflection of their society. Personal and cultural contexts overlap to make people who they are and permeate the whole family system. Every family is located within culture and community but we cannot understand what these mean to them until we ask. In most families the answers we receive to questions about identity, ethnicity, faith, culture and beliefs will be complex and, so long as we listen carefully, these answers will often defy stereotypes. Culture and community can be, simultaneously, both a resource and also a source of stress. Protective factors and risk factors derived from culture and community impact differently on each part of the family system to generate patterns of resilience and vulnerability that can be explored and understood in whole family assessment.

EXERCISE

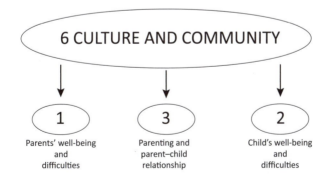

Figure 1.4 Influences in your childhood (adapted from Falkov 2012)

Think back again to your own childhood.

- What were the significant cultural and community influences at play within your family?

- What positive impact did they have on you, your parents, your siblings, and members of your wider family?

- How did they enhance your parents' approach to parenting roles and responsibilities?

- How did they strengthen relationships in your family?

- What problems did they generate for you, your parents, your siblings, and members of your wider family?

- What aspects of culture and community undermined your parents' capacity to parent?

- How did culture and community contribute to any difficulties in the relationships between family members?

Poverty

Many individuals are crushed by the experience of poverty and disadvantage, and it is always the most vulnerable who suffer the consequences. Even the most resilient child from poverty stricken circumstances is finding it more difficult to do well in life than a more ordinary child from a wealthy background. To witness these inequalities one has to ask, what would that resilient child or person have been able to do, what would their contribution to the community or the economy have been if they never had to overcome disadvantage? A society that maximises opportunities for all citizens is also one that makes best use of the many assets for well-being, social and economic development.

(Schoon and Bartley 2008, p.27)

Income inequality has risen more rapidly in the UK than in any other westernised country except New Zealand during the past 30 years. The proportion of children living in poverty rose from 10 per cent in 1979 to 32.9 per cent in 1996. By 2011/12 this percentage reduced to 27 per cent, but it is expected that 4.7 million children in the UK will live in poverty by 2020 (CPAG 2012). Changes to the structure of employment together with planned changes to the tax and benefit system mean that relative poverty and inequality are set to rise continuously until 2020 (Brewer *et al.* 2012) and the Institute for Fiscal Studies expects a surge of 100,000 children falling into poverty each year. The circumstances of individuals and families facing multiple difficulties will worsen as the gap between rich and poor grows (Resolution Foundation 2012).

> ...the experience of poverty is almost overwhelmingly negative, and can have psychological, physical, relational and practical effects on people's lives. Poverty is a highly stigmatised social position and the experience of poverty in an affluent society can be particularly isolating and socially damaging.

> (Ridge 2009, p.2)

Most parents who live in poverty are good parents (Katz *et al.* 2007). Many strive to protect their children from hardship and prioritise their needs, but do so at immense personal cost (Ridge 2009). Most children defined by social workers as 'in need' are living below the poverty line (Bradshaw 2002). Parents are placed under stress, and the care of their children is compromised when their difficulties are exacerbated by poverty (Cleaver, Unell and Aldgate 1999).

> There's people getting by on £50 a week, always worrying, taking off how much they spend on shopping, travel, etc., lying awake at night worrying about how to give their kids enough food. Then you go to court and all sorts of people are getting paid. You can't just starve people into care. Why don't they help? They don't want you to mention poverty.

> (Parent, quoted by Children's Commissioner 2010, p.26)

It is not surprising that assessments rarely focus on families' practical and material needs since very few local authorities provide services to address the impact of poverty (Clark and Davis 1997). Given that so many of the children who are referred to children's services grow up in very poor families, whole family assessment should routinely consider how disadvantage affects parents, children and parenting. For example, children are more likely to care for a parent if their family is poor and isolated, making it difficult to be sure whether the adversities they face are about their role in the family or their disadvantaged circumstances (SCIE 2005a).

Disadvantage

EXERCISE

The Casual Vacancy is J.K. Rowling's first novel written for adults and is set in a small English town. Read *The Casual Vacancy*, either alone or pass it round among your colleagues as the starting point for a structured discussion group and consider these questions:

- Does Rowling's depiction of class and ethnicity in 'Pagford' ring true?

- Do you identify with Kay's experience?

- Have you encountered parents similar to Terri? How did they make you feel?

Assessments also need to consider the fundamental and far-reaching impact of impoverished environments on families (Gambrill and Shlonsky 2000; Shelter 2004, 2005). Around 75,000 children are homeless and more than one million children in England live in poor quality housing (SCIE 2005c; Shelter 2005). Poor housing, homelessness and temporary living arrangements undermine parents' well-being and their ability to meet their children's needs. They contribute to children being unhealthy, unhappy and underachieving at school, as well as increasing the risk of illness in later life (Barnardo's 2008; Jones 2004). Families who are poor and poorly housed are likely to be further disadvantaged because, in towns and cities, their children grow up in areas with problems such as criminal and anti-social behaviour, problem drug and alcohol use, poor quality education, health and childcare facilities, and high unemployment rates (Ghate and Hazel 2002; Lupton 2003; Social Exclusion Unit 1998).

An early ground-breaking study opened up our understanding of depression as a largely social phenomenon and developed a model which explained depression in terms of the presence or absence of stressors and vulnerability (Brown and Harris 1978). This identified the significance of their social standing for women's vulnerability to emotional/mental distress and pointed to the existence of a special group of inner-city stresses. In the countryside poverty is exacerbated by higher living costs, isolation and living alongside much wealthier neighbours.

Disadvantage is often deepened by debt since 'loan sharks' routinely target disadvantaged communities and the poorest families. Refugee families, where adults are prohibited from earning a living but are not entitled to full benefits, are often under extraordinary pressure with no material resources to draw upon. Families in contact with social services rarely enjoy the advantages of social and cultural capital that their social workers take for granted (Bourdieu 1991; Cornell and Hartman 1998, p.213). Since social workers, across all services, operate at the meeting point of the personal and the socio-political, if our interventions do not challenge oppression, inequality and disadvantage they are likely to reinforce it.

Vicious circles

A small number of 'problem families' in each community fill the active caseloads of most social work teams. We have long recognised this phenomenon as resulting from 'cycles of deprivation', but research has not given us much insight into how individual difficulties and general adversity impact on each other (Tunnard 2002a, b).

For example, teenage mothers are widely portrayed as a social problem, even as an indicator of society's breakdown. There is indeed evidence that children born to young mothers are more likely to suffer significant harm and also that the mothers of children who come to serious harm are more likely to have had their first child before the age of 21 (Brandon *et al.* 2012). But is this really evidence that young women make more dangerous mothers? Or is this because well-educated, well-off young women are more likely to postpone parenthood whereas those with little money, and a poor education, who have grown up in difficult or abusive families, may become pregnant earlier and struggle as parents because they are poor, stressed, isolated and do not know what they need to know about child development (Breakwell 1993; Herrenkohl *et al.* 1998).

Some families are exposed to a whole range of problems that may include the effects of poverty, poor housing, poor nutrition, low educational achievement, poor health and ill-treatment (Margolin and Gordis 2000). Around 2 per cent of families in England experience multiple and complex difficulties and social work assessment often fails to meet their needs because unco-ordinated services are not able to take account of the range of problems faced by family members (Kendall, Rodger and Palmer 2011):

> It is likely to be the interaction between a number of factors rather than any specific characteristic that leads to parenting difficulties. Thus most families are able to overcome adversities and provide their children with a sufficiently nurturing environment, although

they may fall down in one or two areas. Only a very small proportion are unable to provide a sufficiently consistent standard of care across all seven (child development) dimensions, but it is they who form the group whose children are most likely to be admitted to care or accommodation.

(Ward 1995, p.85)

Children are most likely to experience poor outcomes in families where:

- adults have poor parenting skills
- parents experience emotional/mental distress
- family members are problem drug/alcohol users
- there is domestic abuse
- the parents were themselves abused or neglected as children
- isolation restricts other social influences.

(Gorin 2004; Tunnard 2004)

When children come to harm, it is the build-up of stressors on families that drives abuse and neglect. The literature on anti-social behaviour, and findings from reviews of child deaths, particularly highlight how a complex interaction between socio-economic and psychosocial factors, adult life difficulties and the child's characteristics increase both the vulnerability of adults and risk to children (Brandon *et al.* 2009; Cabinet Office 2005). Around 140,000 families in the UK live with five or more disadvantages (Social Exclusion Taskforce 2008). The most common combination of problems underlying very serious harm to children is where problem drug/alcohol use, emotional/mental distress and domestic abuse occur together (Brandon *et al.* 2009; Rose and Barnes 2008). Numerous studies of mothers experiencing problem drug use have found that many have low self-esteem, care poorly for themselves and are in poverty (Klee 1998, cited by SCIE 2004). Almost 30 per cent of drug users and more than 50 per cent of problem drinkers face three or more significant life difficulties (Weaver *et al.* 2003). The danger in assessing and working with families facing multiple difficulties is that the complexity of the adult problems can so easily eclipse the child's needs (Fauth *et al.* 2010).

Most parents who have suffered abuse or neglect in their own childhoods manage to break the cycle and go on to parent successfully. However, many parents who harm their children have themselves been the victims of abusive and traumatic childhoods (DoH 1995). Numerous studies have established a correlation, but not necessarily a causal link, between childhood abuse and subsequent problems as parents. We have to conceive of parents' own history of being abused as a risk factor (Calder and Hackett 2003). Social workers in adult services witness the continuing psychological impact of early abuse but may not always be aware of people's childhood histories. Victims of childhood abuse and neglect are also more at risk of a range of physiological problems associated with immunity and inflammatory responses in later life. These include cardiovascular disease, viral hepatitis, liver cancer, asthma, chronic obstructive pulmonary disease, autoimmune disease, depression and poor dental health (Shonkoff and Garner 2012, cited by Brown and Ward 2012, p.69). For example, if parents with poor teeth do not use and do not teach simple dental hygiene routines this impacts on the next generation for their whole lifespan:

> The cranio-facial complex allows us to speak, smile, kiss, touch, smell, taste, chew, swallow and to cry out in pain. It provides protection against microbial infections and environmental threats. Oral diseases restrict activities in school, at work and at home causing millions of school and work hours to be lost each year the world over. Moreover, the psychosocial impact of these diseases significantly diminishes quality of life.

> (World Health Organization 2006)

A study where health visitors collected information around the time of a new baby being born found that 6.7 per cent of children of parents who had themselves been abused were thought to be at risk of harm compared with 0.4 per cent where there was no history of abuse. When three specific additional factors – mental distress, being younger than 21 and experiencing domestic abuse – were taken into account, babies of parents who were themselves abused in childhood were 17 more times likely to experience harm (Dixon, Browne and Hamilton-Giacritsis 2005). Our growing understanding of the neurological implications of emotional abuse and neglect has rested on recognition that many parents who harm their children have themselves been traumatised in their own childhoods, and replicate (usually unwittingly) the damaged and damaging parenting style that they experienced. In families where children's fundamental needs are not met, the 'trauma of absence' is re-enacted when the abused child becomes a parent, creating a cycle of neglect that perpetuates across the generations (Howe 2005). Chapter 6 provides further discussion of the impact of neglect.

Dangerous thinking

Empathy and established relationship skills remain the necessary, but insufficient conditions when working with resistant families; they need to be balanced with an eyes-wide-open, boundaried, authoritative approach aimed at containing anxiety and ensuring that the child's needs stay in sharp focus.

(Fauth *et al.* 2010, p.2)

The public's ambivalence about what it expects of social work mirrors the difficult balance between optimism and cynicism that social workers have to find. There is a good evidence base for the effectiveness of professional practice founded on optimism, respect and tolerance. We know from learning theory that people achieve, change and grow when they are supported by teachers, mentors and role models who expect the best of them. A growing body of evaluative research highlights the value of strengths-based approaches across a range of settings because they build rapport, harness motivation and empower people to reclaim and redefine themselves (Blewitt *et al.* 2011; McAuley, Pecora and Rose 2006).

Optimism also energises and sustains the motivation of practitioners. Cynicism threatens both personal-professional development and good practice. If a team lapses into using pejorative terms such as 'punter', they jeopardise their therapeutic alliance with people. Practitioners sometimes defend gallows humour and laughter at the expense of others as an antidote to stress, but they are early warning signs that the professional ethic of respect and unconditional regard has been set aside.

Points to consider

Think about a time when you worked in a place where some people denigrated others (colleagues and family members) in back-room banter and about another time when you worked in a place where people always showed respect to others in private as well as face-to-face.

- What differences did these two settings make to your own practice?

- How did experiences of back-room banter affect your perception of its victims?

- Did you feel able to challenge jocular negative comments?

- What else could you have said or done to improve the team culture?

On the other hand there is no place for naïvety. The tendency towards a 'rule of optimism' remains evident in contemporary assessment practice (Dingwall, Eekelaar and Murray 1983; Laming 2009). Interpersonal processes, for example 'good' relationships between workers and articulate parents, can lead practitioners to neglect or mirror abuse in families with calamitous outcomes for those we seek to protect (Dale *et al.* 1986; Ward and Rose 2002):

> Be mild with the mild, shrewd with the crafty, confiding to the honest, rough to the ruffian, and a thunderbolt to the liar. But in all this, never be unmindful of your own dignity.
>
> (An old legal maxim of unknown origin associated with cross-examining witnesses in court)

Most parents, however flawed, love their children, want the best for them, and parent the best they can, but there will always be a few people who set out to harm them (Fauth *et al.* 2010). Adults intent on harming others sometimes assert their right to privacy in order to conceal abuse (Ofsted 2011). Social workers have to stay alert to the possibility that some people might have reasons to withhold information or tell lies. They cannot take all they are told either by children or by parents at face value, and need to maintain a stance of 'respectful uncertainty' (Ofsted 2011, p.17). It is not pleasant to have to 'think dirty' and it is not easy to interrogate information. It is notoriously difficult for lay people and professionals alike to distinguish truth from lies (Bond and DePaulo 2006; Vrij 2000, 2004) and since social workers do and should invest in building trusting relationships with parents and children, they can be deceived, misled and manipulated.

Conclusion

> Social work calls for a particular mix of analytical skills, insight, common-sense, confidence, resilience, empathy and use of authority.
>
> (Social Work Task Force 2009, p.17)

Much is expected of social workers. Employers want workers who are confident and able to adapt quickly when the needs of the organisation change. Anyone reading the social work literature might infer we are a profession of super-humans who can combine creativity (problem-solving, unique responses to unprecedented circumstances, original thought, reflection and reflexivity), discipline (intellectual rigour, dialectical thought, independence and personal effectiveness) and humanity (commitment to public service, a generous spirit, anti-oppressive values, kindness and authority) with highly-refined communication skills (non-verbal, verbal and written).

Whichever specialism you have chosen, whole family assessment means re-embracing generic social work principles. Linking with others working with the same family might mean sharing knowledge, collaborating to designing a holistic assessment, or meeting with the family as co-workers.

Further reading and resources

Brandon, M., Bailey, S., Belderson, P., Gardner, R., *et al.* (2009) *Understanding Serious Case Reviews and their Impact – A Biennial Analysis of Serious Case Reviews 2005–2007.* London: Department for Children, Schools and Families. Available at www.education.gov.uk/publications/standard/publicationdetail/page1/DCSF-RR129.

Braye, S. and Preston-Shoot, M. (2010) *Practising Social Work Law* (Third edition). Basingstoke: Palgrave Macmillan.

Falkov, A. (2012) *The Family Model Handbook. An Integrated Approach to Supporting Mentally Ill Parents and their Children.* Hove: Pavilion.

Ferguson, H. (2011) *Child Protection Practice.* Basingstoke: Macmillan.

Jack, G. and Gill, O. (2010) 'The Impact of Economic Factors on Parents or Caregivers and Children.' In J. Horwath (ed.) *The Child's World. The Comprehensive Guide to Assessing Children* (Second edition). London: Jessica Kingsley Publishers.

CHAPTER 2

Respectful Engagement

Key messages

- Parents have a right to be engaged as partners in the design and process of whole family assessments undertaken by adult or children's services.

- Child protection concerns need not preclude children or parents from full participation in assessments undertaken by adult or children's services.

- People are more than just their problems.

- Understanding power dynamics and negotiating how authority will be exercised in the assessment process is crucial to achieving partnership.

- The social worker's authority can be used purposefully to create a healthy balance of power between assessors and family members.

People value a social work approach based on challenging the broader barriers they face... They place a particular value on a social approach, the social work relationship, and the positive personal qualities they associate with their social worker. These include warmth, respect, being non-judgmental, listening, treating people with equality, being trustworthy, open, honest and reliable and communicating well... People value the support that social workers offer as well as their ability to help them access and deal with other services and agencies.

(Beresford 2007, p.5)

EXERCISE

Think back to an experience when you were assessed.

- What did you want/expect of the professional?

- Did the professional live up to your expectation?

- Did you feel able to influence the process?

The terms we use to describe the relationship between those who assess and those who are assessed:

> conjure up differing identities, identifying differing relationships and differing power dynamics.
>
> (McLaughlin 2009, p.1101)

The term 'client' is still widely used and accepted by many people. However, campaigning groups argue that it frames the individual as passive, whereas the phrase 'expert by experience' emphasises the knowledge and authority derived from personal experience. Within adult services, welfare has been constructed as a commodity to be bought or sold to 'consumers', 'customers' or 'service users'. The vocabulary used conveys subtle clues about organisations' concept of partnership with families. For example, 'personalisation' constructs the parent as a consumer whereas 'self-directed support' highlights citizenship and entitlement to rights (Henwood 2008, cited by Braye and Preston-Shoot 2010, p.270). But these terms do not capture the nuances of the social work relationship:

> I consume mental health services like cockroaches consume Rentokil.
>
> (Former mental health patient quoted by Barker and Pack 1996, p.6)

None of these available terms adequately capture the relationship dynamic between social workers and family members during statutory child protection investigations. Respect is indispensable (Family Policy Alliance 2005). Trust, authority and negotiation are identified as three organising principles fundamental to relationship-based practice (Cooper *et al.* 2003; Hetherington *et al.* 2003). These themes recur throughout this chapter.

Case study

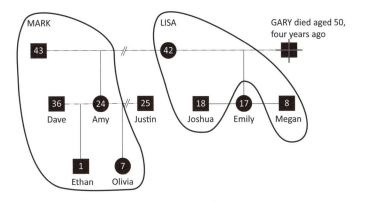

Figure 2.1 The Green family tree

Joshua is bright, funny, sociable when he first asks for help with anxiety during his GCSEs and his GP gives him a short course of mild tranquillisers. Having drunk alcohol in moderation for three years or so, he begins to get very drunk two or three times every week and uses cannabis throughout the summer holidays. He achieves very high grades in his GCSEs but his performance drops steadily throughout AS-level studies and he spends much less time with his friends. In the holidays before his A-level mock exams he is very unwell with a chest infection. During this illness he begins to express bizarre and paranoid ideas. The weekend after the mocks, Joshua swallows most of the tablets in the bathroom cabinet and sets fire to his clothes. After assessment by a psychiatrist, he is discharged from A&E and referred to Child and Adolescent Mental Health Services (CAMHS). Joshua, Lisa and Megan attend three appointments with a family therapist.

Joshua continues to feel anxious and his behaviour becomes even more worrying. Poisoning himself with over-the-counter medications or huge quantities of alcohol, burning himself with cigarette lighters, and violent struggles with Lisa become the norm. Sunday evenings usually culminate in Joshua begging Lisa to take him to hospital. Hoping to keep everyone safe, Lisa has Megan sleep in with her. She puts locks on the inside of her own bedroom door and on the outside of Joshua's.

Soon after he turns 18, Joshua is admitted briefly to a psychiatric ward and discharged with anti-psychotic medication.

Kevin, a social worker from the Community Mental Health Team, conducts a further assessment. Lisa is shocked that Kevin adheres stringently to 'patient confidentiality', saying he is unable to share his assessment/treatment plan. Kevin advises Lisa to keep medication, alcohol, matches and lighters in locked cupboards. Triage nurses in A&E subsequently treat Joshua for any physical injuries and then discharge him straight home. Joshua receives a grant to buy a punch bag.

Lisa is heartbroken to watch her bright, articulate boy lose his place at college and shut himself away, his crises as frequent and intense as ever. She fears for the family's safety.

Lisa's worries are heightened when Megan's school ask to meet with her. Megan has been praised and encouraged for her story-writing since she was five years old but her stories are now very gruesome: frightening story lines involving the paranormal, knives and fire have taken over from her earlier talent for creating magical characters.

- What assessments are needed?
- Which service(s) should be involved in assessment?
- What are the questions for assessment by adult services?
- What are the questions for assessment by children's services?
- What do we need to understand in order to help this family?

Principles of participation and partnership
People who use social services have expertise that encompasses knowledge and understanding of:

- their memories, experiences, wishes and needs
- the significance they attribute to their experiences
- the culture, beliefs and expectations held within their family, network of friends, and community
- their sense of who they are and where they belong
- services and the workers they have engaged with
- the specific difficulties they face
- what works best for them.

Whether based in adult or children's services, social workers are most valued when they can offer support and advocacy. The phrase 'critical fixers' has been coined to express the idea that social workers should engage in a practice:

> which identifies commonalities as well as differences and which utilizes the opportunities created by legal rules…to challenge disabling barriers and to work for structural change as well as individual outcomes.
>
> (Braye and Preston-Shoot 2010, p.26)

Starting from the assumption that social work engages family members as equal participants, assessments can determine the freedom, choice and support afforded to families. The opportunity to experience control and self-efficacy through participation can enhance health and well-being (Leeson 2007). However, various services may take a different approach to participation, sometimes leaving families baffled by the apparent inconsistency they encounter.

Many experts through experience are highly critical of current social work approaches to assessment (Beresford 2007, p.5). Assessment practice in adult services is called to account as:

- led by resources rather than need
- based on deficit models
- incompatible with independent living/self-directed approaches.

In children's services the National Assessment Framework largely neglects the development of supportive partnership-working (Millar and Corby 2006). 'Post-modern' critics of welfare bureaucracy, theorists concerned with professional ethics, and campaigning groups that represent experts through experience agree that current assessment practice is tainted by association with a social work ethos that was:

> invariably exploitative and repressive because of its failure to recognise difference and its reliance on totalising belief systems, be these patriarchal, capitalist or socialist.
>
> (Parton 2002, p.240)

The challenges

EXERCISE

Consider a family that you have assessed recently.

- What level of participation in the assessment process were you able to offer each member of the family?

- What enabled their participation?

- What limited their participation?

- What contribution did they make to designing the assessment process?

- What factors limited the degree of self-determination afforded to each family member?

The degree to which parents are able to engage in assessments can be seen as a stairway leading progressively towards full participation and partnership (Figure 2.2).

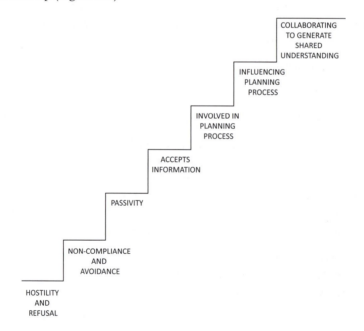

Figure 2.2 The partnership stairway (adapted from Raynes 2003, p.123)

Partnership does not always fit easily with social workers' responsibilities. The welfare system is structured around legal duties to provide certain services, rather than entitlement. This means that people may be refused support they feel they need, experience assessment and securing services as a battle, find their needs are misunderstood, and experience insensitive or inadequate services (Buckner and Yeandle 2011; Robinson and Williams 2002):

> In a society which promotes a self-help, enterprise culture, valuing responsibility and the ability to provide for oneself, to be publicly identified as 'needy' has an inevitably stigmatizing effect. To be chosen for state intervention somehow lowers citizenship status, confirming the neediness as some form of pathology.
>
> (Braye and Preston-Shoot 2010, p.37)

This creates a kind of double jeopardy for parents who need support so that they can parent to their best ability, as well as help in their own right.

Points to consider

In your experience:

- What works best to engage parents as active partners?
- What are your employer's expectations about families' participation?
- What processes are in place to engage parents as active partners?
- What gets in the way of engaging parents as partners?

Whole family assessment addresses a continuum, from supporting families on their own terms to enforcing measures to safeguard some family members from others (Figure 2.3).

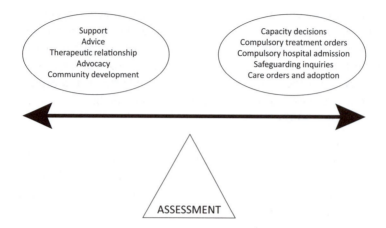

Figure 2.3 The care–control continuum

Using strengths-based approaches

> They said that I failed to protect them, but what was I supposed
> to do? I had no help. I had no support, so I had to manage it my
> way, and of course it was wrong. In fact I thought I was protecting
> them, you just cannot win.

> (Mother quoted by Children's Commissioner 2010, p.23)

EXERCISE
What strategies do you use to maintain:

• good physical health?

• good mental health?

• a healthy work–life balance?

The overwhelming message from families is that they do not want to
be passive recipients of professional assessment, be defined by their
problems, or engage with workers who seem preoccupied with rooting
out dysfunction. People value assessments that can envisage possibilities
and potential (without minimising difficulties) by 'seeing them in the
round'. Like most parents, those facing life difficulties develop a range
of strategies to manage and enhance their daily lives.

Research conducted with people in emotional/mental distress has demonstrated the enormous diversity of approaches they use to take control of their lives (Mental Health Foundation 1996). Disabled parents and parents needing additional support call for social workers to recognise the strengths and resources they and their extended family offer (Morris and Wates 2006, p.xviii). Mothers' accounts of domestic abuse suggest that each creates complex strategies to deal with violence and shelter their children, striving to be 'good mothers' under difficult circumstances (Radford and Hester 2006). Lapierre (2010) found that the most effective intervention and protection plans were based on assessments that identified domestic abuse victims' successful strategies as well as ones that failed. Some apparent 'difficulties' may not be problems at all. For example, deaf children born to deaf parents do better academically, are more mature and have higher self-esteem than deaf children with hearing parents (Morris and Wates 2006, p.3).

Case study

Elaine has had problems with alcohol and heroin since she was 15 years old. She allowed her older sister to raise her first child and her second was removed from her when he was 18 months old. Ten years later she is pregnant with her third child and children's services intend to arrange a pre-birth assessment.

An initial meeting is held involving:

- a counsellor in a voluntary sector problem drug/alcohol use service who has known Elaine for three years

- a social worker in adult mental health services who first met Elaine six months ago after a suicide attempt

- a midwife with a specialist role to support heroin users from their second trimester to six months after birth

- a newly-assigned children's social worker who has not met Elaine but has read the files relating to the removal of her second child.

It is immediately clear that they have very different opinions about the outcome they hope for. Early in their discussion they complete the continuum shown in Figure 2.4.

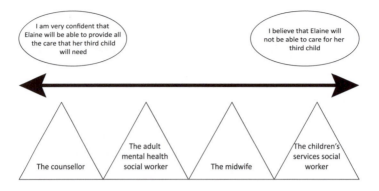

Figure 2.4 Using a continuum to explore disagreements

- What might explain their disagreement?
- What issues do they need to explore in this initial discussion?
- What are the questions for assessment?
- How should the different perspectives of these four professionals be shared with Elaine?

Strengths-based approaches and social work share a foundation in systems theory as well as their emphasis on self-determination and partnership. Different strengths-based approaches have developed in different fields of practice and now play a part in many adult and children's services:

- Motivational Interviewing (MI) is widely used in work with problem drug and alcohol use. MI explores and resolves ambivalence, and elicits and strengthens motivation for change, focusing particularly on the individual identifying their own rehabilitation goals (Miller and Rollnick 1991).

- The Recovery Model now informs much social work practice with people in emotional/mental distress. This means focusing on supporting recovery and building resilience, rather than merely managing symptoms (Copeland and Mead 2000; Davidson 2005).

- Self-directed Support for disabled adults assumes that they have the skills and capacity to identify and manage the support they need (Manthorpe *et al.* 2011).

- Appreciative Inquiry (AI) developed as a tool for organisational development. It is based on the assumption that asking questions about success enables individuals to identify and access their assets and resources (Cooperrider and Whitney 1999).

- Inclusive Solutions has developed a range of tools and techniques for person-centred planning. These tools have been developed in the context of person-centred planning for children and adults, personal and group development. They are often used to address challenging behaviour and meet the emotional needs of children and adults with intellectual impairment. These approaches provide a focus and structure for discussion, bringing together the person concerned with a group of helpers. The process is supported by graphic illustration. A large drawing, like a collective mind map, gradually captures the group's thinking. At the heart of each tool is a commitment to inclusion and a focus on the whole person, transcending the label or diagnosis that might otherwise determine planning (Wilson and Newton 2011).

- The Positive Parenting Programme (Triple P) is widely used in children's services. It aims to give parents simple strategies that prevent problems in families before they arise and create family environments that encourage children to realise their potential (Sanders 2008).

- Solutions Focused Therapy emphasises the strengths people invariably possess and how these can be harnessed to create change. It focuses on helping people identify how they would like their lives to be by 'creating through language an experience of the preferred future'. The therapist eschews claiming expertise and works to create a non-hierarchical collaboration. This approach emphasises active listening and the hypnotherapist Milton Erickson's principle of 'utilisation' – consciously choosing to join with people's passions and ways of being so as to connect with them (Rossi and Ryan 1998). Many social workers in both adult and children's services deploy some of the methods used in a solutions focused therapy (de Shazer 1985; Ratner, George and Iveson 2012).

- The Coaching Cycle is used in some youth services. The assumption is that people possess the necessary resources to resolve their own problems (Iveson, George and Ratner 2012; Laske 2009).

- The Signs of Safety Model is designed to bring solutions focused therapy principles and methods into child protection. It frames risk assessment as a constructive undertaking to explore the problem, at the same time as focusing on building solutions and a safe future. This approach was developed in the context of child protection but can be used equally effectively in families or networks where there is concern for an adult's safety and well-being (Turnell 2012; Turnell and Edwards 1999).

EXERCISE

Watch any episode of the BBC comedy 'The Royle Family' or the Channel 4 show 'Shameless' with a group of colleagues. Agree between you to form two 'teams'. One team should watch out for all the family's protective factors and resources, the other for risks, stressors and vulnerabilities.

- Compare the observations made by the two teams.

- Were the two teams able to achieve a consensus about any specific issues?

- Would you have felt more comfortable in the other team?

If you can do this with colleagues from across a range of adult and children's services, this exercise is a great starting point for a discussion about different priorities and thresholds.

Resilience

Resilience does not constitute an individual trait or characteristic… Resilience involves a range of processes that bring together quite diverse mechanisms.

(Rutter 1999, p.135)

Assessing resilience is always complex. Practitioners from different settings might weight information differently from each other and see the same family's resources and difficulties from starkly different perspectives. Resilience is a complex but important concept in whole family assessment because it can inform planning and action. Children often need help to 'play a bad hand well' (Katz 1997) so that they can thrive despite living with persistent disadvantages.

Reder *et al.* (2003) identified sources of resilience that are particularly valuable for parents facing life difficulties. These include:

- stable relationship with a partner
- success in another unrelated area of life, for example sports, education, work
- self-efficacy – a sense that they are in control of their lives
- ability to reflect
- for those abused in childhood, having had one supportive relationship with a safe adult and being able to confront and reflect on experiences, acknowledge the details of abuse with appropriate affect, gain perspective and integrate the experience, and forgive the abusive parent.

Resilience in childhood derives from a mixture of nature and nurture. Multiple risk and protective factors are involved. Sources of resilience include:

- factors within the individual such as temperament, intelligence, conventional good looks, birth-weight and gender (girls are more resilient up to adolescence, boys from adolescence onwards)
- warm, positive, close relationships
- support from the wider community, for example from neighbours, a faith community or social services.

The International Resilience Project (Grotberg 1997) concluded that across different cultures, the building blocks for resilience in children are:

- a secure base, where the child feels a sense of belonging and security and will grow up able to say 'I have people that I trust and love'
- good self-esteem, an internal sense of their own worth and competence that enables the child to feel 'I am a lovable person'
- self-efficacy, a sense of mastery and control, along with accurate understanding of personal strengths and limitations so that the child has confidence in their ability to solve problems.

Case study

Alison Lapper is an acclaimed artist. Her autobiography, *My Life in My Hands*, describes her experiences as a disabled child, adult and parent.

- What are the sources of Alison's resilience in childhood?
- What adversities has Alison faced?
- What strengths has Alison harnessed to empower her as an adult?
- What are Alison's needs as a parent?
- What are her son's needs and rights?

Children who have been helped to develop resilient strategies are better equipped to resist stress, manage adversity and cope with change (Gilligan 2007). They are able to recover more quickly and completely from any traumatic experiences (Newman and Blackburn 2002).

There is some truth in Nietzche's adage 'what doesn't kill you strengthens you' ('Was dich nicht umbringt macht dich stärker') implying that adversity has a 'steeling' effect (Nietzche 1992; Rutter 1999). But beware of resilience as a double-edged sword! Parents and children who are demonstrably successful may still need help and support. It would be naïve to assume that evidence of coping indicates resilience. For example, children may cope with their parents' problem drinking but this does not necessarily equate with healthy and positive outcomes (Adamson and Templeton 2012, p.9). Factors or processes that seem positive in the short term may be less helpful, or even harmful in the longer term. For example, at 16, Sabine presents as a strong and competent young woman, but toward the end of her interview in *Being Seen and Heard* (Royal College of Psychiatrists 2004) speaks poignantly about her inability to be playful and describes herself as 'suicidal, really suicidal'.

Case study

Cynthia has experienced emotional/mental distress throughout her adult life but holds the view that medication is harmful to her. She did not have children until her early 40s and is a single parent. Whenever the stresses of lone parenting overwhelm her she slides into manic behaviour and is usually admitted to hospital at least once a year. As soon as she receives medication her mood stabilises, and she soon feels ready to return to the challenges of parenting. As a black mother of children with mixed ethnic origin, on a predominantly white estate, she often experiences overt racism. Cynthia's daughters Alyssia and Danielle perform well academically at school, maintain close friendships and are generally popular. They always present at school immaculately groomed, impeccably dressed and are invariably polite and co-operative towards staff, children and parents. The only obvious problem that has ever come to light in school is that Alyssia has very regular, positive contact with her father whereas Danielle has never met hers and sometimes feels jealous of her sister.

- What evidence is there of resilience in this family?
- What stressors and vulnerabilities would an adult mental health worker be concerned about?
- What different interpretations might explain the children's presentation?
- What are the questions for assessment in adult services?
- What are the questions for assessment in children's services?
- What would be the benefits of adult and children's services working together to assess this family?

Fonagy's definition of resilience as 'normal development under difficult conditions' (Fonagy *et al.* 1994) draws attention to the importance of thinking about children's resilience in terms of their developmental potential. We have a good research evidence base (Jones, Hindley and Ramchandani 2006, cited by Brown and Ward 2012, p.22) to help us understand how certain protective factors can help to mitigate the impact on children where a parent's behaviour is harmful. These include:

- a non-abusive partner
- a supportive extended family
- parents' ability to recover from harmful experiences in their own childhood
- parents' ability to recognise and take responsibility for the harm their behaviour causes
- parents' willingness to engage with services.

The cumulative build-up of stressors undermines resilience in children living in troubled families. Horwath's resilience/vulnerability matrix is a tool you can use to map the adversity children in a family face, protection they experience, resilience they enjoy and vulnerabilities they have to overcome (Figure 2.5). This enables you to analyse the complex interaction between vulnerability and resilience with protection and adversity to identify need and design helpful interventions.

The Scottish government created an expanded version available on-line at www.scotland.gov.uk/Topics/People/Young-People/getting itright/national-practice-model/resilience-matrix.

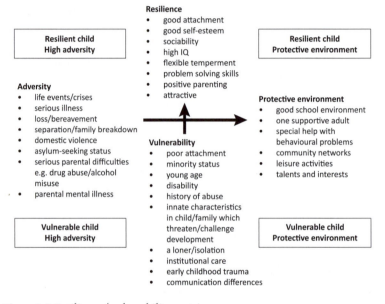

Figure 2.5 Resilience /vulnerability matrix

Case study continued

Use the resilience matrix to map what you know about Alyssia and Danielle's circumstances.

- To what extent do protective factors offset the adversities they each face?

- What resilience factors does Alyssia benefit from?

- What adversities does Danielle face?

Meeting together to share the differing perspectives of the parents, a worker involved with the adults and a children's social worker can deepen understanding of both the parents' and the children's experience.

The dynamic between family strengths and vulnerabilities

> The concept of child protection automatically pits the child against the parent...this thinking leads to the adversarial practice that has dominated the field, but we are finally coming to recognise that 'blood is thicker than child protection services'.
>
> (Turnell and Edwards 1999, Foreword by I.K. Berg)

Social workers' perspectives on protective factors and vulnerability within a particular family may be different depending on their role. Social workers sometimes have to assert children's and adults' right to protection from more powerful family members and this in turn can have implications for how best to engage families in assessments where there is a risk of harm.

Case study continued

Look back again at the Green family case study.

- Which members of this family have experienced harm?
- Who is at risk of future harm?
- What will be adult services' top priority?
- What will be children's services top priority?
- What dangerous behaviours need to be reduced or eliminated?
- What goals for change might Lisa identify?
- What is working well?
- What protective factors are already in place?

Assessments that simply enumerate reported or perceived strengths and weakness are pointless and dangerous (Kelly 1996). Searching for strengths should not distract workers' attention from the impact of parents' harmful behaviour on their children. There is a danger of confusing evidence of strengths with evidence of protection or safety (Parton and O'Byrne 2000). In whole family assessment it is helpful to ask 'How might this particular strength or resource help this family overcome the difficulties it faces?'

The definition of safety as 'strengths demonstrated as protection over time' (McPherson, Macnamara and Hemsworth 1997) enables assessors to elicit information about strengths and resources available to families and give respectful weight to these, whilst interrogating whether and how these strengths translate into positive family experiences and protection. Bear in mind that any strengths and stressors might have complex and different implications for each family member. For example, when a couple have separated acrimoniously, contact with the family of the estranged parent may be a positive resource for the children but a source of stress for the main carer; meanwhile, finding a new partner might provide welcome support to the parent but create difficulties for the children.

You can begin to interrogate these processes, by asking parents and children for their insights as well as drawing on information elicited from colleagues working with the family.

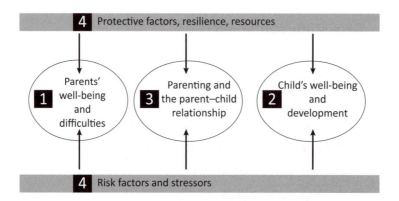

Figure 2.6 Exploring the protection Lisa provides, Megan's vulnerability and resilience, and the adversities the family faces (adapted from Falkov, 2012)

Case study continued

Look back again at the Green family case study.

- What resources does Lisa benefit from?

- In what sense do these resources serve as a protective factor for Megan?

- What stressors have impacted on the relationship between Lisa and Megan?
- What are the risk factors for Joshua?

Assessing denial and ambivalence

A parent who has harmed their child, particularly in the case of sexual and/or physical abuse, faces a challenging dilemma. An admission of responsibility will leave the parent liable to criminal prosecution. But an unexplained injury and denial of responsibility makes it much more likely that the civil court will find significant harm in care proceedings and remove children from the family. A non-abusive co-parent/partner can be caught in the same dilemma. Seeking to understand what might drive a parent to deny or minimise what they have done need not mean colluding with what they have done (Dale 2004).

Jenkins (1990), working in Australia with men who had committed serious violent or sexual offences, 'invites' people to take responsibility for their actions, by pursuing the 'grain of honour' that might enable the offender to begin to see his behaviour through a more self-critical lens. The concept of externalising problems (White 1995) can help get to the heart of parents' perspectives where they present as both personally troubled and harmful to others. Exploring family 'scripts' (Byng-Hall 1995) may help make sense of any contradictions between how parents perceive themselves and unwanted, harmful patterns of behaviour.

Skilfully managed, honest, gentle, subtle discussions can sometimes enable parents to shift from outright denial to taking responsibility for a safe family future, so that workers can create conditions of 'safe uncertainty' (Robinson and Witney 1999). Families need to be willing to address the concerns even if they do not agree with them. Sometimes this willingness amounts to little more than wanting to 'get the social workers off our backs'.

EXERCISE

To get a sense of the conflicted position parents can get caught up in, watch *The Woodsman*. Directed (and co-written with Steven Fechter) by Nicole Kassell in 2004, it portrays Walter, a convicted child sex offender recently released from prison. Walter is befriended by Vickie, a single parent he meets in his new workplace. He is distrusted and shunned by his sister and brother-in-law and closely watched by a suspicious police officer, Detective Lucas. The film explores the ethical dilemmas they each face.

- What evidence is there of the 'grain of honour' within Walter?
- What evidence is there to justify surveillance by Lucas?
- How does Vickie reconcile her affection for Walter with her feelings about his past?
- What might 'forgiveness' mean in this context?

Social workers can find it very hard to conceive of parents as partners in assessment if they believe the parent to be implicated in harming their child, and this sometimes causes disagreements between workers. When families simply deny abuse it cannot always be formulated as a family matter. For example constructive approaches to working with denial are not relevant when families are targeted and abused by an intrusive predator. Social workers are necessarily drawn into a more forensic, investigative approach:

- if a parent is believed to have harmed a child but denies responsibility
- if a parent is unable to provide a plausible explanation for harm a child has experienced
- if a parent does not take steps to protect a child from harm
- if a parent is believed to have fabricated or induced illness in a child.

Social workers might, understandably, respond at a human, emotional level with anger or disgust and need to acknowledge those feelings but consciously set them aside in order to design assessments that are both participatory and rigorous.

Wherever there is a concern that children could be harmed, workers have to fulfil responsibilities that inevitably involve varying degrees of coercion. Skilful exercise of authority is needed to ensure that families retain as much control as possible without compromising the worker's role. This might involve simple measures such as encouraging parents to use advocates and offering hostile parents a choice between negotiating when, where and how meetings will take place, or, alternatively, knowing that professional discussions will take place in their absence. The Resolutions Approach applies systemic perspectives and solutions focused methodology where parents deny or minimise their responsibility for children who are or have been harmed. It aims to reduce risk of harm despite uncertainty and ambiguity so that families can stay together. Assessment focuses on understanding what changes can be made to promote safety (Essex *et al.* 1996; Turnell and Essex 2006).

Generating knowledge and expertise

> If you don't know what's wrong with a patient, ask him, he may tell you.
>
> (Kelly, quoted in Bannister and Fransella 1980, p.75)

Personal construct theory describes 'self-characterisation' as a first principle for assessment. If past behaviour is, indeed, the best indicator of future behaviour then families, knowing their own track record, are in pole position to predict what might work best. Families generally understand a great deal about the difficulties they face and assessment processes can give them opportunities to articulate this knowledge.

Even young children can offer rich understanding and straightforward information that might otherwise be missing: just ask them! Assessors need not fear that involving children in assessment will be detrimental to them. Children of problem drug/alcohol users parents say that being involved in finding solutions to problems helps them to cope, especially in the context of a strong relationship with a support worker (Bancroft *et al.* 2004). Young people don't necessarily want a professional to sort out all the problems but prefer to help plan changes alongside someone they trust so that they can still feel some sense of control (Cossar, Brandon and Jordan 2011, p.10).

If trust has been created, direct, probing, explicit, questions (put tactfully!) enable parents to voice their own concerns about family life. Many parents will give an honest account of how their difficulties impact on their children (Daniel, Taylor and Scott 2010). For example, problem drug users are generally aware of safety issues as well as how their own emotional state impacts on their children (SCIE 2004). Parents describe asking for help when they knew they needed it, long before the crisis that precipitated social work assessment (Bostock *et al.* 2005; Children's Commissioner 2010; Dale 2004; Scottish Executive 2002).

In reviews of child deaths it often emerges that parents had already talked about the danger they posed, by saying things like 'I'm at the end of my tether' or asking for children to be accommodated (Reder and

Duncan 1999). This means embracing the possibility that families may conceptualise danger in ways that differ from researcher and professional constructs of risk (Adams 2001; Clarke 2000). Misdirected worry about causing offence, and avoiding embarrassing or culturally sensitive questions can leave families with unmet needs and even put them in danger. For example, Fiona Pilkington killed herself and her disabled 18-year-old daughter after years of harassment that went unrecognised as disability hate crime (Independent Police Complaints Commission 2011).

Family group conferences often elicit a rich understanding of the history and extent of a family's problems, and new insights into its strengths, as well as identifying resources and ways forward. They originated in New Zealand where families, white European and Maori workers collaborated to develop a narrative model that perceived culture, belief and personal experience as a source of strength (Tamasese and Waldegrave 1994). Despite academic interest in narrative approaches, assessments still silence families if undue power is invested in professionals:

> I was always told that you couldn't challenge it, as it's always used against you.
>
> (Parent quoted by Children's Commissioner 2010, p.16)

The frustrations parents and children express about having no influence in assessments are backed up by evidence from audits and inspections. One review of case records found that fewer than 20 per cent of families were provided with basic information about the assessment process or with written agreements (Scottish Executive 2002, cited by Fauth *et al.* 2010, p.37). Assessment agreements sometimes amount to a set of instructions. No wonder parents and children subsequently feel angry when they sign up to an agreement they have had no say in and disagree with (Bostock *et al.* 2005; Dale 2004).

The social work relationship

> It took some time, but I think finally she understood. I was making choices, weighing up the options. Thinking about what was safe for my children. She seemed to stop seeing me as this battered woman, and moved to thinking I was someone who she could

work with. I don't know what made the difference, but it was great. It meant that we could work together.

(Parent quoted by Children's Commissioner 2010, p.41)

Points to consider

- What personal qualities do you bring to building social work relationships?
- How do you negotiate the assessment process?
- How do you describe your assessment role?
- Where/when are you least likely to engage well?
- What are the differences between how adult and children's workers build relationships with people?

Spratt and Callan (2004) looked into how parents feel about children's social workers and found that successful working relationships were usually formed even though they felt apprehensive. They concluded that:

Social workers display considerable skills in monitoring risks while engaging with families...and...the subtleties involved in such activity are not captured by official measures of performance which concentrate on more abstract indicators...

(Spratt and Callan 2004, p.199)

Shiatsu practitioners and other body therapists learn to 'listen' with their fingers and see with the 'third eye'... Perhaps, social work experience teaches us listen with a third ear.

These subtle skills include bringing awareness of how stressful being assessed can feel and recognising that stress interferes with listening and communication (Dickenson, Johnson and Samson Katz 1993). If this is not taken into account, assessments can generate misleading information because the family behaves differently from usual. When workers from both adult and children's services are involved in statutory assessments, it is easy for the adult worker's support role and the children's worker's investigative role to polarise them as 'good' or 'bad'. Children's social workers are most likely to err towards a more forensic and confrontational approach to assessment during child protection inquiries. This is a problem because partnership and relationship-based work are essential where there is risk of harm so that the assessment can set the pace for positive change – and all the more so where families feign compliance or present as difficult to engage, hostile, evasive or actively deceitful (Barlow and Scott 2010; Brandon *et al.* 2009; Platt 2006a, b, 2008).

Points to consider

- What 'subtle skills' do you employ to create helpful relationships with individuals and families at the same time as monitoring their safety?

- How do you manage the tension between your statutory duties to investigate harm and the need to engage with families?

- Have your relationships with families ever broken down?

- How were these breakdowns resolved?

Not surprisingly, parents and social workers share a sense that it is easier to form a constructive relationship in informal assessments than in formal investigations (Platt 2008, cited by Fauth *et al.* 2010, p.43). But this relatively simple account of the power dynamic is not the whole story. In all our relationships, our interactions are determined by the meaning we have for each other. Past experiences, for example of poverty, mental illness, social/cultural factors, or our current context all impact on how we engage in relationships. Assessment relationships can be overwhelmed by unresolved 'care and control' conflicts (Reder and Duncan 1999). Experience of damaging relationships with previous assessors who used power destructively can colour the family's approach to social workers they meet later:

> They want you to give up everything, to come out and say, you are right, I am a bad parent, I have made all the wrong choices, and then they would be happy. But I can't, because I do not think it's true.
>
> (Parent quoted by Children's Commissioner 2010, p.20)

Research with parents in Ontario found it is how parents perceive the *use* of power that determines their response to workers (Dumbrill 2006). When power is used coercively *over* parents they either battle with the social worker or take a line of least resistance by appearing to co-operate. When professionals use power *with* and to support parents, for example by advocating on their behalf, a collaborative relationship is generated.

Parents tend to put the difference down to the style or personality of their social worker. However, Dumbrill found that one family might describe a social worker as frightening and coercive, but another family might report that the same worker had used power authoritatively to support, advocate and arbitrate for the family. This study concluded that a complex mix of variables produced the parents' perception of how power was played out with the worker and determined how their relationship developed.

The implication of these findings is that, rather than launching into discussions about the family's problem when they first meet, social workers need to start by exploring how the family anticipates power will play out between them and then asking how they feel about this. Practitioners report that explaining their role, their responsibility and the assessment process enables parents to identify shared goals and feel fully involved (Saint-Jacques *et al.* 2006, cited by Fauth *et al.* 2010). This idea fits with the social theory that 'noise-free' communication relies on an ethical commitment to addressing power dynamics (Habermas 1984). It should come as no surprise to social workers trained as 'skilled helpers' to address power issues via immediacy process questions such as 'How are you and I doing?' and 'What's going on between you and me right now?' (Egan 2002).

The assessment relationship as ecosystem

> Speech is not what one should desire to understand, one should know the speaker.
>
> The deed is not what one should desire to understand, one should know the doer.
>
> Mind is not what one should desire to understand, one should know the thinker.
>
> (Kaushitake Upanishad, 3:8)

Wherever families have contact with several different professionals, with different public agencies and with both adult and children's services, they are caught up in a complex web of relationships. Workers they meet may have quite different expectations of the degree of autonomy and partnership each family member should exercise. Every social worker brings their own personal style of practice as well as a set of specific responsibilities that will affect the way they relate to each family member and how their role in the family is perceived.

Ecological approaches to social work practice emphasise the importance of the worker paying attention to his/her own place in the world of the persons/people being assessed (Bronfenbrenner 1979).

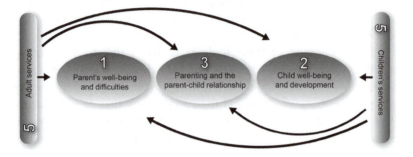

Figure 2.7 Taking into account the impact of services in the families you work with (adapted from Falkov, 2012)

Points to consider

Think about an assessment you are currently undertaking.

- What is the impact of your involvement with the family on the parent's health and well-being?

- How is your involvement in the family perceived in their culture and community?

- Has your involvement contributed to the family's strengths and resources?

- What effect do you anticipate the assessment process will have on parent–child relationships?

A systemic approach to assessing family difficulties requires the worker to focus on relationships, and on how each individual is both a participant and a contributor in their social environment. From this perspective the assessor becomes, however temporarily, a participant in the family ecosystem and impacts on it. Pre-verbal children and family pets can be very sensitive to mood and act out feelings they pick up in the home. For example pets may distract assessors from their purpose, overwhelming them (whether with friendliness or hostility) at key moments of stress in home visits.

The process of assessment is to describe, and to decode, the complex barrage of information that flows when people meet. It should be a shared review of the family's past and present experience and a shared anticipation of the future. Personal construct theory frames assessment as an interactive process of communication in which we endeavour to understand the other person. The full significance of what others want to convey is filtered through the meanings we attribute to what we can see, hear and sense. Workers' ability to secure rapport and a shared language with individual family members is crucial to accessing useful information. Understanding relies on the assessor investing wholeheartedly in this engagement. The quality of the social work relationship becomes part of the story and inevitably influences the quality of the assessment (Calder and Hackett 2003, p.35).

People are constantly confronted with choices and each choice made, in turn, places the chooser in new conditions and produces new consequences. It is how we make sense of these experiences that makes us unique, and how we construe others and ourselves accounts for our sense of identity. It is therefore not enough to look at someone in terms of reported facts about their history and circumstances. Assessment demands that we see these through their eyes, and try to understand what they say and do now in the light of how they make sense of their experiences.

Alongside being sensitive to the power they wield in the assessment process, social workers also need to take into account the power dynamics within each family. For example, using a child as interpreter or translator for their parent creates a whole new dimension to their relationships during and after the interview. Similarly, social workers need to consider the particular dynamics within a family when they decide what questions to ask a child and what information it is appropriate to share with each family member (Cossar *et al.* 2011).

Case study continued

For example, thinking again about the Green family, we can map key aspects of Kevin's role as a social worker from the Community Mental Health Team who conducted an assessment of Joshua at home following his discharge from psychiatric hospital.

	Priorities	Responsibilities	Authority
Joshua	To assess Joshua with a view to making a full recovery from this initial episode of illness To minimise Joshua's experience of stigma and labelling To prevent Joshua becoming institutionalised	To assess Joshua and refer for further psychiatric treatment as needed To assess and implement a plan of intervention to enhance Joshua's recovery To respect Joshua's right to confidentiality	To implement Mental Health Act and secure hospital treatment for Joshua if he represents a risk to himself or others
Lisa	To elicit relevant information from Lisa about Joshua's behaviour and progress To engage her support in enabling Joshua to remain safely at home	To consider whether Lisa is at risk from Joshua	
Ethan	To ensure Lisa's care of Ethan does not compromise her ability to meet Joshua's needs	To consider whether Joshua poses a risk to Ethan	To refer to children's services as needed
Emily	To ensure that family relationships do not jeopardise Joshua's recovery	To consider whether Joshua poses a risk to Emily	To refer to children's services as needed
Megan	To ensure that Megan's behaviour does not exacerbate Joshua's distress	To consider whether Joshua poses a risk to Megan	To refer to children's services as needed

Amy	None	None	None
Sophie	None	None	None
Dave	None	None	None
Mark	None	None	None

Figure 2.8 The web of responsibility

- What priorities would be in the forefront for:
    1. triage nurses in A&E?
    2. a social worker in problem drug/alcohol use services?
    3. the support worker in Megan's nurture group?
- What are the responsibilities of:
    1. the head-teacher at Megan's school?
    2. the family GP?
    3. Lisa as Emily's parent?
- What authority can be exercised by:
    1. the CAMHS family therapist?
    2. the psychiatrist that admitted Joshua to hospital?
    3. Lisa as Megan's parent?
    4. What are Kevin's responsibilities towards Amy's family?

Setting off on the right foot

She started off by saying 'I am going to be honest with you' and this led to a ten minute look at what was wrong with our family. I was tempted to say 'I am going to be honest with you' but you cannot do it can you? So we all sat there and listened to how bad we were as a family. And secretly, as this was my only power, I thought I am not going to tell you anything.

(Mother quoted by Children's Commissioner 2010, p.32)

Social workers sometimes meet families who are described as hostile, avoidant, manipulative, dishonest or 'playing the game'. Meanwhile some families describe workers who are rude and aggressive, using power *over* rather than *with* them (Dale 2004; Dumbrill 2006; Scottish Executive 2002). Workers and families can get stuck in vicious circles where they become more hostile or more mealy-mouthed, and mutual distrust deepens (Children's Commissioner 2010):

> They call us reluctant, but they make us like that. We are resisting oppression. Fear makes us defensive. I will never have children as both me and my partner have been in care and I think that they (the social workers) will take the child away. I cannot risk it.

(Young person quoted by Children's Commissioner 2010, p.20)

Unfortunately, the evidence that resistance is a reaction to aggressive social workers and inadequate practice is borne out by research evidence and reviews of child deaths. Some workers bring negative, judgemental, confrontational and aggressive attitudes to the assessment relationship (Cameron and Coady 2007; Dale 2004). A series of connected studies found that workers tended to slip into directly challenging, contradicting or ignoring people who they perceived as resistant, whereas the more someone disclosed, the more workers reflected with them and explored their strengths (Forrester *et al.* 2008a, b, cited by Fauth *et al.* 2010, p.45). Social workers tended towards confrontational, even aggressive communication styles and did not listen! This pattern is mirrored when organisations avoid families perceived as 'difficult' by closing cases, switching workers, losing files. These processes often account for how social workers fail to meet the needs both of adults at risk of harm and of neglected, disabled and older children (Brandon *et al.* 2008; Ofsted 2011).

It is normal for parents to feel anxious and distressed under scrutiny and distressed or angry when their family life comes under theat. This means that social workers' perceptions of parents' attitudes and attributes may not be a good source of assessment information. If a parent is articulate, plausible, apparently committed, and concerned we are more inclined to see them as safe and open to change (Holland 2000). But is a parent who is inarticulate, passive or unco-operative necessarily more dangerous to the child than someone who is friendly and likeable? The question should be 'Why have I failed to engage with this family?' not 'Why is this family so difficult to work with?'

EXERCISE

Next time you start an assessment:

- Ask about previous experiences of being assessed.

- Ask whether the person feels you are more likely to use power over them or with them.

- Acknowledge and accept whatever feelings are expressed about your power.

- If you sense that someone is fighting you or is only pretending to collaborate with you, talk again about the power dynamic.

These ideas are not new! Rees (1978) found that difficult social work relationships arise when workers and families have different goals and do not communicate. Negotiation is the way forward. Don't imagine that taking this approach will give you and the family equality. You are still the more powerful partner, but addressing the power dynamic increases the chances of reaching a good whole family assessment.

Trust

EXERCISE

Think back to a relationship you have had with a professional helper that you trusted.

- What personal qualities in that person encouraged your trust?

- What did that person do to gain your trust?

- How did that trust make you feel about your situation?

- What did your trust in that person enable you to achieve?

If we want to negotiate ideas and understand another's worldview we have to create trust. Going out of the way to help, keeping promises, being consistent and reliable all earn respect as well as trust (Hopkins and Niemiec 2007). Trust can only exist in relationships that are honest and workers therefore have a responsibility to demonstrate openness and transparency. The Johari window (Figure 2.9) is a communication model that is used to improve understanding between individuals (Luft and Ingham 1955). There are two key principles behind the idea:

- You can build trust with others by disclosing information about yourself.

- With the help of feedback from others you can learn about yourself, identify issues and set goals for change.

Known to self and known to others OPEN *You decide to tell the family that you feel anxious.*	Known to others but not known to self BLIND SPOT *You have decided not to mention this to the family and believe that you have successfully overcome any signs of anxiety. In fact, the family sense your anxiety – including their dog!*
Known to self but not known to others HIDDEN *You never sleep well when you have to do something new or difficult. You know that your anxiety about this form will keep you awake tonight.*	Not known to others and known to self UNKNOWN *Your immune system is compromised by the anxiety. One of the children picked up a stomach bug at school today, is contagious but not yet unwell. You will be ill over the weekend.*

Figure 2.9 The Johari window (adapted from Luft and Ingham 1955)

The open area represents all the things that you know about yourself and the things that others know about you, such as how you behave and any personal information you choose to share. The blind spot represents all the things about yourself that you are unaware of but that other people do know. The hidden area represents things that you know about yourself but that you keep private. The unknown area represents things that you don't consciously know and that others are unaware of. As you share information, the open area expands vertically so that the hidden area gets smaller. As the family give you feedback, your open area expands horizontally and the blind spot gets smaller.

Points to consider

- Which of your personal qualities do parents most appreciate?

- Which emotions are you least likely to express to others?

- Do you identify more closely with the experience of parents or children?

- How do you contain strong feelings (your own and others) when they arise during assessments?

Self-awareness is the foundation of relationship-based practice and mindful use of self is a powerful social work tool. People who choose to share information are usually easy to talk to. Their honesty and openness build trust and make others feel more comfortable. This does not mean that you have to share information that you wish to keep personal. Deciding what to share and when is a professional judgement.

Rights, responsibilities and needs

Human rights and social justice serve as the motivation and justification for social work action.

(The International Code of Social Work
Ethics, IASSW and IFSW 2005)

Case study

Nadia is a young woman of mixed heritage who suffered serious neglect in early childhood, and at 11 years old was physically and sexually abused by her stepfather. The whole of her extended family live on the same estate and are all involved to a greater or lesser extent in selling drugs. She and her six siblings have been in and out of care all their lives; only the youngest sister has achieved stability in a long-term placement. Nadia has problems with both alcohol and drugs, binge-drinks and uses heroin and cocaine as well as cannabis. Nadia is three months pregnant when she turns 18. She has to leave supported lodgings and has no realistic option but to return to her family. Children's social services refer her to SafeHaven, a voluntary organisation working with mothers who are problem drug users. After a pre-birth conference her new social worker asks Nadia to sign a written 'contract of expectations'. This document underpins a plan for the baby to stay in Nadia's care providing she uses neither alcohol nor any non-prescribed drugs. The document is explicit that should she fail to achieve this a care application will be made.

- What would you think about this intervention if you were the social worker at SafeHaven?

- If you were a family solicitor what legal advice would you give Nadia?

- What evidence base informs the approach adopted by children's services?

- What does Nadia need?

Campaigning groups have led the way in demanding changes to the relationship between the individual and the state. The eventual introduction of personal budgets for both adults and children who need support to enhance independence is the result of disabled group campaigns for their entitlement as citizens. Organisations such as YAYPIC and the Family Rights Group have long harnessed the rights perspective to challenge poor social work practice. Much of what is best about contemporary social work is attributable to the pioneering work of organisations led by experts through experience.

A human rights approach challenges the role of the state in family life by empowering individuals both in relation to others and in relation to the state (Brayne and Carr 2010). Social workers across all services have to take regard of individual rights but also exercise a responsibility to ensure the safety and address the needs of each individual within a family. Schofield and Thoburn (1996) suggested it is helpful to integrate these two perspectives by considering children's rights and welfare alongside each other rather than allowing them to compete for attention. For whole family assessment we need to go a step further to integrate the parents' rights and welfare as well.

Case study continued

Use Figure 2.10 to map the respective needs, rights and responsibilities of each member of the Green family.

	Rights	Responsibilities	Needs
Emily			
Joshua			
Amy			
Megan			
Ethan			
Olivia			
Lisa			
Dave			
Mark			
Justin			

Figure 2.10 Considering rights and responsibilities and needs

- What further information do you need?
- What fundamental issues still need to be addressed?
- What issues are likely to be contested?

Parents and children alike struggle to exercise their rights and responsibilities without the information they need. Colmer (2010) found that children of psychiatric patients felt excluded and bewildered, often misunderstanding the illness and their situation. Meanwhile psychiatric professionals said they did not feel equipped to talk with children. Children need to be given accurate and age-appropriate information about emotional/mental distress and psychiatric interventions (Roberts *et al.* 2008).

Case study continued

- Write down in a few sentences exactly what you would say:

     ∘   to explain Joshua's behaviour to Megan?

     ∘   to Megan about her new preoccupation with the macabre?

Conclusion

You've got to trust (the social worker) and she's got to trust you. Otherwise there's no point.

(Child quoted by Cossar *et al.* 2011, p.4)

Social work has long struggled with its identity. Is assessment a technical-rational process, a social science where decisions and intervention rely wholly on evidence-based practice or is it about building relationships to form subjective judgements and influence change? When any of us have to rely on professionals we usually value their humanity and simply want to take for granted that they will offer relevant knowledge and expertise. The contribution of experts through experience leaves us in little doubt that they mostly recognise and are affected by the person within the social workers they meet. Rapport is created when people recognise the self in each other. Social work demands a professional ability to act as a chameleon, to mirror the other while remaining true to the social work role and to the authentic self. If we hide behind our professionalism we cast away opportunities for heartfelt engagement and without that engagement there can be no understanding or benign influence. This approach is congruent with the principles on which social work and public service are founded, but its emphasis on the nurturing of compassionate and caring relationships has its roots in the 'ethics of care' (Banks 2006).

Further reading and resources

Akhtar, F. (2012) *Mastering Social Work Values and Ethics.* London: Jessica Kingsley Publishers.

Beresford, P. (2007) *The Changing Roles and Tasks of Social Work from Service Users' Perspectives: A Literature Informed Discussion Paper.* London: Shaping Our Lives.

Children's Commissioner (2010) *Family Perspectives on Safeguarding and on Relationships with Children's Services.* London: The Office of the Children's Commissioner.

Hart, A., Blincow, D. and Thomas, H. (2007) *Resilient Therapy. Working with Children and Families.* Hove: Routledge.

Turnell, A. and Edwards, S. (1999) *Signs of Safety: A Solution and Safety Oriented Approach to Child Protection.* New York: Norton.

CHAPTER 3

Constructive Collaboration

Key messages

- Working across adult and children's services rests on building honest, respectful relationships.

- Communication is key to creating and sustaining productive collaboration.

- Investing in collaborative professional relationships 'adds value' to whole family assessment.

- Working together improves the quality of information available, provides a sound knowledge base for designing effective assessments, and affords opportunities for robust critical analysis.

> They never speak to each other…like the mental health team never spoke to my mum's social worker…just pick up the phone you know? There's fax! There's th'internet! Why don't you just use it!
>
> (Carly, aged 21, a mother of baby twins, reflecting on her own childhood experiences in Royal College of Psychiatrists 2004)

The gulf between different services interferes with our capacity to assess the needs of both children and their parents. The use of eligibility criteria and thresholds to restrict access to limited resources only widens this gap (Blewitt *et al.* 2011). Research carried out in all areas of parenting difficulty warns against the dangers of adult and children's services failing to co-ordinate their work and evidences the positive impact of working in partnership (Asmussen and Weizel 2009; Moran, Ghate and van der Merwe 2004; Olsen and Clarke 2003; SCIE 2009). Reviews of both child and adult deaths repeatedly highlight how the endemic failure of working together places them at risk of harm (Sinclair and Bullock 2002).

Case study

After a sex and relationship education session in his final year of primary school, Jack talked with his best friend about 'doing it' with his mum and this resulted in a referral to children's services. As part of her Initial Assessment, Amanda (a social worker in a children's duty and assessment team) learns that Jack lives at home with his mother Kimberley. His two older brothers and his older sister all left home when they were around 17 years old. Record checks indicate that Kimberley received services from the adult mental health team until recently. When Amanda contacts Chris (Kimberley's former social worker in adult mental health services) she learns that Kimberley had talked with him at intervals over a period of several years about her sexual thoughts about children, but Chris had never considered discussing these conversations with children's services.

- Why might Chris not have considered making a referral to children's services?

- If Chris had made a referral, how might children's services have responded?

- What are the questions for assessment now?

Many barriers interfere with working across the interface between adult and children's services but social workers can rely on having much in common:

- Core principles: individualisation; purposeful expression of feelings; controlled environment; acceptance; non-judgemental attitude; self-determination; confidentiality (Biesteck 1961).

- Statutory mandate and duties (Braye and Preston-Shoot 2010).

- Responsibility for both care and control and the dilemmas of doing society's 'dirty work' (Thompson 2000).

- A commitment to social justice (IASSW and IFSW 2005; Banks 2006).

- A shared code of conduct (HCPC 2012).

- Shared understanding of psychosocial approaches to assessment (Healy 2005).

- Mutual grounding in core theory and method, for example systemic and psychosocial (Watson, Burrows and Player 2002).

- A 'practice wisdom' approach to blending intuition and analysis (Munro 2008; O'Sullivan 2011).

- Ambiguous status within the professional hierarchy.

- Mutual grounding in core theory and method, for example systemic perspectives (Watson *et al.* 2002).

The systemic principle that individuals cannot be understood in isolation from one another, but rather as part of a network of relationships, is generally accepted across all services. Systemic approaches in social work practice encourage practitioners to direct their focus beyond individuals to consider the environment and context in which their difficulties have arisen.

Points to consider

- How does your organisation promote whole family assessment?

- What gets in the way of whole family assessment?

- What protocols are in place to support whole family assessment?

Social work's legal mandates generally demand minimal intervention. The principle that decisions about psychiatric interventions should adopt the least restrictive alternative is mirrored in the 'presumption of capacity' and the 'no order' principle enshrined in children's legislation, as well as in the 'presumption of capacity'. Similarly, law and guidance embody the rights to independence and family life and these aspirations are instilled as part of the professional culture (Brown and Ward 2012, p.71). Families' greatest fear is that social workers will exercise their power to destroy the life they have together (Dale 2004; Hadley Centre 2008; SCIE 2005c, 2008a; Totsuka 2008). This fear is often shared and supported by professionals and sometimes stands in the way of trust and collaboration across service divides:

> Collaboration will not be realized without discussion of values, power, objectives, expertise, knowledge, attitudes to information exchange, and structures.

> (Braye and Preston-Shoot 2010, p.9)

When organisations put these discussions in place, collaboration 'generates social capital, benefits other types of partnerships and seeps into other pieces of work' (Williams and Sutherland 2010, p.11). Ultimately, organisations that assess whole families to support their complex needs are able to meet performance indicators more effectively and perhaps even more cost-effectively than when individuals in the family are assessed separately (Gopfert *et al.* 2010, p.42). Working together to generate whole family assessments means operating within boundaries (retaining respective roles and responsibilities) but without unnecessary barriers (Aldridge 2006; Arksey *et al.* 2002; Cree 2003; Roberts *et al.* 2008).

Ultimately, whole family assessment relies on individual practitioners from different services getting their heads together. This might be as minimal as just sharing information but, at best, can enable workers to agree joint assessment processes. Whatever form it takes, whole family assessment is distinguished by its focus on the interrelationships between family members and how these impact on individuals within the family. A study of pilot projects undertaken by the Department for Education (Kendall *et al.* 2011) found that the key strengths of the whole family assessment models examined included engagement, transparency, comprehensive family support/action plans, and avoidance of duplication.

Case study

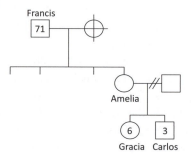

Figure 3.1 The Garcia family tree

Gracia has multiple sensory impairments. She has always been very wakeful at nights and sometimes screams and thrashes around, apparently angry and frustrated, in the early hours of the morning. One night, Amelia hits Gracia so hard around the head that she causes a brain haemorrhage. Amelia also cares for Francis who has Alzheimer's disease.

- What are the questions for assessment?
- Which professionals need to be involved in assessment?
- How would you engage the family?

Relationship-based collaboration

People working together rely on sharing power and expertise, pursuing mutually agreed person-centred goals, and committing to work together as active participants in a dynamic process (Gottlieb, Feeley and Dalton 2006, p.8, cited by Wallace and Davies 2009, p.111). Making real human connections is essential because:

> tacit knowledge is not easy to capture, translate or transfer because it is internalised within individuals, acquired through experience and difficult to communicate and does not readily move between cultures and professions.
>
> (Williams and Sullivan 2010, p.1)

Simple strategies form the foundations of successful collaboration:

- Making time to share relevant information and explore insights about the family face to face.

- Negotiating shared supervision with one or both of your practice managers so that you can ensure support for your collaborative approach.

- Agreeing to co-work with the family sometimes so that they are not caught in the middle between you; and you in turn are able to make sense of different perspectives.

- Ensuring meetings are held at times and venues that work best for your counterpart so that no opportunities for shared thinking are lost.

- Agreeing how and when to keep in touch in order to minimise drift.

- Listening actively to break down barriers and deepen mutual understanding of different perspectives and insights.

- Adopting a stance of appreciative enquiry by valuing the different knowledge and skills your counterpart brings.

- Mapping the collective knowledge, expertise and skills available, think about how you can most effectively bring these together, and design a plan for an integrated holistic assessment of the whole family.

- Agreeing a crisis contingency plan.

- Explicitly agreeing the boundaries around your respective roles and making these clear to the family and other colleagues.

- Understanding your counterparts' professional context, for example the particular pressures they are under, the priorities that drive their service.

Points to consider

Think about an assessment that involved colleagues from a different service.

- Which of your professional colleagues held the most reliable information about the family?

- Who contributed most theoretical knowledge?

- Who had the most responsibility?

- Who had the most authority?

- How did you negotiate the assessment process?

Each individual brings expectations and patterns of behaviour that are familiar and comfortable to them. Previous attachment experiences in family and personal life, as well as in learning and working contexts, colour interpersonal behaviour and so influence the strategies brought to each new working relationship as it unfolds (Baim and Morrison 2011). Since 'it takes two to tango' no working partnership will be quite the same as any other. Just as children thrive in families where generous unconditional support goes alongside well-defined boundaries and high expectations, we all need this balance in our working lives. Most practitioners have experienced the creativity that a challenging and supportive working partnership can generate (Jackson, Firtko and Edenborough 2007; Wilson and Ferch 2005).

Collaboration across service divides rarely feels straightforward. Theory and research cannot hope to capture the uncertainty, unpredictability and ambiguity of working alongside colleagues, because it hinges on complex webs of relationship between imperfect human beings. The heart and soul of working together is about colleagues building authentic relationships based on sharing aspects of their real selves. Strengths-based teamwork, relationship skills and intuition are more effective in complex and contested contexts than control, rationing and competition. The holistic model emphasised throughout this book understands assessment as a shared process of exploring uncertainty. The social worker's task is to integrate the different insights afforded by each perspective contributed, and to make sense of dissonance. This moral-relational approach demands skills and qualities traditionally associated with the 'feminine'. These are all too readily trumped by more 'masculine' discourses, for example models that seek to avoid complexity and prefer simple answers to problems (Claire Blake, Senior Paediatric Nurse, personal communication, July 2013). The personal qualities, values and skills on which the tradition of humanist social work rests can be re-framed and properly recognised as 'emotional intelligence' (Goleman 1996; Howe 2008; Mullender and Perrott 2002).

> The thing that makes it work in any type of structure is the personal commitment of the people…it isn't organisations getting together, it's individuals sitting around a table.
>
> (Nurse Director quoted by Williams and Sullivan 2010, p.13)

Communication, consensus and conflict

> Communication is the process by which information is transferred from one person to another and is understood by them.
>
> (Reder and Duncan 2003a)

Our perception and understanding of the world hinges on definitions and meaning. We make sense of our experience and others through language (Lightfoot, Cole and Cole 2008). Language is always a creative expression of the individual, and meaning is a dynamic interaction. Communication is therefore crucial to collaborative practice. Working across the service divide demands 'active listening', the attempt to understand not just what is said in words but also the 'meta-communication' – thoughts and feelings articulated through the use of voice and body, unconscious emotional messages and the decisions about what not to say (Moss 2008; Reder and Duncan 2003a). This means that colleagues should not assume shared knowledge and understanding but should question and challenge each other.

EXERCISE

- Have you been involved in a disagreement with colleagues that escalated into a row?
- What was the context of the disagreement?
- How did it unfold?
- How did you feel?
- What was the real reason for the row?
- How was it resolved?

Understanding and working with subtle differences in the language we use can build trust within professional relationships. It is pointless to aspire to creating a single shared language. Different vocabularies exist because our knowledge-base and skills, methods and interventions differ (Hetherington *et al.* 2003). Collaboration works when we understand these differences, and reach shared understanding about families' experiences and needs (Hallett and Birchall 1992). Working together provides an opportunity to assert social work values and anti-oppressive principles, and influence the practice of other disciplines (Braye and Preston-Shoot 2010, p.270).

Each practitioner's capacity to understand the significance of information is easily undermined by all kinds of extraneous personal/professional factors. In the stressful uncertain context of assessment practice, anxiety can both cause, and result from, misunderstandings and disagreements. Hierarchy and status have a part to play in this.

EXERCISE

Have you witnessed or experienced occasions when:

- the emotional impact of assessment work has got in the way of keeping a child or an adult family member safe?
- an email exchange has escalated into a row because an emotional charge has been read or written into the message content?

- the views of a low-status worker with extensive knowledge of a family have been outweighed by the expert opinion of a professional based on a single contact?

Meanings cannot be absolute and universal. In order to make sense of families, and of each other, practitioners have to be alert and work hard to ensure clear communication (Hetherington *et al.* 2003). Language reflects and perpetuates the individual's worldview and differences in gender, class and ethnicity mean that we all organise and express our experience differently (Bernstein 1964). It is important not to get caught up in specialised professional language. For example:

- 'being safe' and 'protection' do not mean the same thing

- parents and adult services workers may be alienated by assessments described as 'investigations' since this implies that a crime has been committed

- to talk about 'sectioning' someone is a very strange use of language.

Working together means checking out extra layers of ambiguity and meaning.

EXERCISE
How would you define these phrases/words:

- a reasonable standard of health and development

- harassment

- likelihood

- degrading treatment

- love

- care that it would be reasonable to expect a parent to give

- power

- consistent with sexual abuse?

Sometimes misunderstandings arise, quite simply because of differences between the language, vocabulary, concepts and syntax used from one discipline or organisation to another.

Case study

Aimee was born with a heroin dependency and has been in a mother and baby placement within a hospital ward for three months. A discharge plan has been drawn up and recommends close monitoring.

What would the term 'close monitoring' usually mean to:

- a ward sister?

- a social worker in a children and families support team?

- a general practitioner?

- a worker in a problem drug/alcohol use service?

Jargon and acronyms develop to enable workers to take short cuts in familiar areas of practice. Unfortunately they provide insufficient information for anyone outside the closed communication loop and can even exclude, de-skill and confuse them. Appendix 1 provides 'translations' of acronyms you are most likely to come across in whole family assessment.

Ideas and language deemed unhelpful and derogatory in one social care context (for example describing a colleague as 'passive-aggressive' or a father as 'manipulative' or a mother as 'a typical victim') may be employed without compunction in another.

Points to consider

- Have you ever taken issue with the way you heard someone describe you?

- How did this feel?

- Have you ever been challenged because you used words that caused offence?

- What led you to use the words that caused offence?

- Were you able to reach a shared understanding and agreement about the right language to use?

- Are there any words that could cause offence but are nevertheless useful in assessment reports?

How ideas are presented and communicated can make a huge difference to practice. For example, these two versions of the National Assessment Triangle present the dimensions of the child's world in ways that elicit quite different conversations.

Points to consider

- How do they differ?

- Which would you prefer to use?

- Which is more likely to engage parents and children?

NAF triangle
England and Wales

Figure 3.2a The National Assessment framework triangles

This is the version presented in the government guidance for England and Wales and is very familiar to social workers in children's services.

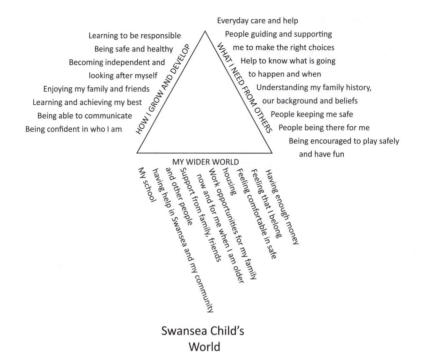

Swansea Child's
World

Figure 3.2b The Swansea triangle

This version was developed in Swansea. It is based on Scotland's *My World Triangle* (www.scotland.gov.uk).

Assumptions, bias and stereotypes

I am young and black with five children, and a social worker came round and made the assumption that the children all had different fathers. She was then surprised when they didn't. She just kept putting her foot in it and didn't even realise it!

(Parent quoted by Children's Commissioner 2010, p.32)

Points to consider

- What accurate assumptions do people make about you?

- What mistaken assumptions do people make about you?

- How do these assumptions make you feel?

It is inevitable that professionals are biased and hold stereotypes. As a species, human beings are ever alert to difference. We are all flawed and our practice may be affected by our own experiences, for example as parents, carers, service users or as 'wounded healers' having overcome harm and trauma. It is each practitioner's responsibility to recognise our biases and ensure that prejudice does not interfere with our ability to create relationships and understand others' experiences. These experiences can be a great source of motivation, sincerity and insight but only if we develop self-awareness, remain open to honest self-exploration, and are willing to learn from others throughout our working lives (Milner and O'Byrne 2009). In whole family assessment, workers across services particularly need to explore the assumption that parents find it too difficult to look after children because of the problems they face. The traditional family welfare model implies that children of parents facing any kinds of life difficulty inevitably 'need' state intervention (Braye and Preston-Shoot 2010, p.269).

In whole family assessment these questions, adapted from McCracken's cultural review (1988), make a challenging, useful foundation for building partnership by prompting honest conversations with families and colleagues:

- What do I know about families in this situation?

- Where does my knowledge come from?

- What prejudices might I bring?

- What do I expect about children/parents in this situation?

- What might surprise me about this situation?

- Why would this be a surprise?

- How might the children/parents in this situation perceive me/ my organisation?

- What impact might this assessment have on the children and parents in this family?

- What agency norms and practices will influence my assessment, for example thresholds, practice standards, team expectations?

Case study

Charmian, aged 32, and Ed, aged 22, have known each other for less than a year when their daughter Elise is born and Ed moves into her flat. Charmian has neurofibromatosis (NF1), an inherited condition that can result in cognitive impairment, epilepsy, sensory impairment and is associated with increased risk of childhood leukaemia. When Elise is two months old, Charmian takes her to the health visitor's clinic and describes how she has been quiet and floppy since left in Ed's care for an hour or so yesterday. On further questioning she shows some old bruises on her legs and implies that Ed inflicted them. Charmian is offered a mother and baby placement as temporary refuge from Ed and he is refused contact. The plan is that Charmian and Elise will be rehoused with support from children's services. When Elise is five months old, Charmian unexpectedly fails to return to the foster home after going out with friends for the evening. Several weeks later she phones the foster carer to say she has moved to another part of the country with a new boyfriend.

Within a few days, Ed contacts social services. He has heard that Elise is in foster care and asks if he can look after her now. Children's services have already made plans to place Elise for adoption but Ed takes legal advice and joins care proceedings. Ed belongs to a large Barbadian family. His mother uses a wheelchair following a car accident and is cared for on a rota basis by Ed and his younger sisters. Ed has only been known to social services in his role as a carer, has no history of violence at school or work and has had no contact with the police. A paediatrician meets with Ed to explain the risk that Elise too may have NF1 and could have health problems and special needs in the future. His response is that he and his family know how to deal with disability and love Elise whatever her future holds. His account of the day Charmian left him is that Elise had a cold. Charmian had been trying to feed her without success, wanted to give her a second dose of Calpol and became increasingly agitated and frustrated before leaving the house. Ed had been able to soothe Elise and she was asleep by the time Charmian returned.

On investigation it emerges that Charmian endured childhood abuse. Police records indicate that she has formerly made many unsubstantiated allegations of sexual or physical assault against teachers and friends. Research into Charmian's medical records indicates that she has a seven-year-old son, who lives with his father's family. Elise's GP discloses that Charmian expressed ambivalence throughout her recent pregnancy. Ed describes how he had gradually come to realise that she was less able than he assumed when they first met, that she has some significant cognitive impairment and perhaps some hearing loss.

- With the benefit of hindsight what would you do differently?
- What could adult services have contributed to assessment and planning for Charmian and Elise?
- What are the questions for assessment now?

The professional system initially acted on legitimate concerns. Quite properly, credence was given to Charmian's testimony; she and Elise were actively protected from all risk of harm and resources were harnessed to support attachment between them. All the agencies involved acted upon professional knowledge informed by the unpalatable history of institutional negligence towards victims of domestic violence, the increased risk of violence for women who are pregnant or have recently given birth, and evidence that contact with violent fathers is risky. Unfortunately this professional narrative about domestic abuse blinded professionals to the particular stories of the individuals involved, led them to plan their intervention in the absence of a full family assessment and consequently undermined Ed's place in Elise's life.

- What other assumptions may have been made about Ed's role in Elise's life?

The unique universal and universal unique

EXERCISE

This is the opening line of Tolstoy's novel *Anna Karenina*:

All happy families are alike: each unhappy family is unhappy in its own way.

- Do you think Tolstoy got this right?
- What types of unhappiness do you see in the families you work with?

Each family has particular values and beliefs, rooted in cultural contexts such as community, class or faith. Child-rearing practices and expectations about autonomy, achievement and independence vary across different cultures but also from family to family. The onus is on assessors to think about how families' unique experience and identity influence how people behave and relate towards each other. No assumptions can be made, as family relationships rest on a complex negotiation of different, sometimes competing, family histories and cultural traditions:

> Every assessment should reflect the unique characteristics of the child within the family and community context. The Children Act 1989 promotes the view that all children and their parents should be considered as individuals and that family structures, culture, religion, ethnic origins and other characteristics should be respected.
>
> (HM Government 2013, p.21)

Assessment is about interpreting families' narratives and therefore involves managing the tension between 'exegesis' (drawing meaning out), and 'eisegesis' (putting meaning in) (Habermas 1973). Thinking about assessment in this way refers us back to theories about development, linguistics and attachment to explain how each family member constructs an idea of 'self' (Bowlby 1988, 1998; de Shazer 1994; Erickson 1959/1980). However, individuals are not always free to create our own 'personal myth' because we all have to locate ourselves amongst narratives we have little power over, for example gender, sexuality, class, race, community:

> …there is nothing inevitable about identities. Instead they are products of people's efforts to understand and respond to the situations in which they find themselves, using such resources as they command. Identities are human creations, existing only in the ways that we come to think about ourselves and others. Ultimately, the construction of an identity occurs as an on-going act of interpretation…human beings have to make their own sense of their conditions, and in the process, make themselves.
>
> (Cornell and Hartman 1998, p.231)

EXERCISE

Take a trip back in time to think and feel as you did when you were eight years old.

- How would you have described your family to an interested adult?

- What made you who you were then?

- Create two drawings to represent your identity: one of you as a child and another as you are now.

- What of your sense of identity has changed and what remains the same?

Assessment is not just about using knowledge, but also thinking from each person's perspective, and stepping into their shoes to experience their concerns and dilemmas (Lindsay Hill, Senior Lecturer in Social Work, personal communication, April 2012). Social work is informed by the technical-rational contributions of research but demands a practical-moral approach so that judgements and decisions rest on understanding the unique circumstances of each family. Research attempts to derive general principles from individual experience. Social workers have to harness knowledge drawn from theory and research with what they can learn from each family's experiences and worldview. Together, these enable social workers to understand each family's needs and analyse what harm individuals might experience.

This echoes the Taoist dialectical principle of yin and yang (Figure 3.3). Simultaneously thinking about universal principles and unique experience in this way supports subtle analysis of complex and interacting needs within each family.

> In this system of thought, all things are seen as parts of a whole. No entity can ever be isolated from its relationship to other entities; no thing can exist in and of itself. There are no absolutes. Yin and Yang must, necessarily, contain within themselves the possibility of opposition and change.
>
> (Kaptchuk 1983, p.8)

Figure 3.3 Yin/yang symbol

Simultaneously thinking about universal principles and unique experiences in this way supports subtle analysis of complex and interacting needs within each family. The added value of working together across services is that you can rely on your counterpart for in-depth knowledge of research and theory in their own field. This enables you to focus together on what is unique and different about this family and each individual within it. As experts through experience, families sometimes integrate formal knowledge with their sense of self. The beliefs families hold about the nature of the problems they face, and their experience of seeking and receiving help, need to be explored. For example, some problem drinkers find it helpful to frame alcoholism as illness, whereas for others medicalising the problem undermines their sense of self-efficacy.

Conceptualising the unique-universal and the universal-unique captures the paradoxical injunction to use research/evidence-based practice (the universal) whilst holding in mind the individuality of the person in their situation and context (the unique):

> Every child's case reveals a multitude of different factors and variables making predictability difficult and leading to a quality of unexpectedness. Cases are, therefore, confusingly, both similar and different to each other.

> (Brandon *et al.* 2009, p.40)

Making children's identity the starting point helps ensure a focus on each individual's needs. This dimension of children's development is often overlooked when it is interpreted as only requiring a brief note about ethnicity or culture. This can also happen if assessments focus on arguing a case for particular interventions, for example securing a specific service or a legal mandate.

Failure to get to grips with children's experience and sense of self is a huge lost opportunity because assessments are the medium through which other professionals now and in the future come to know them. Social workers often have in-depth and balanced knowledge about individual children. However, this is not always conveyed in assessments reports that fail to capture the rounded and grounded sense of the real child held in workers' heads (Thomas and Holland 2010; White, Hall and Peckover 2008).

EXERCISE

Look back over an assessment you wrote recently, putting yourself in the shoes of different family members.

• Would each of the adults recognise themselves fully in your description of them?

• Would each of the children feel that you understood them fully?

• Could your description of the adults damage their reputation in any way?

• Could your description of the children undermine their self-esteem?

Theories of change and the assessment process

Assessment is not an end in itself. Its purpose is to identify need and provide a basis on which to plan interventions to meet the family's need, enhance their life together and reduce risk of harm. This means that we must be able to explain the theory of change on which each assessment rests.

Several distinct issues need to be clarified in the design of parenting assessments (Holland 2004):

1. Should there be assessment of the *potential* of parents to change (in the future)?

2. Should there be change *during* the assessment?

3. How is change understood?

4. Are we looking for behavioural or attitudinal change?

5. Is the focus on the past, the present, the future, or all three?

Social work practice in children's services tended historically to rest on psychodynamic theory and therefore emphasised change in terms of self-understanding. This influence is still evident in the application of attachment theory in children's services. Contemporary social work has also been influenced by learning theory and recent research into cognitive behavioural interventions. For example dependency and addiction services often use approaches that focus on enhancing motivation for change. Cognitive behavioural therapy and 'mindfulness' training have been widely adapted in the field of adult mental health.

Sometimes social workers hope that families will be able to achieve both behavioural and attitudinal change. Their assessments might use the concrete language of measurement to capture behavioural change alongside nebulous ideas about acknowledgement, motivation and aspiration to describe attitudinal change (Holland 2004). Designing assessments carefully with counterparts across services enables you to identify the kind of changes needed, how you will discover whether these are achievable, and how they might be achieved, and what recommendations to make. For example assessments of neglect need to consider whether poor parenting has arisen:

- for practical reasons associated with poverty and deprivation (these can mainly be addressed with practical, common-sense interventions)

- because the parent does not know or understand what their children need (these parents may benefit from parenting programmes such as Triple P)

- because of social isolation (community-based interventions may be helpful)

- because the relationship of care is missing or has broken down (in these circumstances neither practical, educative nor social interventions will make a difference; assessment must focus on how/whether relationship-focused work can achieve lasting change).

Collaboration across adult and children's services affords opportunities to design well-informed assessments based on explicit, well-considered analysis of the questions that need to be asked, and what must be understood, in order to consider what changes are needed and what interventions will promote well-being. Different situations need different timescales. Assessment is a process, not an event (Calder and Hackett 2003, p.36; DoH, DFEE and Home Office 2000a; Holland 2004). Assessment timetables can be planned together to ensure that each process takes into account:

- managing parental ambivalence

- developing trust with children

- matching the needs of parents and children with learning impairments
- testing out capacity for change
- testing out the impact of change
- ensuring that assessment will not be destructive and/or compromised by poor timing, for example during illness, late pregnancy or a period of upheaval.

> The distinction between treatment and assessment is unhelpful and has always restricted the vision and creativity of social work staff.
>
> (Walker and Beckett 2003, p.4)

Assessment responsibilities are often separated from therapeutic roles in health and social care services, but assessments should be designed as helpful interventions, in anticipation that the process will trigger improvement (Ward and Rose 2002). Feeling heard and respected creates an environment in which insight and transformation flourish. Although assessment inevitably explores past behaviour as the best predictor of future behaviour, it should not ignore development and progress:

> Undertaking an assessment with a family can begin a process of understanding and change by key family members. A practitioner may, during the process of gathering information, be instrumental in bringing about change by the questions asked, by listening to the family, by validating the family's difficulties or concerns, and by providing information and advice. The process of assessment should be therapeutic in itself.
>
> (DoH *et al.* 2000a, pp.15–16)

Whole family timelines

> Life can only be understood backwards but it must be lived forwards.
>
> (Soren Kierkegaard, 1813–1855)

Snapshot assessments that freeze the family in time are meaningless. The family model encourages you to think about the family's journey from the past, in the present and ahead into the future.

EXERCISE

Use Figure 3.4 to explore your own journey.

- What aspects of your early relationship with your parents affect how you behave in your closest adult relationships now? (past → present)

- What are you doing in the here and now that takes you towards your goals for the future? (present → future)

- Are there any limitations you experienced as a child that you wish to address now in order to fulfil your potential? (past ↔ present ↔ future)

Social work has often been criticised for failing to take historical information about families into account during assessments. 'Start-again syndrome' results in assessments losing sight of the detail and significance of incidents, failing to notice recurrent patterns, repeating unnecessary assessment. Working together at the interface between adult and children's services enables assessors to draw up meaningful, comprehensive accounts of family history. Jointly mapping information, reflecting and analysing in a continuous, systematic, iterative process should result in well-informed, well-judged recommendations and seamless interventions.

Thinking together about the past

Case study continued

What happens next in the Green family...

When the head-teacher shares the teacher's worries about Megan, Lisa agrees to a Common Assessment Framework assessment led by the school. While this is still under way the police are called to a neighbour's home. Megan has elaborated a 'make-believe' game that culminates in her tying her friend to her bed, setting a fire and barricading her in. During the subsequent joint investigation conducted by police and children's social services further information is gathered:

- Amy, her partner Justin and two children share their home with her father, Mark. Lisa looks after Ethan two days a week while Amy works as a recently qualified community psychiatric nurse.

- According to Lisa, Gary, the father of Emily, Joshua and Megan, was highly-strung and often argumentative if he went drinking after football. Nevertheless, she considered their marriage reasonably successful until seven years ago when he began to drink more heavily and became abusive towards her. She changed the locks on the front door after an incident when Gary threatened Joshua on Christmas Eve. They did not get back together after this. Gary was subsequently found drowned in a pond near his local pub.

- Emily and Joshua never got on well together as children and she is angered by all the trouble he has caused. She now 'sofa-surfs' with friends.

- Joshua received a Statement of Special Educational Needs (SEN) when he was aged eight that identified dyslexia.

- Emily is not expected to achieve any passes at GCSE. She has never received a statement but Lisa feels that she is 'if anything, even more dyslexic than our Josh was'.

- Although Megan is very clever, a real all-rounder, she had been included in a nurture group since Year One.

- Megan has always been seen as the most difficult of the children, with a strong personality and a need for clear boundaries. Lisa finds Megan hard to manage and she irritates Joshua and Emily.

- Lisa was diagnosed with ovarian cancer when Megan was three months old. She had a hysterectomy and chemotherapy and was given the 'all clear' but subsequently developed rheumatoid arthritis. Chronic pain interferes with her sleep and she has frequent flare-ups. Although Emily left home some time ago, she continues to help with housework and shopping for the family.

Conventional calendar chronologies are often found in children's files. Figure 3.5 provides a chronology for tracking Megan's history adapted from a template routinely used in adoption assessments. Chronologies help us to understand and keep track of how events have unfolded.

Figure 3.6 shows information about the Green family set out as a timeline. Creating a timeline can help assessors focus on patterns, trace the significance and meaning of events, and identify further questions about process.

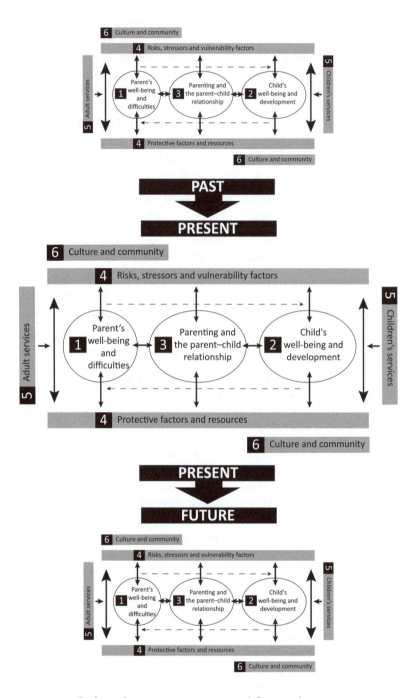

Figure 3.4 Thinking about your past, present and future: a long term perspective on family experiences (adapted from Falkov, 2012)

Figure 3.6 shows information about the Green family set out as a timeline. Creating a timeline can help assessors focus on patterns, trace the significance and meaning of events, and identify further questions about process.

Points to consider

- What patterns can you see?
- What new insights/understandings emerge from this?
- What are the questions for assessments?
- What are the implications for how the assessment should be designed?

SE3R (**S**kim, **E**xtract, **R**ead, **R**eview, **R**ecall) is a systematic method for extracting, collating, processing and memorising narrative detail from continuous text devised by Dr Eric Shepherd in 1987. An SE3R represents the narrative visually as an 'event line' – a hand-written linear representation of the passage of time presented in the present tense, with 'identity bins' providing detail about people, places, etc. This method was originated to facilitate communication in forensic investigation of specific incidents. Figure 3.7 presents the discussions at an inter-agency meeting held soon after Megan's 'game' is reported to the police, collated as an SE3R. Creating an SE3R usually highlights gaps in the information held and helps assessors to identify further factual questions.

Timeline date	Age	Significant individual/family events/history	Significant changes of address	Education/employment	Relationships history	Service interventions
24th December 2003		Megan born				
March 2004	3 months	Lisa diagnosed with ovarian cancer				
24th December 2004	1 year	Gary assaults Joshua, leaves home. Lisa changes locks				
February 2005	1 year 2 months	Gary drowns				
June 2005	1 year 7 months	Olivia born				
January 2007	4 years 1month			Megan attends pre-school		
May 2009	5 years 6 months	Joshua first reports anxiety				
September 2009	5 years 9 months			Megan attends Year One		

December 2009	6 years			Megan begins to attend nurture group
January 2011	7 years 1 month	Joshua's first admission to A&E		
March 2011	7 years 3 months	Emily leaves home		Megan attends CAMHS x3
April 2011	7 years 4 months	Megan's bed moves into Lisa's room		
October 2011	7 years 9 months			Joshua assessed by CMHT
December 2011	8 years			Common Assessment Framework initiated by school because of concerns about Megan's gruesome imagination
March 2012	8 years 3 months			Police investigation of Megan's harmful behaviour towards friend
April 2012	8 years 4 months	Ethan born		

Figure 3.5 Individual chronology: Megan Green

	2003	2004	2005	2006	2007	2008	2009	2010	2011	2012
Gary										
Born 6.6.1958										
Died 27.12.2008	Age 45									
Third child born	Escalating use of alcohol and aggressive behaviour	Age 47								
Leaves family on Christmas Eve		Drowns on Boxing Day								
Lisa										
Born 5.9.1970	Age 33 Fourth child, Megan, born									
on Christmas Eve	Age 34									

					Age 35					
Diagnosed with ovarian cancer and has a hysterectomy in June										
Develops rheumatoid arthritis										
First grandchild born		Age 41								
2nd grandchild born										
Amy										
Born 21.1.1987	Age 18									
Married Justin										
First child, Sophie, born		Age 24								
2nd child, Ethan, born										
Joshua										
Born										

cont.

	2003	2004	2005	2006	2007	2008	2009	2010	2011	2012
9.10.1993	Age 10	Age 11	Age 12	Age 13	Age 14	Age 15	Age 16			
Year 12										
Anxious during June										
Begins binge-drinking and use of cannabis during summer	Age 17									
1st psychotic experience New Year	Age 18									
Escalating disturbed behaviour										
Emily										
Born 5.9.1994	Age 9									
Year 5	Age 10									
Year 6	Age 11									
Year 7										

Begins to take responsibility for household tasks and shopping	Age 12						
Year 8	Age 13						
Year 9	Age 14						
Year 10	Age 15						
Year 11	Age 16						
Year 12	Age 17						
Leaves home							
Megan							
Born							
24.12.2003	Born on Christmas Eve	Age 1	Age 2	Age 3	Age 4	Age 5	
Year 1	Age 6						
Year 2	Age 7						
Year 3	Age 8						
Year 4	Age 9						
Year 5							

	2003	2004	2005	2006	2007	2008	2009	2010	2011	2012
Escalating disturbed behaviour										
Olivia										
16.6.2005			Born in June	Age 1	Age 2	Age 3	Age 4	Age 5		
Year 1	Age 6									
Year 2	Age 7									
Year 3										
Ethan										
6.6.2012										Born in June
Justin										
16.8.1988			Age 19							
1st child born										
Dave										
21.1.1978										Age 36
1st child born										

Figure 3.6 The Green family's timeline

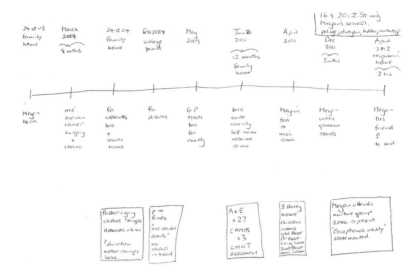

Figure 3.7 SE3R

Inter-agency incident charts (Figure 3.8) record key information about each harmful incident and are most valuable as an inter-agency information tool when completed collectively at, for example core group meetings and conferences (Raynes 2003, pp.127–128).

Date	Incident	Explanation given by parent	Explanation given by child	Advice given	Action taken

Figure 3.8 Inter-agency incident chart (adapted from Raynes 2003, p.127)

Each of these approaches is helpful because they show up patterns and highlight gaps, enabling practitioners to articulate questions and identify issues for assessment.

Thinking together about the future

Thinking together about a family's future demands empathy, imagination and willingness to have both immediate and very long-term outcomes in mind. The key question when meeting a family, regardless of whether they minimise their difficulties, manage them stoically, or seem overwhelmed by them, is 'What will be the outcome if nothing changes?' Research from the field of neuro-science lends weight to the argument that assessment has to look at long-term impact of parental behaviour rather than merely describing or even capturing why the parent's behaviour is compromised. (The long-term impact of impoverished family relationships on children's development is discussed further in Chapter 6.)

Case study

The police are called out at 10 pm on a Tuesday night in March by neighbours concerned about six-year-old Richard and his sister five-year-old May playing out in the street with older children. When police officers take the children home they find their flat cold, grubby and sparsely furnished. Several young adults are watching TV and are obviously drinking alcohol. The children's mother is not drinking with them but is fast asleep in another room. She tells the police officers that she has no idea what time it is, and that she sleeps very heavily because of medication prescribed by her GP. She seems disoriented and confused.

- What are the most serious immediate risks to the children?
- How likely is it that Richard and May will be seriously harmed?
- What immediate impact does playing outside so late have on Richard and May?
- What will be the impact on Richard and May if nothing changes?
- Think about how the impact will affect them as they grow into adolescence and adulthood. What will be the long-term consequences for Richard and May if nothing changes?
- What are the questions for assessment?

Once assessors have a sense of what might happen if nothing changes, they can begin to consider the preferred future. Thinking about all the possible futures that lie ahead of a family, and permanency planning for children, at the early stages of assessment processes helps assessors to identify evidence-based interventions that will stand children in good stead, whatever the immediate outcome (Brown and Ward 2012).

EXERCISE

Look back over one of your recent assessments.

• What adversity is faced by the person it centres on?

• What are this person's unique talents and potential?

• What is your worst fear for this person?

• What is the best, realistic future you can anticipate for this person?

Assessment models, tools and instruments

Three distinct practice models inform assessment by different social workers and in different social work settings:

• *Questioning*: The assessor defines the problem, need, or risk and drives the content and process of assessment. Expertise and power is embraced by the practitioner.

• *Procedural*: The assessor uses standardised tools to determine eligibility for services/match needs to services/identify risk. Needs are often conceptualised in terms of deficit, that is, what people cannot do (Gurney 2004).

• *Exchange*: People are perceived as experts about their situation and the assessor has responsibility to bring problem-solving resources to an interaction. Rests on partnership and attention to the family's narrative (Smale *et al.* 1993).

When social workers design and conduct assessments collaboratively from across various contexts, they need to be able to identify when, how and why these different approaches have been, or will be, adopted and explore how to integrate the different types of information elicited.

Social workers often have to synthesise assessments made by other disciplines working in the fields of criminal justice, health or education. Working together across the service divide enables assessors to make sense of specialist input from unfamiliar fields and discuss the implications of insights afforded by other disciplines with their social work counterpart.

Assessment can be thought about in two distinct ways: either as a rational, scientific, technical task, supported by tested, objective, consistent protocols; or as a reflective process where professionals seek deep understanding of complex situations to form judgements. Assessment tools therefore fall into two broad categories:

- *Actuarial approaches* emphasise the identification of factors that can be shown as statistically significant predictors. Much research has been invested in the effort to create assessment instruments that accurately identify and predict risk. These are now widely used throughout social care in the US, but are most commonly used only in specialist settings within the UK.

- *Consensus-based or clinical instrument tools* place greater emphasis on practitioners drawing on information gathered through interviews, experience and theoretical knowledge to form a clinical judgement. This mode of assessment dominates British social work practice.

Actuarial approaches might be conceived of as more scientific and reliable set against the more reflexive and intuitive approaches implicit in clinical assessment. Many assessment tools have been designed to support assessment. Appendix 2 provides an overview of assessment instruments, tools and models used by the professional disciplines most likely to contribute to whole family assessment.

Both actuarial and clinical approaches have their advantages and disadvantages. Clinical assessments are often flawed and 'gut feelings' can, for example, perpetuate racist social work practice unless supervision and a healthy team climate encourage practitioners to explore and challenge their assumptions (Kemshall and Pritchard 2005; Munro 2002; Wonnacott 2012). The value of actuarial assessments is also questionable and not all have been empirically validated. They may not help assessors weight individual risk factors or volatile combinations of risk factors. Many were developed in the US, and have been based on research with specific populations. This means that they may not translate well into UK practice and may not take into account differences of culture and context. Above all, they cannot capture the complexity of families' experience. It is usually helpful to see the two approaches as complementary (Munro 2002).

Managing information

Good quality information is vital to effective assessment and decision-making. It is often only when information from different sources is pieced together that families needs and any risk of harm become apparent. Provided there is consent, information must be shared whenever doing so will benefit the family.

All workers have a duty of care, responsibility to identify children wherever there are clear concerns about safety and an obligation to act appropriately (DfES 2005, 2006). The duty to share information is explicit and guidance is intended to cut through difficult inter-professional dynamics.

However, when you are considering preventative interventions, it can be hard to decide whether and when it is legitimate to share information with counterparts in other services. The fear of breaking trust with the family is sometimes cited as a significant barrier to whole family working.

Practitioners also feel constrained by legislation and local guidance on recording and sharing information. The restrictions on exchanging information set out in the Data Protection Act mean that if someone is unable or refuses to give consent to information-sharing this should be honoured and documented with their reasons for refusal. Workers employed within the NHS are further limited by accountability to the Caldicott Guardians for patient information. Workers in adult services may feel inhibited from acting on general or nebulous concerns about emotionally abusive or neglectful parenting because of uncertainty about whether there are legitimate grounds to share information without consent in the absence of a clear incident or event (Calder and Hackett 2003). The law of tort enables people to seek damages should they experience a breach of confidentiality. Government guidance deals with this apparent contradiction by setting out seven 'golden rules' for information sharing where the decision to do so is difficult (HM Government 2008):

> The key factors in deciding whether or not to share confidential information are necessity and proportionality, i.e. whether the proposed sharing is likely to make an effective contribution to preventing the risk and whether the public interest in sharing information overrides the interest in maintaining confidentiality. In making the decision you must weigh up what might happen if the information is shared against what might happen if it is not and make a decision based on professional judgement.

> (HM Government 2008, p.21)

When workers in different contexts contribute contradictory information, this need not be a problem or a source of conflict but an opportunity to secure a richer assessment. The strength of whole family assessment is that social workers can achieve understanding of people's functioning in several environments and in the context of different professional relationships. These usually generate new information; for example, an isolated under-confident parent might appear more able in their local family centre than at home (Bronfenbrenner 1979).

Working together across different services not only enables practitioners to gather more complete information from a range of sources, it can also open up discussion about the quality of information available. Morrison and Wonnacott (CWDC 2009) stressed that it is not enough for assessors simply to gather information:

A careful consideration of assessment practice is likely to reveal that, regardless of any frameworks, information is gathered according to the bias of the worker, and will be affected by the quality of relationships with service users and professionals across the network. Information is too often gathered without being evaluated for quality or relevance, and there is little consideration of the all important questions 'What don't we know?' (Wonnacott 2012, p.106)

Morrison developed a matrix to help highlight information that is missing, to separate out clear factual information from information that is ambiguous, and to identify where the assessment has been led by assumptions rather than factual information.

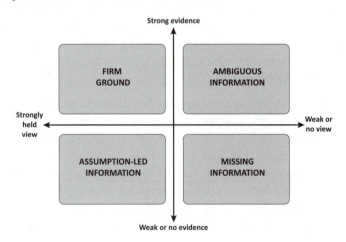

Figure 3.9 The discrepancy matrix (adapted from Morrison and Wonnacott 2009)

Case study continued

What is the quality of what we know so far about the Green family?

- What information is missing?
- What information needs further clarification?
- What are the questions for assessment?
- What is your assessment plan?

Using this tool to share information with a colleague across services often identifies crucial information that is missing. The matrix encourages you to interrogate the quality of information available about the family. It may help you identify assumptions that, along the way, have been incorporated into 'knowledge' shared between professionals as if they were facts. Very often meeting with colleagues to map what you know about a family reveals that almost everything you each think you know is ambiguous and open to interpretation. Recognising flawed information usually enables you to draw up a purposeful plan to fill in gaps. The assessment team is better equipped to tolerate initial uncertainty and ensure that recommendations and decisions will rest on the best information available.

Planning together and deciding where to start

Assessment procedures and protocols help social workers conduct assessments with consistency and fairness. However, since each family's circumstances are unique, whole family assessment also demands creativity.

Points to consider

- Have you ever been asked to undertake an assessment that you did not feel was needed?
- Have you ever made a referral for a special assessment, only to be told that the family's current circumstances make assessment impossible?

- Have you ever read a specialist assessment and thought 'I already know this!'?

Robust joint planning across service divides ensures that assessment attends to fundamental questions and bypasses unnecessary or irrelevant tangents.

When you need to think about risk, it is helpful to differentiate between 'predisposing hazards' and 'situational hazards' (Brearley 1982). Predisposing, background hazards are general factors in a family that make an undesirable outcome more likely to occur. Situational hazards are specific factors in the current circumstances that further increase that likelihood. This distinction sharpens the focus on where the problems are and how to alleviate them (Kelly 1996).

You can map what you know about a family onto a matrix to help identify the focus of different issues for assessment, avoid investigating dead-ends, and set aside factors that are irrelevant to decision-making (Figure 3.10).

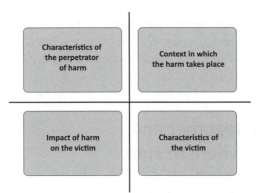

Figure 3.10 Making sense of the facts: a model for preliminary analysis

Exploring the context of harm

Case study continued

Think again about the Green family. Joshua has threatened Lisa and made physical attacks on her. Map what you know about their circumstances and begin to analyse what you already know.

- What more do you need to find out about these experiences?
- Does it feel right to describe Lisa as Joshua's victim?
- Will it be helpful to focus on Lisa's victimhood?
- What is the impact of Joshua's violence on Lisa?
- Is Joshua's behaviour driven by the need/desire to disempower Lisa?

In this instance, as is usually the case in situations where children are violent towards their parents, there is little point in getting tangled up in trying to understand which person is victim or perpetrator. Often people are neither or both. The problem is rarely binary – it is usually fruitless to look for a single cause and since there is rarely a simple explanation for how this issue arises in families. The assessment task is to identify the complex web of reasons behind the incidents.

EXERCISE

Dangerous Child is a film directed by Graeme Campbell and written by Karen Stillman.
Sally keeps quiet about her teenage son's escalating violence until she finds herself suspected of child abuse.

- How does Jack's violence fit into Sally's story?
- How would the story unfold if told from Jack's perspective?
- Whose story is this?

Children's violence towards parents is typically mentioned in passing as just one facet of a complicated history. Most parents who are assaulted by their children are more concerned about repairing the relationship than about the impact of violence on themselves. Boys aged 13–14 are most likely to become perpetrators of violence within their family: 70 per cent of assaults are made by boys and 70 per cent of parents experiencing violence are mothers. Divorce/separation is the most common background factor but children's violence towards a parent usually has its roots in multiple situational factors and is usually best understood by exploring the context in which it arises.

The reasons behind this phenomenon are always complex and particularly challenging to assess since it turns our usual beliefs and expectations about parenting and power dynamics upside down

(Gallagher 2008; Holt 2012). The central message for Lisa and for many parents like her is that change remains possible. Assessment usually involves identifying how best to re-empower the parent. Different models for treatment are beginning to emerge, especially drawing on ideas from the field of restorative justice (Helen Bonnick, independent social worker/consultant/educator, personal communication, April 2013; see also www.holesinthewall.co.uk).

Considering the characteristics of abusers

Sometimes harm arises primarily because of a family member's characteristics. For example, in the Garcia family discussed earlier in this chapter, Amelia has a heavy burden of responsibility. She is isolated and unsupported. Her daughter has already suffered very severe harm. Fundamentally both she and Francis will remain at risk in Amelia's care because of her inability to manage under conditions of stress. Overwhelmed by Gracia's distress, Amelia lashed out at her. She is likely to experience similar circumstances as sole carer of Francis and he too could suffer the consequences of Amelia's poor impulse control.

This book assumes that most parents want to parent well, and that few people actively choose to harm others. From this strengths-based perspective it is not usually appropriate to describe parents whose behaviour harms their children as abusers or perpetrators of abuse. There are exceptions to this rule. A more forensic approach to risk assessment is needed when parentsdeploy their authority and power destructively to inflict emotional, physical or sexual harm on their children.

Case study

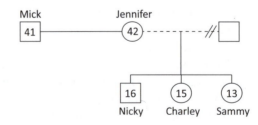

Figure 3.11 The Gray family tree

Jennifer has a history of emotional/mental distress and in her thirties sustained serious injury to her spine after jumping from a road bridge. It was clear that she would no longer be able to manage her home or raise her three children without help. She is pleased when she meets Mick and he soon moves in with her. Over five years or so, Mick proves a dedicated advocate/carer for Jennifer and competently heads up his new household. He soon gains the trust and admiration of professionals involved with the family. Nicky and Charley seem to enjoy life in and out of school. Only Sammy gives cause for concern with challenging behaviour and occasional soiling. Mick takes the lead in seeking help on Sammy's behalf and attends numerous appointments with her at CAMHS. He often voices worry that she too will succumb to emotional/mental distress. When Sammy asks her GP for the pill it finally emerges that Mick has sexually abused her throughout. It is not until long after they have separated that Jennifer confides that Mick raped her on at least three occasions.

- What should be the focus of assessment?
- What are the questions for assessment?
- What are Jennifer's needs as a single adult?
- What are Jennifer's needs as a single parent?
- What are the children's needs?

When children are sexually abused within their family, a co-ordinated multi-disciplinary, assessment needs to explore three dimensions:

- the experience and vulnerability of the child
- the breakdown of protection and safety within the family
- the abusive parent's behaviour, motivation and drivers.

In this case the heart of the story lies in Mick's characteristics as a predatory perpetrator. Jennifer's personal needs and needs as a parent did not cause these events but this family's vulnerability gave Mick an opportunity. When adults sexually abuse children they have already:

- put aside their knowledge that their actions are illegal and morally wrong
- resolved internal inhibitors, for example the fear of being found out

- overcome external inhibitors, for example gained other adults' unconditional trust

- planned how, when and where to commit the offences and 'groomed' the child to accept abuse.

Assessing the continuing risk posed by any perpetrator of child sexual abuse requires a pluralistic approach: it is not safe to rely on either clinical judgement or actuarial assessment alone. Assessment involves gathering information from a number of sources including historical records, clinical interviews, psychometric profiles, and assessments using actuarial tools that measure static, unchangeable risk factors such as negative family history, previous offending and relationship history (Browne, Beech and Craig 2010). Sexual abuse very rarely comes from nowhere. It can be driven by sexual attraction (to pre-pubertal or pubertal boys, girls or both) power, control, revenge or anger; sadism; affection/intimacy needs; and sometimes re-enact the perpetrator's own childhood experience.

In cases of sexual abuse, assessors need to look out for warning signs that a non-abusive parent like Jennifer may not be able to provide protection in the future. Assessment involves identifying the patterns, both positive and negative, that have made the family unsafe (Bentovim 2010). If a parent decides to live with an adult who poses a risk to children, assessment should be geared to designing a plan that empowers the non-abusive parent to:

- be aware and in control

- stay open-minded but sustain some mistrust

- listen/watch/observe

- notice the perpetrator's behaviour/moods

- recognise grooming behaviour

- believe children's accounts

- ask for support.

Focusing on victims' experiences

Case study

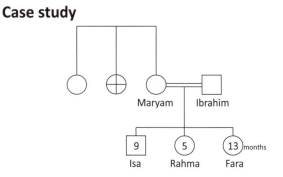

Figure 3.12 The Inuwa family tree

Maryam's first contact with mental health services comes when children's services refer her for assessment. Maryam trained as a nurse in Nigeria before marrying Ibrahim, an accountant whose firm requires him to move every six months. Isa and Rahma are both healthy and strong babies. When Rahma is 18 months old, Maryam takes her to hospital reporting that Rahma had a sudden severe and prolonged convulsion. Although an ECG shows normal brain function she is still prescribed a low dose of anti-convulsant medication based on her mother's reporting. This apparently does little to control the reported seizures and the dosage is steadily increased over the next few years. Maryam reports that her younger sister suffered from severe epilepsy until she died at 16 but no medical records are available.

Rahma gradually becomes more physically infirm and her behaviour more challenging as her medication levels escalate. At four she is enrolled in a school for children with physical and learning impairments. Maryam secures a personalised care budget and organises a roster of daytime care for weekends and holidays. The possibility of Fabricated or Induced Illness (FII) is never raised until the couple request funding for an expensive more specialist school placement for Rahma. A few weeks later Fara is admitted to hospital having apparently stopped breathing.

- What should be the focus of assessment?

- What are the questions for assessment?

- If the epilepsy is Maryam's fabrication, what impact has this had on Rahma?

- Has Rahma suffered physical harm from Maryam inducing illness?

- What are Rahma's needs now?

Most social workers will feel emotionally overwhelmed by the need to 'think the unthinkable', often about parents who have engaged as constructive partners with services and present as caring and competent (Precey 2003). FII is best framed as a continuum where the focus should be on exploring the impact of the parent's behaviour on the child. For example, an older first-time mother with a medical background whose baby was conceived after many rounds of IVF takes her new-born infant to the GP at least once a week and regularly phones her health visitor about very minor concerns. Although she is unduly anxious she is not requesting medication or medical intervention or describing life-threatening events such as apnoea.

Her over-presentation for medical help and advice, failure to be reassured and reported medical background could be seen as fitting the profile of an FII perpetrator. But there could be many other explanations for her behaviour as well: post-natal depression; extreme anxiety because of the significance of the child; isolation and loneliness that can come with new motherhood; or an over-active imagination based on her own medical knowledge. Whatever her motivation, the fact she is not seeking any services that would have a direct impact on the baby's health or development means that the focus of concern is better directed at her than considering a child protection investigation on the baby. Eminson and Postlethwaite (1992) conceptualise FII as being on a spectrum, helpfully highlighting how a range of explanations may need to be considered for the mother's behaviour and its intentionality (Figure 3.13).

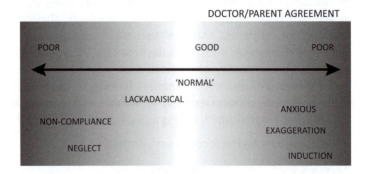

Figure 3.13 Spectrum of illness behaviour (Eminson and Postlethwaite 1992)

In another example, a child may present as chronically underweight with no apparent medical cause. This could be due to a parent not understanding about good nutrition and regular meals, or a delusion about the child's body image, or a deliberate deception where they knowingly starve the child but insist that he has consumed enough food and the child is either too young, too confused or too intimidated to contradict her. Rather than speculating on motivation, action needs to be taken to establish what is happening. One possibility would be to admit the child to hospital, ensure that feeding is undertaken by staff and see what happens. If the child gains weight the parent can be asked how she makes sense of the discrepancy in his weight when he is fed at home.

FII is not easily understood or identified – perpetrators are usually very plausible and often trigger disagreement between the different services involved. Partnership principles and strengths perspectives must be tempered with recognition that overt compliance and care can conceal covert deceit and harm. There are worries that by going down the psychosocial route a genuine medical condition may go untreated. Time can elapse between the identification of a concern and action being taken, and sometimes action is never taken at all because the evidence is too uncertain.

As in Rahma's case, assessment often centres on the parent suspected of harming the child. Sometimes many months or even years go by in fruitless efforts to understand the parent's motivation, and attenuated efforts to secure a psychiatric diagnosis that might explain their behaviour or prove pathological dysfunction. The government has published guidance outlining the causes/impact of FII and providing inter-agency procedures for assessment and intervention (DfE 2008). The overriding message of this guidance is that the impact of FII on the child should be the focus of assessment no matter how bizarre or compelling the parent (Gretchen Precey, independent social worker/consultant/educator, personal communication, April 2013).

Similar processes often affect social work with families where a parent's behaviour is difficult and irrational. When a parent's behaviour seems to indicate emotional/mental distress but is not attributable to an easily treatable psychiatric condition, they may be diagnosed as having borderline personality disorder (indeed, with FII, if there is a psychiatric diagnosis at all, it is likely to be personality disorder). In these circumstances assessment must focus on children's experience and whether the parent's behaviour is harmful to them. Personality disorder is a complex aspect of psychiatric care where the diagnosis itself rarely helps take whole family assessment forward. A productive exchange of information and knowledge between children's workers and mental health social workers should focus on the meaning of the parent's presenting behaviour for the family, its detrimental impact on family members, and what children need to protect them from harm.

Thinking holistically about vulnerability and harm

Theories of risk are complex and hotly contested (Power 2004; Webb 2006). Workers across different services may take quite different approaches to risk assessment, risk management and risk-taking. Talking about risk, how you perceive risk within the family you are working with and your respective approaches to risk assessment, risk management and risk-taking is fundamental to effective collaboration.

Assessing risk and harm is at the heart of most qualified practitioners' workloads and is always complex and challenging. Workers in adult and children's services are equally affected by anxiety when undertaking assessment since it always carries with it the possibility of making mistakes. Uncertainty is inevitable, but its burden can be shared across the service divide: 'a trouble shared is a trouble halved'.

Donald Rumsfeld, US Secretary of Defence, said to a press briefing on 12 February 2002:

> There are known knowns; there are things we know we know. We also know there are known unknowns; that is to say we know there are some things we do not know. But there are also unknown unknowns – the ones we don't know we don't know.

Rumsfeld failed to mention the unknown knowns: reviews of both adult and child deaths repeatedly find that indicators of risk were already known, but not by the worker responsible for assessment! In social work we have to accept that there will be precious few known knowns. Unfortunately, as human beings we have a strong preference for certainty and feel uncomfortable with uncertainty (Goddard *et al.* 1999). Government often colludes with the media by insisting that we should be able to foresee all risks. Practitioners can feel pressurised to provide simple answers and unable to assert the value and necessity of uncertainty.

Ambiguity about the relationship between the individual, family and state lies at the heart of problems in our social care system. UK legislation attempts to marry paternalism with a rights perspective. Social workers bear the brunt of a widespread feeling that state intervention is unnecessary and intrusive. Consequently, only a small proportion of the children who actually experience abuse are ever reported to statutory agencies (Cooper *et al.* 2003). Some workers in adult services share this view and there is some truth in it. Many families get caught up in child protection enquiries compared with a very small number of children experiencing abuse (Cawson *et al.* 2000). Sometimes assessments fail to discuss families' needs because procedures have driven practice into knee-jerk reaction to a specific incident. Thresholds for assessing child protection concerns can be inconsistent. Similar interventions might be recommended regardless of whether children are perceived as in need or at risk. Social workers are better at predicting outcomes where risk is low than in high-risk situations (Hayes and Spratt 2009, 2012).

Case study

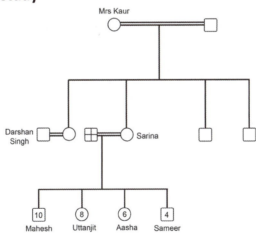

Figure 3.14 The Singh family tree

Dr Bradford and Janeka, an Approved Mental Health Practitioner (AMHP), visit Sarina at home at 10 pm on Friday night at her GP's request. Sarina has had depression for several months and has now sunk into catatonia. When they arrive, Sarina's four children are all in bed. Dr Bradford and Janeka talk with Mrs Kaur and

Darshan before they see Sarina. They easily reach agreement that Sarina needs immediate compulsory treatment in hospital. An ambulance is called to take Sarina to hospital while Dr Bradford and Janeka follow her in Janeka's car. On Monday morning Aasha is admitted with severe splash burns to her eyes and face caused by a pop-tart exploding as she took it out of the microwave. Mahesh is distraught. On investigation, it emerges that Janeka assumed Mrs Kaur would stay behind with the children. Mrs Kaur and Darshan believed that since a social worker was involved in arrangements for Sarina, responsibility had passed to social services. They went home as soon as they saw Sarina safely into the ambulance. The children have been alone all weekend.

- What were the immediate causes of the social worker's mistake?

- What were the fundamental causes of the social worker's mistake?

- What underlying factors contributed to the social worker's mistake?

In this scenario, the children's inherent vulnerability has been overlooked and catastrophically amplified. Root cause analysis is used in many different contexts to identify how mistakes like this arise (Fish, Munro and Bairstow 2008; NHS 2004). It assumes that systems and events are interrelated and that by tracing back how a story has unfolded it is usually possible to discover where the problem started. This tracing back involves investigating patterns, finding flaws in the system and uncovering specific actions or events that contributed to the problem.

Root cause analysis encourages investigators/assessors to look for multiple causation and how different factors have interacted with each other rather than accepting one-dimensional, linear explanations for events. When complex family problems need to be untangled, colleagues thinking together across service divides are in a strong position to reach a deeper understanding of how problems have emerged and how to intervene. Applying root cause analysis across the service divide ensures that assessments address underlying problems rather than just describing symptoms. This in turn enables assessors to formulate constructive recommendations and plans for whole family interventions. Using this approach also encourages assessors to be aware of how separate factors can interact to increase risk.

Mutual challenge and critical thinking

Whole family assessments aim to integrate competing, complex information: families' own expertise; individual members' differing perspectives; contributions from other disciplines; personal and professional values; empirical research; psychological and sociological theory; and the legal and policy framework. Uncertainty and ambiguity are inevitable. Social workers are not super-human, and just as assessment may be affected by assumptions, bias and stereotypes, it may also be flawed by poor thinking processes (Brandon *et al.* 2009; Holland 2004; Laming 2009; Manthorpe and Martineau 2010; Munro 2008, 2011b; Reder and Duncan 1999).

Points to consider

- What errors of thinking did you often make in the past?
- How did you overcome these?
- What mistakes are you still most likely to make?

Workers can lose sight of important information because of how memory and suggestibility function; for example, most people are better at remembering first impressions, vivid experiences and recent events. It is not unusual for workers to feel muddled, confused, overwhelmed or distracted. It is easy to turn away from the unbearable, and particularly difficult to 'see the wood for the trees' when you are worried or anxious (Ferguson 2011). Practice supervisors are most social workers' first port of call when help to think through the assessment process, to analyse the information gathered and to hypothesise about its significance is needed. Skilled supervision helps practitioners bring together specific information about the family; research-based knowledge; theory; and to practice wisdom and intuition by providing space and stimuli for reflection and analysis (Wonnacott 2012). Opportunities to think together across the service divide, with colleagues and their supervisors, increases complexity because more information and ideas are available.

Clear thinking is often compromised by detrimental patterns commonly seen in both adult and children's services, such as:

- identifying events/incidents rather than searching for patterns
- focusing on problem behaviour rather than understanding its causes/drivers

- forming an opinion and sticking to it despite dramatic changes of circumstances or new information

- giving too much weight to gut feelings

- hearing parents' accounts of problems but not children's; that is, the most vulnerable family members are disempowered

- focusing on thresholds and throughput therefore losing sight of professional purpose

- confusing roles/responsibility/accountability

- mirroring families' behaviour (e.g. conflict, neglect, passivity)

- feeling overwhelmed by having too many problems to solve and not enough support/resources

- feeling frightened of a family member (most commonly of a man)

- feeling reluctant to judge families, especially if they are in dire straits

- feeling reluctant to judge families acting on values/beliefs (cultural relativism)

- imposing a personal interpretation of families' experience because of the need to find meaning/explanation

- colouring observations of families with previous personal/ professional experience

- focussing more on risks to self, and to the need to demonstrate defensible practice than on harm experienced within the family.

At root these are all cognitive mistakes (Brandon *et al.* 2008, 2012; Munro 2008, 2011b).

Social workers often have to integrate and mediate different information and ideas from different sources. Whole family assessment demands critical analytical skills. Once qualified, social workers need to gain in confidence and refine the ability to reflect, make sense of complex information and share thinking coherently in meetings and in writing. Talking things through enables assessors to hypothesise and test out the significance of information from different perspectives as well as generate sophisticated analyses of complex problems. The process of sharing and challenging ideas about the family before reaching conclusions expands each worker's capacity for critical reflection. Interrogating each other's ideas can safeguard assessors against errors of thinking.

There is also a place for intuition and gut feeling provided it can be brought into conscious awareness, scrutinised and challenged, whether in supervision or in discussions with colleagues. Experimental psychology and neuroscience join with the psychotherapeutic tradition in a new field of neuro-psychoanalysis that focuses on issues such as motivation, affect, personality, consciousness and dreams (Turnbull 2003). We need to pay particular attention to ensure that these are not undermined by more conventional and analytical approaches to forming judgements.

EXERCISE

Find an assessment report you have written.

- Take four coloured pens to highlight:
    1. descriptive writing
    2. analytical writing
    3. your conclusions
    4. recommendations.

- For each descriptive section answer the question 'So what?'

- For each analytical section answer the question 'What does this mean for the person concerned?' and 'What does this mean for other family members?'

- For each conclusion answer the question 'What is the specific evidence for this conclusion?'

- For each recommendation you have made answer the question 'What research/theoretical knowledge is this recommendation based on?'

Analytical writing is a skill in its own right. You may not have had a chance to develop this fully before you qualified as a social worker. General study guides can enhance your ability to write effective analytical reports.

Defensible recommendations can be achieved when workers across the service divide challenge each other to:

- differentiate between diagnosis, assessment and prediction. It is difficult to predict risk. Overall, assessments are only slightly better than guessing

- understand how risk factors interact with each other (Brown and Ward 2012)

- use tools that help distinguish between high and low risk situations (Hayes and Spratt 2012)

- relinquish the need to predict, in favour of structured clinical decision-making and indicative assessment (Horwath 2010)

- focus less on the detection of abuse and more on the design of effective intervention

- be proactive and decisive in assessments and intervention (Barlow and Scott 2010; Hayes and Spratt 2012)

- acknowledge that the unexpected can and does happen

- explore 'safe uncertainty', design risk-management strategies and be courageous about positive risk-taking.

Conclusions

Working together across the service divide strengthens assessment not least because 'two eyes are better than one'. Collaboration can bring depth and balance to social work assessments by challenging the effects of bias, providing a safeguard against errors of thinking, and shedding extra light on uncertainty and complexity. Different models and approaches to gathering and analysing information can complement each other. Constructive partnerships rely on appreciation and respect for each other's perspective, knowledge and skills, and a willingness to name and explore assumptions and prejudices. Constructive, honest communication and authenticity are essential. Just as partnership between families and social workers relies on a healthy recognition of the power dynamic, so too collaboration between professionals from different parts of health and social care services can be undermined by inequalities of status, whether these are explicit or implicit.

The power dynamic between an authoritative professional and a lay person with no formal knowledge but a crucial role in the family can skew the value of the insights they offer.

Further reading and resources

Bentovim, A. (2010) 'Safeguarding and promotion of the welfare of children who have been sexually abused. The assessment challenges.' In J. Horwath (ed.) *The Child's World. The Comprehensive Guide to Assessing Children* (Second edition). London: Jessica Kingsley Publishers.

Browne, K.D., Beech, A.R. and Craig, L.A. (2010) *Assessments in Forensic Practice. A Handbook.* Chichester: Wiley.

Cleaver, H., Unell, I. and Aldgate, J. (2011) *Children's Needs – Parenting Capacity. Child Abuse: Parental Mental Illness, Learning Disability, Substance Misuse and Domestic Violence* (Second edition). London: The Stationery Office.

Cottrell, S. (2005) *Critical Thinking Skills. Developing Effective Analysis and Argument.* Basingstoke: Palgrave Macmillan.

Gast, L., and Patmore, A. (2012) *Mastering Approaches to Diversity in Social Work.* London: Jessica Kingsley Publishers.

Howe, D. (2008) *The Emotionally Intelligent Social Worker.* Basingstoke: Palgrave Macmillan.

Power, M. (2004) *The Risk Management of Everything: Rethinking the Politics of Uncertainty.* London: Demos.

Precey, G. (2003) 'Children and Risk of Illness Induction or Fabrication (Fabricated or Induced Illness).' In M. Calder and S. Hackett (eds) *Assessment in Child Care. Using and Developing Frameworks for Practice.* Lyme Regis: Russell House Publishing.

Titterton, M. (2004) *Risk and Risk Taking in Health and Social Welfare.* London: Jessica Kingsley Publishers.

CHAPTER 4
Exploring Parenthood

Key messages

- The challenges of parenting can be detrimental to adults' well-being.

- Some people need support in order not to be overwhelmed by the demands of parenting.

- Parents assign special significance to each of their children.

- People struggle to fulfil their potential in the parental role when their own needs are not met.

- The term 'capacity assessment' is used in social work to refer to three quite different processes (mental capacity, parenting capacity, capacity for change), and each can have a part to play in whole family assessment.

Case study

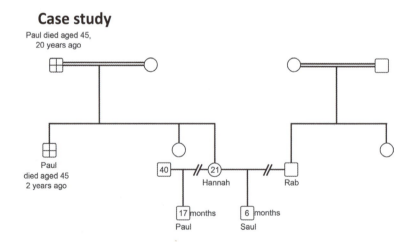

Paul died aged 45,
20 years ago

Paul
died aged 45
2 years ago

40 — Hannah (21) — Rab

17 months — Paul

6 months — Saul

Figure 4.1 Paul and Saul's family tree

Anne, a health visitor, refers Hannah and her family to children's social services. Anne has never before had any concerns about the family and used to see Hannah, Rab and Paul very regularly at her clinic. Hannah stopped going to the clinic for routine checks within weeks of Saul's birth and home visits prove unsuccessful until Anne briefly gains access to a dirty and chaotic living room. Anne hears several young men leaving via the kitchen on her arrival. The room smells of cannabis smoke. Beer cans and takeaway boxes litter every surface. Paul is sitting on the settee under a piece of blanket watching TV. Saul is asleep in his pushchair. Hannah has been unwilling to name Paul's father. Saul's father, Rab, aged 20, lived with them until three months ago.

Ben, a duty social worker, makes a home visit by appointment. He finds the home clean and tidy and sees Paul playing nicely with Saul. Hannah is quite cagey. She tells him she has family nearby, a mother, an uncle and a sister, but that they are all snobs and she only ever liked her brother, who died two years ago aged 45. Her own father also died at 45 soon after she was born. She is unwilling to share information about Paul's father other than that he still lives nearby, has children who are now young adults, and is about 40 years old. She says she was pleased when Rab 'f...ed off back to his mum in Scotland, because he's not all there and he's no use to me'. Hannah tells Ben that she stopped attending the health clinic because she felt too tired to go out but has now been given anti-depressants by her GP. Hannah says she is not interested in joining any local groups because she has plenty of friends, some with children the same age as hers.

- What are the questions for assessment?
- Who else does Ben need to engage with?
- What will happen to Paul and Saul if nothing changes?

Parenting

The rewards of parenting can be especially meaningful, and creating a family can be a powerful driver to live well when adults have other difficulties to overcome. For some, however, its challenges add stresses that can overwhelm both parents and/or families. Parents may fear that professionals will assume they are inadequate and harmful to their children. There is little research on the experience of adults in their role as parents rather than in their own right, or about support they might need to enable them to look after their children as fully as they can (Morris and Wates 2006, p.17).

The social role of parenting is fundamental to the identity of most people when they become mothers and fathers. For women in emotional/mental distress, their sense of self and self-esteem can be powerfully wrapped up in their identity as mothers (Wagstaff 2010). Domestic oppression creates a context that complicates motherhood, particularly as abusive partners often deliberately target mothering and mother–child relationships. Women in these circumstances believe strongly that they are responsible for their children's protection, safety and care, but given their desire to be good or even perfect mothers, they are devastated when others perceive them as failing to protect or meet the emotional needs of their children (Lapierre 2010).

Within the literature on fatherhood, there is remarkably little consensus. Much has been made of the contemporary 'flight from fatherhood' and absence of fathers in children's lives but there is also evidence many men are interested and invested in fathering. Social work assessments often fail to focus on the significance of fathers and their role in families' lives (Brandon *et al.* 2009; Ofsted 2011). Fathers can be excluded from assessment processes because of traditional expectations or by logistical considerations, by workers' preference for focusing on mothers, by identifying fathers only in terms of risks they represent, by their absence, and by their own reticence (Waterhouse and McGhee 2013). When social workers' engagement with fathers is poor, their potential as a resource in the family may not be used and/or the risks they pose in the family may not be properly assessed (Maxwell *et al.* 2012). Sometimes the key to gaining fathers' engagement in assessment is to focus on practical challenges, goal-setting and problem-solving rather than encouraging rumination.

Children's temperaments, personalities, and specific needs impact on how parents perform in their role, on the 'fit' between them, and on how their relationship unfolds (Bogenschneider, Small and Tsay 1997; Maccoby 2000; both cited by Calder and Hackett 2003, p.159). Some children are easier to look after, care for and love than others but this is not to say they are to blame. For example, a baby with colic might leave a parent feeling exhausted and inadequate, or a child's anxiety could have a detrimental impact on both partners' health and on the couple relationship. Sometimes well-meaning parents prove unable to set boundaries for an older child whose misdemeanours outside the home bring troubles to their door. Children's offences can lead to a parenting order or eviction, giving rise to acute distress and parents feeling powerless (Henricson 2003; Hollingsworth 2007). Whole family assessment enables social workers to take into account any physical, temperamental or behavioural difficulties that children bring to the family and how these might affect parents, parenting, family relationships and ultimately children's well-being (Hoghughi and Long 2004).

Case study continued

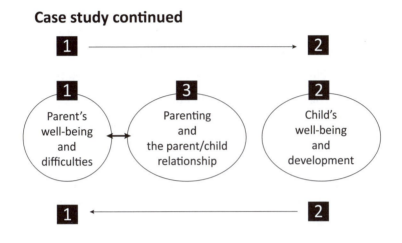

Figure 4.2 Getting to grips with the dynamic between Hannah and Rab's well-being and difficulties, their relationship with their children, and Saul and Paul's well-being and development (adapted from Falkov, 2012)

- What is the impact of parenting on Hannah?
- Can you hypothesise about the significance of Rab's departure for Paul's experience of parenting and the parent–child relationship?

The meaning of the child

The more that human beings are able to envision mental states in the self or other (and thus what is internal to the self and particular to the other) the more likely they are to engage in productive, intimate and sustaining relationships, to feel connected to others at a subjective level, but also to feel autonomous and of separate minds.

(Slade 2005, p.271)

Social workers sometimes sense that something is not right in a family, or for a particular child. This can arise when a child holds special 'psychological significance'. It's as though the child is:

an actor in someone else's play.

(Britton, personal communication, quoted by
Reder, Duncan and Gray 1993, p.52)

For the parent, the child's real identity, personality, and qualities are hidden behind the role they are playing in the parent's story. Children can take on special significance if, for example:

- their birth coincided and is associated with a difficult time

- they compensate for, or remind the parent of, a loss

- their personality, looks or manner remind the parent of someone who abused them

- they fulfil needs arising from unresolved difficulties in the parent's childhood, for example the parent expects unconditional love in this relationship and feels distress when the child opposes them or seeks independence.

Parents caught up in these processes may feel guilty and inadequate, or perhaps angry, presenting the child as the problem. When children are perceived negatively by a parent their capacity for reflection and sense of self is compromised (Fonagy and Target 1997).

EXERCISE

The Illustrated Mum is a novel by Jacqueline Wilson written for a young teenage readership and has been dramatised in a production by Julia Ouston, directed by Cilla Ware. It tells the story of Marigold, who drinks heavily and has bipolar disorder, and the dilemmas faced by her two daughters, Star and Dolphin. Read the book and/or watch the film with some colleagues.

- What role and meaning does Marigold attribute to Star?

- What role and meaning does Marigold attribute to Dolphin?

- How does Marigold's behaviour impact on the relationship between Star and Dolphin?

- How does Star's sense of responsibility affect Marigold?

- How would you describe Dolphin's relationship with Marigold?

Children who are seriously injured or killed by a parent often held a very particular negative significance for them (Laming 2003; Reder *et al.* 1993; Reder and Duncan 1999, p.71):

> Disturbed and abusive parents obliterate their children's experience with their own rage, hatred, fear and malevolence. The child (and his mental states) is not seen for who he is, but in light of the parents' projections and distortions.

(Slade 2005, p.273)

Clues to understanding the child's significance in the family lie in how able parents are to reflect about and tune into what children feel and think. Assessments therefore need to explore parents':

- motivation for having the child
- attitudes and feelings about the child
- capacity to empathise and think about the child's experience.

The Parent-Development Interview is designed to assess these issues and interrogates parents' experience of joy, pleasure, neediness and anger. Social workers can explore these themes with questions such as:

- When do you and your child really 'click'? Give me an example. Can you tell me more? How did you feel? How do you think your child felt?
- What about being a parent gives you the most joy?
- Tell me about a time in the last week when you felt really angry as a parent. How did you feel? What did you do? What effect did your feelings have on your child?

Case study continued

- Can you begin to hypothesise about how Hannah perceives Paul?
- What significance does Rab's absence have for her relationship with Saul?
- What further questions for assessment arise out of considering the meaning Hannah attributes to Paul and Saul?

Parents' needs

Case study continued

- What are Hannah's unmet needs?
- What resources does Hannah have?
- How will you know when Hannah's needs are met?

Assessments sometimes overlook how family life is undermined by the parents' unmet needs (Farmer and Owen 1995; Hetherington *et al.* 2003). Parents' needs can be conceptualised in various ways. Maslow's concept of a 'hierarchy' of universal human needs underpins much social work practice in adult services but is less frequently referred to by children's social workers. Maslow (1970) proposed that people look firstly to meet physiological needs such as food and shelter, and then for safety. They can only engage in love, belonging, intimacy, family and friendship when these basic needs are met. Without good self-esteem it is hard for parents to develop the personal qualities they need, such as confidence, self-respect and respect for others. These in turn are the foundation for self-actualisation, lived out in the parent's capacity to be creative, solve problems and exercise moral judgements. When the basic needs are met, people fulfil their potential. If the basic needs cannot be met or are swept away, the motivation and capacity for maturity and personal growth are lost, with profound implications for parents' ability to meet the demands of family life (Figure 4.3).

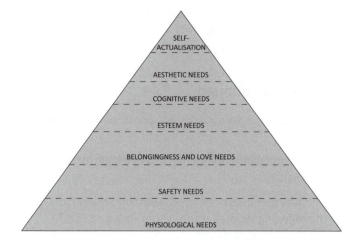

Figure 4.3 Hierarchy of needs (based on Maslow 1970)

The 'human givens' approach (Griffin and Tyrrell 2003) draws upon neuro-scientific insights into the emotional brain and human development. It recognises the basic physical human needs for food warmth and shelter, and Maslow's ideas about intimacy and self-esteem. It also identifies further universal emotional needs that when fulfilled increase self-esteem and the capacity to love and be loved. These basic human needs are for:

- security – safe territory and an environment which allows us to develop fully
- attention (to give and receive it)
- sense of autonomy and control
- being emotionally connected to others
- being part of a wider community
- friendship and intimacy
- sense of status within social groupings
- sense of competence and achievement
- sense of meaning and purpose.

Getting these needs met relies on people already having certain personal qualities:

- the ability to develop complex long-term memory
- the ability to build rapport, empathise and connect with others
- imagination
- a conscious rational mind
- the ability to understand the world intuitively
- an observing self
- the ability to defuse emotional arousal through REM sleep.

This approach provides a helpful framework for understanding what might be missing in an adult's emotional and physical experience and what could be mobilised for them to parent to the very best of their ability. This is about working with parents in assessment to identify, in ways that make sense to them, how their needs might be met.

To support them in fulfilling responsibility for children parents also need to have:

1. Knowledge (e.g. they need to know how to meet children's care needs and interpret their cues, and about their developmental potential and sources of harm).

2. Motivation (e.g. they need to have the desire to protect their child and to sacrifice their personal needs if necessary).

3. Resources (e.g. enough to provide material care and some personal resources to draw on).

4. Opportunity (e.g. they need enough time to be able to be with and focus on their child and a physical space in which they can spend time together).

(Hoghughi 1997, cited by Reder *et al.* 2003, p.5)

Case study

Rona came to the UK from Kurdestan at the age of 15. When she came into care in the UK as an unaccompanied minor, she had not reached puberty and was severely undernourished. She remained in care until aged 18 when she found employment as a nanny. At 19, she met Alain, a PhD student from France and had three children, Henri, now aged 6, Yvette aged 5, and Anne-Marie aged 4. She stayed with Alain for three years, during which he became increasingly abusive toward her, but eventually left him after a particularly violent incident that culminated in rape.

Rona's immigration status came under question when Anne-Marie was born. During a meeting with the Home Office, she made a dramatic call to God for a miracle to reverse the threat of expulsion, and was admitted later that day to a mental health ward for assessment. She was initially diagnosed as psychotic but a subsequent assessment by the same psychiatrist identified her behaviour as a stress response and raised the possibility that she had suffered, undiagnosed, from post-traumatic stress disorder since childhood.

Alain looked after their three children while she was in hospital and subsequently secured custody of them. Two years later she fell pregnant again. She has been unwilling to name the father of this child, but Jon, now three months old, bears a strong physical resemblance to Alain.

The local authority makes an application for a care order at Jon's birth and Rona is required to live with him in a mother and baby foster placement. Gizem, the foster carer, is Turkish but has a working knowledge of Rona's birth tongue. However, the local authority social worker requires them to speak with the baby only in English, and advises Rona that she should even not sing to Jon in her first language. Rona engaged in a parenting assessment two years ago and does so again. Neither of these assessments indicate real concerns about her capacity to care for her children or about her parenting skills.

Jon is thriving and there is evidence of a good attachment between Rona and Jon. Gizem reports that she never feels any need to intervene or to offer support, and that Rona is effectively self-reliant in her care of Jon. Rona has no practical autonomy. Her immigration status is still under question and she is prohibited from seeking employment. While she and Jon remain in foster care she has no access to cash at all – she has to rely on Gizem to buy even personal items such as sanitary products from the foster care allowance.

The local authority now proposes moving Rona and Jon to a residential mother and baby unit for further assessment of Ron's capacity to parent Jon in the longer term.

- What are the questions for assessment?
- What can adult services workers contribute to assessment?
- What can children's services workers contribute to assessment?
- What adversities does Rona face?
- What are Rona's needs?
- How could you ensure a more ethical approach to assessment that will enable Rona to articulate her needs?

Peer support has long-proven value in organisations such as Gamblers Anonymous and 'buddy' systems are now widely used across other kinds of self-help organisations (e.g. MyelomaUK). The effectiveness of 'recovery-partners', led and sustained by people with a history of emotional/mental distress and experience of using mental health services, is the focus of a growing body of outcome-evaluation (Repper and Carter 2011). This research suggests that the benefits of peer-support include reduced hospital admissions, empowerment, improved social support and functioning, empathy and acceptance, reduced stigma and increased hope. Recovery-partners aim to promote well-being and provide a positive role model for recovery by helping people to develop a support plan, and encouraging other helpful relationships. A few new initiatives such as the Strength and Wellbeing for Families Programme work alongside families using peer support, person-centred thinking, and personalisation to co-design bespoke self-help programmes.

Points to consider

Think about parents you have assessed recently:

- Do they have all the informal support they need to parent well?

- What might someone who has lived through similar difficulties be able to offer them?

Mental capacity

Within adult services, social workers use the word 'capacity' to refer to an individual's ability to make specific decisions about their lives; for example, a parent who is unable to manage family finances, or to act on their expressed wish to leave an abusive partner, might prompt concerns about their mental capacity. The Adults with Incapacity (Scotland) Act 2000 and Mental Capacity Act 2005 in England and Wales provide frameworks to empower and protect adults who may not have capacity to make certain decisions for themselves. In Northern Ireland decision-making is still governed by common law. Assessing capacity has become a key issue across the whole of adult services.

Case study

When Aisha first attends the local health centre eight months into her pregnancy her new GP is concerned that she seems completely out of her depth. Aisha comes to her appointment with her aunt, who mostly speaks for her. The community midwife visits the family home and is even more concerned when she attempts to engage Aisha in plans for her delivery. Aisha's family prove reluctant to involve her husband and when the midwife eventually meets Saajid it is clear that he is very worried about their future. He explains that their marriage was arranged according to Hindu tradition by their families. He and Aisha barely met before their wedding and he soon realised that she has very few everyday skills and cannot cope independently. Saajid believes her family is either dishonest or unrealistic about the level of support she needs and fears that Aisha will be unable to care for their baby when he is out at work. The more she gets to know Aisha the more the midwife shares his worries. She wonders whether Aisha even has the capacity to enter into a marriage contract or to give informed consent to medical intervention. The midwife makes a referral to children's social services.

- What are the questions for assessment from the perspective of a social worker in adult services?

- What are the questions for assessment from the perspective of a social worker in children's services?

- How should adult and children's services work together to secure an assessment of this family's needs?

It used to be rare for children's services to give formal consideration to a parent's mental capacity. However, reforms within the family justice system now mean that children's social workers in care proceedings need to:

- anticipate queries about the mental capacity of parents who have not formerly been party to proceedings

- engage with counterparts in adult services with responsibility for mental capacity assessment

- be sufficiently well-informed to raise relevant questions about whether and how the parents' capacity might vary or change

- be prepared to raise detailed questions about parents' capacity in relation to specific decisions or responsibilities.

(Richard Agar, Queen's Counsel, personal communication, February 2013)

The five key statutory principles in the assessment of an adult's capacity are:

1. Every adult has the right to make his or her own decisions and must be assumed to have capacity to make them unless it is proved otherwise.

2. A person must be given all practicable help before anyone treats them as not being able to make their own decisions.

3. Just because an individual makes what might be seen as an unwise decision, they should not be treated as lacking capacity to make that decision.

4. Anything done or any decision made on behalf of a person who lacks capacity must be done in their best interests.

5. Anything done for or on behalf of a person who lacks capacity should be the least restrictive of their basic rights and freedoms.

The mandate to consider capacity inevitably intersects with adult protection processes. In England and Wales, adult protection work is subject only to statutory guidance, *No Secrets* in England and *In Safe Hands* in Wales (DoH 2000a; Welsh Government 2000) in relation to adults defined as 'vulnerable'. However, in Scotland the Adult Support and Protection (Scotland) Act 2007 provides a legislative framework for adult protection and specifies the 'three point criteria' specifying that the 'adult at risk' must be:

1. unable to safeguard their own well-being

2. at risk of harm

3. affected by disability mental disorder, illness or mental infirmity and so more vulnerable to being harmed.

An inspection undertaken by the Commission for Social Care in 2006 found that adults receiving services want more control over their lives, to be able to make real choices and to take control of everyday experiences that most people take for granted. Whether or not direct payments and individual budgets prove effective in achieving these aspirations, adults' social workers will always face dilemmas about individuals who choose to take risks in their lives (Milner and O'Byrne 2009). Whereas the Single Assessment Process used in adult services takes a 'tick-box' approach, the Supported Decision Tool (DoH 2007) is intended to help social workers make informed judgements about capacity and risk. This can also be useful when a parent needs help to think about the best course of action they can take for their family. Its questions encourage a conversation that can enable parents to reach balanced, safe decisions:

1. What is important to you in your life?

2. What is working well?

3. What isn't working so well? What could make it better?

4. What things are difficult for you?

5. Describe how they affect you living your life.

6. What would make things better for you?

7. What is stopping you from doing what you want to do?

8. Do you think there are any risks?

9. Could things be done in a different way which might reduce the risks?

10. Would you do things differently?

11. Is the risk present wherever you live?

12. What do you need to do?

13. What do staff/services need to change?

14. What could family/carers do?

15. Who is important to you?

16. What do people important to you think?

17. Are there any differences of opinion between you and the people you said are important to you?

18. What would help to resolve this?

19. Who might be able to help?

20. What could I do to support you?

21. Agreed next steps – who will do what?

22. How would you like your care plan to be changed to meet your outcomes?

23. Keep a record of any disagreements between people involved.

24. Has a date been agreed to review how you are managing?

The self-help organisation Bipolar UK have long recommended that people who experience mood swings prepare a 'relapse plan' and draw up a written agreement to be implemented if their usual level of competence is temporarily lost. For example, if someone knows that they drive recklessly and at dangerous speeds when they experience a mood swing towards mania, they might agree in advance that their partner should contact the psychiatrist and lock the car keys in a secure place as soon as specific indicators of elevated mood are noticeable. This same principle of agreeing written contingency plans can be helpful for families where it is possible to anticipate how parenting might be compromised by a health relapse, medical crisis or by an escalation of problem drinking/drug use.

Parenting capacity

The assessment of parenting is a notoriously, and perhaps inherently, value-laden area of child welfare practice.

(Calder and Hackett 2003, p.156)

Children's services used to rely on the concept of 'good enough' parenting, but since 2000 (DoH, DFEE and Home Office 2000b) have focused on 'parenting capacity'. Assessing parenting capacity is complex because, at its best, parenting is a highly dynamic process that has to respond to the particular demands and needs of each child. Enabling children to become independent is parenting's fundamental goal, so it can be defined as any and all activities and behaviours that achieve this (Jones 2001; Reder *et al.* 2003). Many different forms of parenting work well. Black children continue to be over-represented in the child protection, care and youth justice systems (Owen and Statham 2009) and yet we still see children with similar backgrounds left unprotected (Brandon *et al.* 2008; Laming 2009). It seems that some social work assessments perpetuate and assert Euro-centric models of parenting, whereas others are dangerously timid about challenging poor parenting where there is cultural difference. Practitioners have to strike a difficult balance to achieve genuinely anti-discriminatory assessments that perceive and understand parents' behaviour as well as focus on how well their children's fundamental needs are met. Models for understanding diversity, discrimination and cross-cultural communication can help practitioners work confidently with diversity (Gast and Patmore 2012). It is important that social work assessment should go beyond simply giving information about ethnicity, nationality, culture, language and religion to explore and make sense of how these influence each parent's parenting style, and expectations of family life (Brophy 2008, cited by Braye and Preston-Shoot 2010, p.39).

The Assessment Framework Triangle (HM Government 2013, p.20) starts by identifying children's needs and invites assessors to explore the extent to which parents meet those needs. It sets out universal expectations about what parenting involves: that parents will provide for the child's basic physical needs, keep them safe, meet their emotional needs, give the child a sense of being specially valued, promote intellectual development through encouragement and stimulation, demonstrate and model appropriate behaviour and control of emotions, and provide a stable family life. Focusing on the interaction between the child's developmental needs and parents' capacity is helpful because it underlines the responsibility not just to prevent children from coming to harm, but also to ensure they will reach their full potential.

Many models have been developed to guide the type of information needed to assess parenting capacity and how to make sense of it. Reder, Duncan and Lucey (2003, pp.15–22) draw on systemic principles, and set out a framework for exploring the interaction between:

- the known history
- the parent (and parent–child relationship)
- the child (and child–parent relationship)
- the context (and family–context interaction).

Farnfield's ecological model of parenting (2008) is rooted in attachment theory and evolutionary psychology (Figure 4.4). It conceptualises parenting as a series of relationship systems.

Hoghughi (1997, cited by Reder *et al.* 2003, p.5) identified three core elements of parenting as:

1. Care (meeting the child's needs for physical, emotional and social well-being and protecting the child from avoidable illness, harm, accident or abuse).

2. Control (setting and enforcing appropriate boundaries).

3. Development (realising the child's potential in various domains).

EXERCISE

Think about a family you have assessed.

- How well does the parent fulfil each of Hoghughi's three elements of parenting?
- If you have found that one of these elements is weak, how will you determine whether this can improve?
- If it is clear that the parent cannot meet a specific need, how else might it be met?

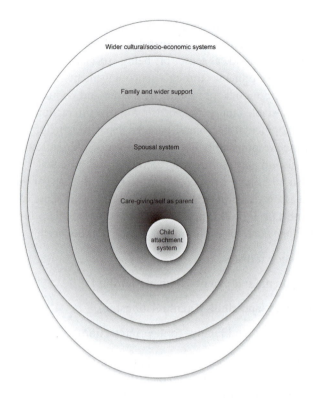

Figure 4.4 An ecological model of parenting (Farnfield 2008, p.1078)

Parenting capacity assessments focus on the concrete evidence of how the parent behaves, but also have to take into account the parents' personal qualities. Belsky and Vondra (1989, cited by Reder *et al.* 2003, p.7) summarised these as:

- Sensitivity to the child's capabilities, developmental tasks and cues; capacity to empathise; a nurturing orientation; realistic intentions; appropriate ascription of child's intentionality.

- Psychological maturity with a stable sense of self; self-esteem; an internal locus of control; belief that own psychological needs are being met; capacity to show affection; ability to enable others; active coping styles; recognition of effects of own behaviour.

- Mental health including warmth; parent-initiated interactions and spontaneity; environment stability and organisation.

- Developmental history of affectionate parenting and an intact family.

Those who experienced poor parenting or abuse do not inevitably repeat these patterns. However, adults' efforts to parent well are compromised by identifiable factors that increase the risk that their children may experience harm (Jones 1997). These include:

- unresolved experiences of childhood abuse
- pervasive problems with power and autonomy
- pervasive problems with expressing emotion
- personality disorder
- problem drug use
- paranoid psychosis
- intellectual impairment
- poor competence in sexual domains
- denial of problems
- lack of empathy for the child
- prioritising their own needs above the child's.

Unfortunately, social work practice has not always made the best possible use of these models or the research that informs them. Indeed, parenting assessments are sometimes not carried out at all (Brandon *et al.* 2008; Woodcock 2003). When assessments of adult's capacity to parent fall short it is often because they:

- struggle to convey the complexity of parenting relationships
- tend to focus on physical care and routines and deal less thoroughly with psychological factors that drive parenting problems
- tend to rely on parents' own reports of how they parent, and stop short of analysing these accounts.

Points to consider

- What does your role enable you to contribute to parenting assessment?

- How well do these models for assessing parenting fit with the assessments you are required to undertake?

- What organisational/professional challenges do you face when you assess parents?

Assessment is more than providing descriptive information about the parents and being well-informed about the difficulties they face. The significance of parents' problems depends on how their behaviour within the family is affected (Brandon *et al.* 2012). Whole family assessments need to ask the questions 'So what?' and 'What does this mean?' to identify the impact of parents' difficulties on the child and vice versa. When you are thinking together across the service divide about parenting capacity, and especially when considering thresholds of harm, you can consider potentially contentious, interconnected questions. For example:

- What does this adult need in order to be a good parent?

- How has the parental role compromised this adult's well-being?

- Has this child experienced good enough care?

- Does this parent have the capacity to meet the child's needs?

- Has this child experienced significant harm?

- Is the harm this child experienced attributable to the parent?

- Has this child been intentionally abused?

- Does this parent have the capacity to keep this child safe?

Each answer in this process is likely to generate further questions for assessment (Rachel Foggitt, independent social worker/consultant/ educator, personal communication, April 2012).

Assessments of families where individuals and relationships have been compromised by several, interacting, life difficulties need to take into account the impact of the past on the present and future. It is also helpful to consider the significance of each separate problem from each child's perspective.

Case study

Brenda has been diagnosed with borderline personality disorder, has a 20-year history of problem drug and alcohol use punctuated by brief periods of abstinence, and has been abused by five partners within the past 12 years. Her life revolves around conflict. Having spent 15 months in foster care at Brenda's request, the three older children demonstrate and articulate the impact of domestic abuse, inconsistent parenting, long periods of neglect and emotional harm. The eldest is thought to have post-traumatic stress disorder and it is very difficult to provide the 12-year-old with 'safe boundaries'. The five-year-old presents as anxious by day and wracked with night-terrors. Family life was extremely chaotic throughout Brenda's most recent pregnancy and during the the youngest child's first three months. Mother and baby have been in a specialist psychiatric placement for 10 months, and during this time Brenda has successfully completed a 16-session cognitive behavioural programme. Her psychiatrist's report indicates that, whereas she previously did not believe that her thinking or behaviour were unusual, Brenda now understands and is able to manage her personality disorder. Brenda is due to return home this week and wants all her children back with her. The psychiatrist supports this plan.

- How does Brenda's recent treatment alter her vulnerability to domestic abuse and problem drug/alcohol use?

- How can a whole family assessment determine Brenda's parenting capacity in the future?

- What can adult services contribute to this assessment?

- How will returning home now impact on the children?

Parenting capacity cannot be assessed once and for all in families affected by the interaction of several life difficulties. The fundamental issue is to anticipate the impact of renewed/continuing difficulties on the children. When a parent's care of their child has been flawed but is considered 'good enough', assessments often recommend 'monitoring'. Subsequent practitioners might interpret this as 'popping in to check things are okay'. You can pre-empt this risk by spelling out what the threshold of 'good enough' looks like in this particular family. This means anticipating the different ways in which difficulties are most likely to arise, and specifying how deterioration might be indicated. Monitoring is better understood and framed as continuing assessment of parental capacity to sustain behavioural change. This, in turn, should raise questions about how to assess adults' motivation to become and remain the best parents they can be.

Capacity for change

Where whole family assessment raises concerns about well-being or safety it is helpful to differentiate between:

1. the parents' theoretical potential to fulfil their role

2. their readiness to change

3. their demonstrable achievement of change in everyday family life.

(Cassell and Coleman 1995)

Case study continued

Think back to Paul and Saul's experience of Hannah as a parent.

*   Are there reasons to think that Hannah cannot be a good parent to Paul and Saul?

*   What is Hannah's motivation to make lifestyle changes?

*   What specific changes would you want to see within six weeks of the initial assessment?

*   What difference will these changes make to Paul and Saul?

*   What recommendations would you make for further intervention?

*   What difference will those interventions make for Paul and Saul?

There are several perspectives on why personal change is notoriously difficult to achieve. Reluctance to change can be understood in psychodynamic terms as a response to loss and as a measure of the human need to retain a sense of control and agency (Griffin and Tyrrell 2003). Systems theory describes how families' systems often prefer stability and to avoid change, and seek to achieve, 'homeostasis' (Minuchin and Fishman 1981). Prochaska and DiClemente (1982) provide a model for understanding universal processes that drive and sustain personal change, but can also undermine it. This helpful model for understanding five stages in the process of change highlights how altering behaviour hinges upon intention and motivation (Figure 4.5).

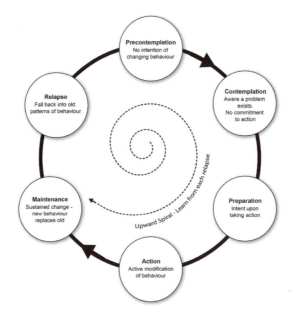

Figure 4.5 A comprehensive model of change (Prochaska and DiClemente 1982)

Several helpful approaches can be used to explore parents' motivation to change their behaviour. Morrison (2006) applies Prochaska and DiClemente's model to parenting, describing seven sequential elements of motivation, as necessary first steps towards genuine and lasting change:

1. I accept there is a problem.

2. I have some responsibility for the problem.

3. I have some discomfort about the impact, not only on myself, but also on my children.

4. I believe things must change.

5. I can be part of the solution.

6. I can make choices about how I address the issues.

7. I can see the first steps to making the change/can work with others to help me.

It is inevitable that parents will feel ambivalent and might even disengage from the change process. When social workers watch out for indicators of ambivalence they can support parents to persevere. Indeed, it is helpful to think of motivation as a product of the interaction between the parent, the assessor and the context in which the assessment is taking place. How much pressure is the parent under? How much support is on offer? Do the parents stand to lose anything if they engage in change? Morrison (1991) described how motivation is driven by the interaction between factors on a long continuum from internal to external drivers for change.

It is unusual for any of us to set about personal change without some external driver. Remember how even small changes that we genuinely want to achieve, such as eating less chocolate or going to the gym, prove exasperatingly difficult to maintain! Horwath and Morrison (2001) developed a model that identifies four possible responses to interventions intended to promote change (Figure 4.6).

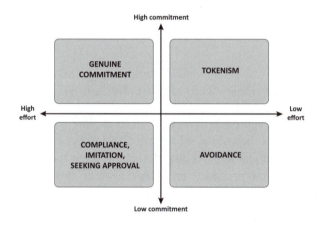

Figure 4.6 A model for recognising ambivalence (adapted from Horwath and Morrison 2001)

Case study continued

- Does Ben have the information he needs to form a judgement about Hannah's motivation to provide for Paul and Saul's needs?

- What do you think Hannah really wants?

Explicit, detailed conversations about their goals can help explore how ready parents are for change. Motivational interviewing focuses on goals and outcomes and has been widely adopted in the field of problem drug/alcohol use (Miller and Rollnick 1991; Scales, Miller and Burden 2003). Motivational interviewing demands tolerance, patience and optimism and a willingness to accept the inevitability of relapse. In order to harness this approach in whole family assessment, social workers need to relinquish the temptation to instruct or advise. It rests on interviews that are simultaneously gentle and challenging where the worker:

- expresses empathy

- avoids arguing

- detects and 'rolls with' resistance

but also:

- highlights discrepancies in history

- raises awareness about contrast between expressed aims and actual behaviour.

Asking parents direct questions about faith, religious practice or spirituality might feel uncomfortable, intrusive or too normative. However, open questions that elicit parents' ideas and fundamental values can elicit conversations that afford useful and immediate insights into their aspirations and drivers. Even in the secular West, the search for meaning and purpose remains a significant driver for most people (Frankl 1984). Questions such as:

- What do you think life is really all about?

- What do you hope your children will tell your grandchildren about the childhood you gave them?

- When you look back at this time in your life what will you see as your biggest achievement?

- What enables you to keep going in the face of difficulties?

can help parents consider their priorities and think purposefully about the future. Their reflections can then inform further discussions about goal-setting and planning for the future. Sometimes parents' answers clarify the need for intervention where it becomes apparent that they will not be able to make the changes their children need.

EXERCISE

Next time you have to meet with family where there are concerns about safety ask a colleague to observe your meeting and make time for discussion afterwards. Ask your colleague to notice your interventions and give you feedback about:

- how comfortable you seemed with holding open, non-judgemental discussions about harmful behaviour within the family

- what skills you used in order to highlight discrepancies between what was described and the concerns that were raised.

Where there are concerns about a child's well-being or safety, social workers have to consider whether a parent's inevitable ambivalence about change is a 'deal-breaker'. It can never be assumed that new parenthood inevitably provides the impetus to reverse entrenched problems. Sometimes 'family scripts', that is, ideas and beliefs carried forward from people's childhood, inject unwanted patterns of behaviour into family life, and stifle their intention to be good parents (Byng-Hall 1995). Children grow up fast and need their parents to fulfil their responsibilities now, not on a promise. Assessment of motivation can make it clear that a parent will need many months or years to change, or even that relapse is inevitable. However, parents who address issues during pregnancy and before their child is six months old, are more likely to sustain a safe environment for their families (Ward, Brown and Westlake 2012).

Motivation is a key issue for assessment in families where a parent is a problem user of drugs or alcohol. There is a widespread assumption that becoming a parent should provide problem users with the motivation to quit but little discussion of how the pressures of parenting might lead some deeper into self-medication.

Social workers conducting whole family assessments can use awareness-raising questions to test motivation such as:

- Never mind me or your family/friends. Do YOU think you have a problem with alcohol/drugs?

- Are you unable to remember some of yesterday?

- Have you argued with family or friends about alcohol/drugs?

- Have you used alcohol/drugs to face problems?

- Have you become physically or emotionally unwell as a result of alcohol/drugs?

- Have you had money problems as a result of alcohol/drugs?

- Have you given up hobbies or work to drink/use drugs?

- Have you been arrested through alcohol/drugs?

- Have you needed to use drugs first thing because of withdrawals?

- Have you felt guilty about your drinking/drug use?

- What are the good things, the enjoyable things, about drinking/ using drugs for you?

- What are the drawbacks/problems, drinking/drug use cause for you?

It is not easy for problem users to get their behaviour into perspective. Using these questions to explore motivation can also help parents move from pre-contemplation through contemplation and towards determination. If a problem user can't think of any downside to drinking/using, then it will be an uphill struggle for them to stop (Rob Jackson, Consultant Psychiatrist, personal communication, April 2006).

Where parents are not fulfilling their aspiration to be better parents because of poor childhood experiences, it is impossible and unfair to assess their motivation to parent differently until they understand why and how they need to change. How this is achieved will depend on the parent's learning style. Many need practical guidance and someone to model better approaches to parenting. Some parents respond well to watching popular TV programmes about parenting. Wildlife programmes can serve as useful starting points for discussion about parenting patterns, beliefs and values. Others will be prompted to reflect on and hopefully be empowered by books about parenting such as:

- Helen Sanderson and Maye Taylor's *Celebrating Families. Simple, Practical Ways to Enhance Family Life.* This is a practical guide for parents and is all about appreciating the individual and enhancing communication.

- Margot Sunderland's *What Every Parent Needs to Know. The Remarkable Effects of Love, Nurture and Play on Your Child's Development.* This is written for parents. It explains neuro-science and child development without losing sight of practical realities.

The double jeopardy of parenting and emotional/mental distress

More than one in three adults diagnosed with psychiatric illness have dependent children living with them. A small but growing number of people diagnosed with bipolar disorder and schizophrenia are parents (Morris and Wates 2006). Around 59 per cent of women in contact with community mental health services are mothers. Being a parent generally reduces the risk of suicide and self-harm in distressed adults, so any indication that a parent has self-destructive thoughts is likely to mean they need urgent help (Brandon *et al.* 2012). Suicide and homicide are most likely when emotional/mental distress coincide with acute problem drug and alcohol use. Increased alcohol and drug use frequently occurs in the period leading to suicide or homicide, often in the absence of more obvious indicators of distress (Appleby 2000).

Hormonal changes during and after pregnancy, compounded by altered lifestyle, relationships and routines, lead to post-natal depression for one in ten new mothers. Lone parents are three times more likely to experience emotional/mental distress than others (CSIP/Barnardo's 2007; Parrott, Jacobs and Roberts 2008). Young women are the group at highest risk of depression because child-bearing and rearing coincide with periods of heightened vulnerability to emotional/mental distress (Falkov 2012, p.27). The NHS does not record patients' parental status, and medical staff may not always recognise its significance, but longstanding research urges social workers to acknowledge and meet the needs of adults in emotional/mental distress *as parents*, and their children as carers, in a positive and supportive way (Aldridge and Becker 2003; Social Exclusion Taskforce 2008; Hugman and Phillips 1992; Webster 1992).

Intellectual impairment

Around 2.2 per cent of the UK's adult population are defined in law (DoH 2001) as 'learning disabled'. The number of parents defined as learning disabled is growing, but meaningful information about their needs is elusive. A further 6.7 per cent of the general population struggle with reading, writing, making decisions and organising everyday life. These adults with intellectual impairment do not necessarily fit the eligibility criteria for adult support services. Different sources provide wildly varying estimates of how many children grow up with a parent whose parenting may be compromised in these ways. We have very little information about the long-term health and well-being of adults who have grown up in the care of parents with intellectual impairment (McGaw and Newman 2005).

It is not easy to generalise about these families' experiences since individuals will demonstrate skills in some areas of parenting and deficits in others. For adults with an IQ of more than 60 there is no direct link between their IQ and parenting ability. Parents with intellectual impairment may struggle to adapt to their children's changing needs and need help to learn and retain new skills. These parents are more likely than the general population to have been abused as children; and for those whose own childhood experiences were negative, a poor sense of their potential and worth can make raising children even more difficult (Cleaver, Unell and Aldgate 2011). Stigma, reduced opportunities to learn how to parent from friends and family, and lack of support to develop new skills can further undermine their potential as parents (SCIE 2005c).

Parents with varying degrees and types of intellectual impairment can face difficulty in fulfilling family roles and responsibilities. Risks to children can include problems arising out of poor access to ante-natal care, developmental delays that can arise from either genetic or environmental influences, behaviour problems, language delays, and unintentional neglect (James 2004). Long-term, home-based, holistic interventions are often effective in sustaining good parenting when support and education is personalised to the individual's needs and ability. The provision of firmly structured, intensive, reliable, long-term, informal and formal support is the best way of ensuring that parents will succeed (McGaw and Newman 2005). Sound specialist, diagnostic and functional assessment is therefore essential (SCIE 2005c; Morris and Wates 2006).

The model most widely used in the UK is the Parenting Assessment Manual (McGaw et al. 1998). This sets out a competency-based, holistic approach to mapping a family's strengths and needs, taking into account environmental factors, stressors and the support available to the parents. It focuses on empowering parents. McGaw (2000) helpfully emphasises that assessment processes should help parents learn to say 'no' rather than encouraging passivity and compliance.

Without a good quality assessment, families can be caught up in generic, service-led interventions that do not take into account parents' specific needs and are unlikely to enhance parenting. For example, one mother described attending a parenting class:

> I had not got on with any of the other women, so they said I had problems with social things. It was not me. It was the group. They could not accept me. And now it was my fault and was put in my notes.
>
> (Parent quoted by Children's Commissioner 2010, p.24)

These families are over-represented in statutory children's work. Around 50 per cent of parents with intellectual impairment lose the care of their children. Consequently 25 per cent of children on care orders involve a mother and/or father with intellectual impairment and they are almost twice as likely to be adopted as other children.

Some parents are unfairly 'presumed incompetent'. Local authorities and the civil courts sometimes act on the stereotype that parents with intellectual impairment cannot learn the necessary skills and will pose risk to their children (McConnell and Llewellyn 2002). On the other hand, evidence also suggests that high referral and intervention thresholds leave the needs of children in some families neglected far too long. Assessments are often delayed until crisis-point, too few skilled and robust social work assessments of parents' latent capacity are undertaken, and specialist assessments of developmental potential and specific needs are rarely commissioned (Cleaver and Nicholson 2008). These children therefore suffer the double blow of prolonged harmful experiences within their families followed by removal into the care system. This is a tragedy for parents and children alike.

Disabled parents and parents with sensory impairment

UK labour force surveys suggest that around three million children live with disabled parents, parents with limiting longstanding illness and parents with sensory impairments. There is, though, remarkably little research about the impact of parental disability on children (Blewitt *et al.* 2011; Dearden and Aldridge 2010). These parents say they most want help with childcare, domestic tasks, and transport, and report that their needs are not met for a number of interconnected reasons:

- Children and adult services fail to co-ordinate with each other and the quality of assessments undertaken is sometimes poor (Morris 2003).

- The community care provisions for parenting support to disabled parents are not clear about entitlement and the law is difficult to understand (Goodinge 2000).

- The artificial divide between adult and children's services increases fear, anxiety and vulnerability and discourages parents from requesting help (Wates 2002).

- Social isolation means that many disabled parents miss out on support and information (Blewitt *et al.* 2011).

Case study

Sally has been blind from birth and was raised by blind parents. She has a poor relationship with her parents but is close to Paul, her sighted older brother. Paul is married with two young children. At just 15, Sally realises that she is pregnant and immediately decides the baby should be adopted. Her son Ethan, a healthy sighted baby, is placed at birth with well-matched parents but within weeks Sally regrets her decision. She asks for contact with a view to Ethan returning to her care. Children's services reluctantly agree to contact, and undertake an assessment. This concludes that she is too immature to fully appreciate Ethan's needs, and that her support network is insufficient to enable her to parent well.

Sally's solicitor instructs an expert witness who explores these issues and concludes that Sally has the potential to parent successfully, that her brother and his wife are committed to offering active support, and that Ethan has the right to be raised within his birth family. Children's services do not accept these recommendations, citing new concerns about Sally's ability to parent a sighted child. They emphasise that at supervised contact in a family centre Sally has looked unkempt, tripped over toys while holding Ethan, held a spoon too far away from Ethan's mouth for him to reach his food, and sat in the dark with him as the light faded.

- What are the questions for assessment?

- What contribution can adult services make to this assessment?

- Is it fair to asses Sally's potential on the basis of formal contact sessions in an unfamiliar setting?
- What is driving decision-making in children's services?
- How can children's services progress this assessment?

The emphasis within adult social care legislation and guidance on assessing what people can or cannot do underpins a deficit approach to disabled parenting rather than addressing the social and economic factors that create and exacerbate disability. Human rights legislation requires that all parents should be judged by the same standard. However, assumptions and misunderstanding about how disability affects families and lifestyles can drive a negative spin on parents' reasonable requests for help (Crawshaw and Wates 2005; Goodinge 2000; Lapper 2005). Disabled parents continue to highlight problems created by inaccessible environments and forms of communication. They often incur unavoidable additional costs not covered by disability benefits (SCIE 2005b).

Adult social workers, especially if they work in multi-disciplinary teams, may be able to engage psychologists, physiotherapists and occupational therapists as contributors to whole family assessments. Accessing this specialist expertise can introduce innovations and modifications that make parenting easier for disabled parents. Individual budgets and personalised plans can be designed to differentiate people's personal needs from what they might need to meet their family responsibilities.

Conclusion

The traditional Yoruba worldview is that children are the *summum bonum*, the chief good in life (Zeitlin 1999), and for most parents having children is at the heart of their identity. It is usually a devastating blow for parents to realise they have failed to meet their children's needs. Most parents are heart-broken to lose their children. Every assessment, whether led by adult or children's services, has to reach an understanding of what being a parent means to each adult, with a view to supporting them to parent to the best of their ability. Assessments that inform the earliest, best possible, most powerful interventions to address the needs of families facing difficulties have the potential to transform troubled lives. Since children's welfare and needs must always be paramount, all social workers have no option but to scrutinise parenting through the lens of the child's experience.

Further reading and resources

Blewitt, J., Noble, J. and Tunstill, J. (2011) *Improving Children's Outcomes by Supporting Parental Physical and Mental Health*. London: Centre for Excellence and Outcomes in Children and Young People's Services (C4EO). Available at www.c4eo.org.uk, accessed on 19 July 2013.

Cleaver, H., Unell, I. and Aldgate, J. (2011) *Children's Needs – Parenting Capacity. Child Abuse: Parental Mental Illness, Learning Disability, Substance Misuse and Domestic Violence* (Second edition). London: The Stationery Office.

Griffin, J. and Tyrrell, I. (2003) *Human Givens: A New Approach to Emotional Health and Clear Thinking*. Chalvington: HG Publishing.

Reder, P., Duncan, S. and Lucey, C. (2003) 'What Principles Guide Parenting Assessments?' In P. Reder, S. Duncan and C. Lucey (eds) *Studies in the Assessment of Parenting*. London: Routledge.

CHAPTER 5

Understanding Children's Experiences

Key messages

- The behaviour of parents with difficulties impacts differently on each child in the family.

- Each child is unique, has unique needs, and has their own personal identity.

- Each child's potential is affected by the unique challenges they face.

- Growing up with parents whose capacity is compromised by problem alcohol or drug use is harmful from conception, throughout adulthood and into adult life.

- The combination of problem alcohol and drug use alongside parental emotional/mental distress is particularly toxic to children.

Case study continued

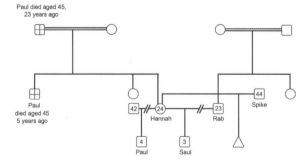

Figure 5.1 Paul and Saul's family tree three years later

Hannah is referred to both the community mental health team and a specialist midwife by a voluntary sector problem drug/alcohol use clinic. Hannah has attended the methadone clinic for 18 months. The clinic workers have longstanding concerns about her well-being: they recognise that Hannah often uses alcohol, heroin, cocaine and cannabis alongside her regular prescription and that her friends are all street-drinkers. They have noticed that Hannah's mood and behaviour are increasingly erratic and are worried that she talks about being pregnant but has sought no medical advice. The referrals include information about Paul and Saul but little detail about Hannah as a parent because she does not bring them into the methadone clinic.

Doreen, a social worker from the community mental health team, meets with Hannah by appointment at the clinic. Hannah is tearful and talks very rapidly and incoherently about how she feels completely overwhelmed by a whole list of worries: rent arrears, neighbour disputes, Saul's behaviour, and her mother's recent death all feature in her tirade. She discloses that her partner Spike, aged 42, expects her to have sex with his 'friends', that she is unsure when she fell pregnant and that she wants to terminate the pregnancy. Doreen asks about Hannah's coping mechanisms and learns that her friendships are 'a lifeline'.

When Sue, the specialist midwife, visits Hannah's home the next day, she finds the house in darkness with no heating or light. Hannah is not at home but a group of adolescents aged between 12 and 15 are immersed in a noisy computer game. They let Sue in and offer to text Hannah. Paul has a high temperature and is asleep on the living room floor in a vest. Wearing only a very soiled nappy, Saul insistently climbs up onto Sue making loud noises but does not speak. She can see that Saul has numerous small burns on his arms and back. Sue immediately contacts children's social services.

Cheryl, the duty social worker, arranges to make a joint visit with the police later that afternoon and secures a provisional appointment for paediatric assessment. The police use their emergency powers to remove Paul and Saul. It emerges that Spike has a long history of criminal offences associated with dealing drugs and for domestic abuse. Children's services identify Spike as a pseudonym and realise that he is already well-known to them having been implicated in child sexual abuse over many years. They initiate care proceedings.

- What are Hannah, Paul and Saul's immediate needs?

- What are the questions for assessment?

- What is Doreen's role in the assessment process?

- What knowledge, theory and research must Cheryl refer to as she designs the assessment?

Empowering children's voices

Every child has the right to say what they think in all matters affecting them, and to have their views taken seriously.

(Unicef's summary of Article 12, United Nations Convention on the Rights of the Child, 1989)

This principle applies equally to workers in all services and is enshrined in family law in all three UK jurisdictions:

Every assessment must be informed by the views of the child as well as the family. Children should, wherever possible, be seen alone and local authority children's social care has a duty to ascertain the child's wishes and feelings regarding the provision of services to be delivered.

(HM Government 2013, p.21)

Most children can articulate vital information that adult social workers need to know about their families. Those growing up with parental problem drug/alcohol use or domestic abuse know about their parents' problems even when adults try to conceal and reduce their impact on family life (SCIE 2004). Children can also offer valuable insights about the needs of parents with emotional/mental distress (Armstrong 2002; Dulwich Centre 2008; Riebschleger 2004; Stallard et al. 2004; Totsuka 2008). Young carers say that social workers should ask them about how their parent is and what kind of support would be helpful, as they often know more about this than anyone else. Where there are complex problems, shifting the focus away from the professional perspective to take a 'child's eye view' can be helpful (Cossar et al. 2011, p.9; Jones 1997, p.526):

Some adults can be too busy to listen to what kids want to say – sometimes kids say some amazingly influential and important things because they see the world from a different perspective.

(Child quoted by Morgan 2010, p.32)

Children often express concern that they don't get to know social workers well enough to trust them; they have a sense of injustice that they so rarely have a say; and disquiet about being kept ill-informed (Cleaver and Walker 2004; Cossar *et al.* 2011; Morgan 2006). These complaints are supported by evidence that social workers are not sufficiently or consistently able to observe, engage, play or talk with, and focus on children (CSCI 2005; Horwath 2010). Reviews of child deaths have shown how dangerous this can be (Brandon *et al.* 2012).

Children's perspectives are often ignored or misrepresented, distorted or only partly articulated and there is little evidence that direct work is at the heart of every assessment (Horwath 2010). It seems that even when social workers hear children's opinions, they don't necessarily write these into important reports for case conferences or court hearings (Cossar and Long 2008, cited by Cossar *et al.* 2011; Holland and Scourfield, 2004). Interestingly, practitioners who may have the closest connection to individual children and hear about their thoughts and feelings (e.g. mentors, classroom support workers, play therapists) sometimes report that they are excluded from formal assessment process and their opinions are marginalised:

Too quickly (we) make a child's view true and authentic when it's to our advantage, but if the child disagrees then it's more difficult… then we tend to explain this view by reference to circumstances that reduce the validity of the child's view.

(Archard and Skivenes 2009, p.397)

When it became clear that no social worker had communicated directly with Victoria Climbié, Lord Laming emphasised that:

Seeing, listening to and observing the child must be an essential element of an initial assessment for any social worker.

(Laming 2003, p.238)

However, subsequent reviews of child deaths (Birmingham SCB/ Radford 2010; Westminster LSCB 2006) bear poignant witness to how children are so readily silenced. Ofsted's examination of 67 child death reviews found that:

The child was not seen frequently enough by the professionals involved or was not asked about their views and feelings.

Agencies did not listen to adults who tried to speak on behalf of the child and who had important information to contribute.

Parents and carers prevented professionals from seeing and listening to the child.

Practitioners focused too much on the needs of the parents, especially on vulnerable parents, and overlooked the implications for the child.

Agencies did not interpret their findings well enough to protect the child.

(Ofsted 2011, p.4)

Reviews of child deaths repeatedly identify that social workers still sometimes fail to see children altogether.

Particular groups of children are more likely to be marginalised in family assessments than others, including:

1. children of parents who are unco-operative or overtly hostile towards social workers

2. children of parents whose compliance with social workers disguises the harm they inflict within the family

3. children of parents whose own complex and pressing life difficulties distract social workers' attention

4. children who are hostile, hard to engage or refuse to talk

5. adolescents

6. disabled children

7. siblings who are not presented as having problems

8. children who are unable to speak because of disability, trauma or threats

9. children whose first language is not English.

(Rose and Barnes 2008; Brandon *et al.* 2008, 2009)

Workers can struggle to hear parents' perspectives, let alone the voices of children, for a number of reasons:

- Practitioners' knowledge and training is valued over expertise gained from experience.

- Commitment to keeping children with their families leads workers to conflate children's and parents' identity so that the family law paradigm works against children's rights (Sawyer 2006).

- Practitioners shut off from children (sometimes consciously and sometimes unconsciously) to avoid feeling overwhelmed by their struggles and emotional pain (Ferguson 2011; Rustin 2005).

- Practitioners don't have the skills needed for working with children (Gibb 2009; Munro 2011b, p.112; Taylor and Boushel 2009).

- There is an assumption that caring adults know best and that children have less right to a say because they have no responsibility. Children often do understand their responsibility for their own behaviour and actions, prioritise the right to be protected from abuse *and* value the right to be heard (Butler-Sloss 1988; Morgan 2010).

- There is uncertainty about when and how to take children's views which conflict with those of the parents or other professionals.

- Staff turnover and the lack of venues for direct work compromise social workers' intention to work directly with children (Leeson 2007; Winter 2009).

- Getting to know children feels like an unachievable luxury and lower priority than talking with their parents and other professionals, administrative tasks, recording and filing reports on time (Horwath 2010; Munro 2011a).

You would say to them about something that's happening or how you feel and they would always seem in a rush to get away or feel like you have to hurry the conversation.

(Child, quoted by Children's Commissioner 2010, p.34)

Children often do understand their responsibility for their own behaviour and actions; prioritise the right to be protected from abuse; *and* value the right to be heard (Buttler-Sloss 1988; Morgan 2010).

Case study continued

- What questions should Doreen ask Hannah?
- How can Cheryl ensure that Paul's knowledge and experiences are properly understood?
- Can Cheryl learn anything from direct work with Saul?
- What questions should Cheryl ask Hannah?

Empowering children's voices relies on accurately assessing how able the child is to understand their situation and contribute. A clear picture of the child's psychological and intellectual development is needed if children's wishes and feelings are to be attributed value and meaning. Assessing each individual child's ability to conceptualise the decisions to be made requires careful consideration. Social work assessments have to weigh up a complex constellation of factors such as age, genetic potential, cognitive and neurological development, life experiences, current circumstances and cultural context. Judgements about children's competence can be difficult and complex for legal, psychological, ethical or practical reasons (Lefevre 2010; Reder and Duncan 2003b). The following generalisations drawn from psychological research, applied cautiously, give some helpful pointers:

- Very young children's ability to reason, to consider abstract ideas, to discuss hypothetical 'what ifs' is undeveloped (Hobson 1985). These abilities gradually take shape during middle childhood. By early adolescence, most children can think more flexibly about complex questions and abstract ideas.

- Very young children's limited understanding of time relations makes it difficult for them to consciously contribute to plans. In middle childhood they still rely on adults to order their experience of events in the past, present and future. It is not until adolescence that they can really begin to envisage and therefore make plans for the future (Piaget 1969).

The judgement in *Gillick* v. *West Norfolk and Wisbech Area Health Authority* [1986] determined case law and has been incorporated into the British Medical Association guidance (British Medical Association 2001):

Parental right yields to the child's right to make his own decisions when he reaches sufficient understanding and intelligence to be capable of making up his mind on the matter requiring decision.

Thomas (2002) identified six key aspects of children's participation:

1. the CHOICE the child has over his or her participation
2. the INFORMATION s/he has about the situation and about her or his rights
3. the CONTROL s/he has over the decision-making process
4. the VOICE s/he has in any discussion
5. the SUPPORT s/he has in speaking up
6. the degree of AUTONOMY s/he has to make decisions independently.

EXERCISE

Take five minutes to prepare a statement you could use to explain your professional role to a specific child or young person in a family where you have a responsibility for assessment.

I don't like people looking down on me and I don't like people looking up at me like I'm an adult. I like people talking to me for my age.

(Child cited by Cossar *et al.* 2011, p.4)

Working with children

EXERCISE

- Who did you confide in as a child?
- Can you remember important conversations you had with adults? Where did these take place? Who took the initiative? Who did most of the talking?
- How did you prefer to communicate with adults?

Above all, children want a trusting, stable relationship (Munro 2011b, p.129). They are most likely to trust social workers who come across as warm, friendly, kind and caring, empathic and concerned, open, genuinely interested, honest, non-judgemental, respectful, accessible, consistent, trustworthy and reliable, comfortable playing and talking with children, able to handle strong feelings, and interested in how children think and feel (Bell 2002; Butler and Williamson 1994; Freake, Barley and Kent 2007; Jones 2003; Munro 2001, 2011a, Chapter 3). The descriptions of 'the world's worst Common Assessment Framework assessor' gathered by the National Children's Bureau (2004) are particularly unflattering and telling! Projects such as Kidstime have demonstrated that a forum where children can explore their concerns and begin to develop resources to cope with difficult situations can empower them (Cooklin *et al.* 2012):

> Recognising children's competence and intentionality, facilitating their self-expression and listening carefully to what they convey… requires a real commitment and an anti-oppressive approach to sharing power.
>
> (Lefevre 2010, p.69)

When social workers fail to connect with children, assessments are inevitably, sometimes fatally, flawed by:

> Throughout the studies there was a sense of disconnection from the children themselves: not paying attention to children's emotional development and not thinking about what it's like to be a child living in that family or beyond the school setting; seeing the disability not the child; and most powerfully holding back from knowing the child as a person.
>
> (Brandon *et al.* 2012, p.7)

Finding out what children know and think is best achieved through informal, unstructured exchanges where the emphasis is on listening, and following the child's lead (Reder and Duncan 2003b, pp.134–136). While some children are able and willing to give straightforward verbal accounts of their experiences, most use a much wider repertoire of media to express themselves. Many convey their feelings and needs best in symbolic or non-verbal ways (Thomas and O'Kane 2000). Magaluzzi's poetry (cited by Lefevre 2010, p.64) refers to the richness of children's ability to share and communicate as the 'one hundred languages of childhood'.

EXERCISE

- Spend time with several different children that you know outside of work.

- Notice how many of the 'one hundred languages of childhood' they employ.

- Notice which of these you feel most comfortable with.

Finding out about children's experiences

Whole family assessment relies on learning about children's daily routine, where they go, who they spend time with, how they feel about the people in their lives, whether they regularly benefit from good experiences at certain times, and recurrent difficulties. For example, if a mental health worker usually visits a parent during school hours they may not gain a sense of how stressful a time the whole family has first thing in the morning or at mealtimes. Where several workers from different services are carrying out assessment, perhaps in different settings, there are opportunities to get a more rounded picture. For example, social workers can draw a clock face to map family members' thoughts and feelings at different times of day so that together they can identify any significant patterns and design any changes needed (Raynes 2003, p.129):

> Professionals need to be attuned to the child's world, to pay attention not only to what the child says, but in some cases to what they are not saying and in all cases to how they behave.

> (Cossar *et al.* 2011, p.8)

By contrast with nursery nurses, who usually achieve great expertise in direct observation, social workers do not always develop these skills. Learning to observe children helps to keep the practitioner focused on the child and the child's perspective. Child observation can address crucial questions. For example, does the child play freely, display emotions, play out care-giving/affection or anger/control (Lefevre 2010; McKinnon 2009; Ofsted 2011). There are several different approaches to direct observation including naturalistic, targeted, time sampling, and the Tavistock method. Each of these has advantages and disadvantages (Fawcett 2009).

Children may not be able to recognise, regulate or express how they feel. They can feel a complex mixture of feelings, including loyalty to their parents, and may angrily align themselves with a hostile parent (Cossar *et al.* 2011). Workers can easily unconsciously influence what children say because children can be especially sensitive to the worker's unexpressed desires and feelings (Jones 2003, cited by Lefevre

2010, p.53). Sometimes, abused children develop behaviours as survival strategies, so that what a child does (for example, running away, stealing or telling lies) might convey more than their words can say (Brandon, Schofield and Trinder 1998; Cossar *et al.* 2011; Howe 2005; Schofield and Beek 2006). It is unwise to interpret unusual or distressed behaviour before giving children other opportunities to convey their meaning.

Inevitably, some workers will feel more comfortable and skilled in creating an easy rapport with children than others. This does not necessarily rely on having special techniques or tools, but does demand intuition and flexibility. Some workers come across as friendly and open, inviting children to confide in them regardless of their role or setting. The essential tools are self-awareness and willingness to learn from children, so that communication style can be consciously adapted to meet children's needs (Trevithick 2005).

Boys are less likely than girls to confide in others (Butler and Williamson 1994; ChildLine 2003) and as they grow older, children tend to entrust problems to friends rather than adults (Featherstone and Evans 2004). Children will tell only friends or siblings about their worries unless workers take initiatives to build trusting relationships. Children recognise when social workers relate to them as 'objects of concern' rather than people, for example by bombarding them with questions instead of following the child's lead (Butler-Sloss 1988; Children's Commissioner 2010). Children dislike it when they only see their social workers at meetings, and when decisions are made by professionals they've not met, let alone got to know and trust (Children's Commissioner 2010; Cossar *et al.* 2011).

If parents or children have mixed feelings about meeting with a social worker, children can be enabled to initiate communication privately, for example by agreeing a code word, giving the child a diary to write down worries in, or giving the child a mobile number to send texts to (Cossar *et al.* 2011; Hutton and Partridge 2006; Morgan 2006a; Ofsted 2011). Social workers can help children feel comfortable by setting aside their power and status, such as making appointments that suit the child's schedule and in places that meet their needs, using advocates or interpreters, spending time with the worker in a playground, or window shopping (Lefevre 2010, p.73).

Child-centred, relationship-based practice means doing whatever it takes to:

- help children feel safe and build trust
- match the child's pace

- communicate in ways that children are familiar and comfortable with, for example play, activity, symbolic, creative and expressive techniques

- find methods and tools that engage children and help them communicate, for example ecomaps, rating scales, questionnaires, life-story books.

Appendix 3 lists just some of the many resources and toolkits intended to support practitioners' engagement and communication with children.

EXERCISE
Look back over an assessment you have completed recently.

- How did you engage with children in the family?

- How did you report their understanding and knowledge of the family?

- Prepare two brief letters to explain the outcome of your assessment, and any decisions or recommendations you have made: one for the oldest child and one for the youngest.

Hearing about children's experiences

Children figure out their own ways to resolve worries. Social workers need to ask about these to help strengthen children's own positive strategies, and develop alternatives to any harmful strategies (Cossar *et al.* 2011, p.9). Children sometimes withhold their views because of stigma and discrimination, or loyalty, respect for and protectiveness towards parents (Totsuka 2008). Sometimes, cultural differences, negative experiences or media portrayal of social workers generate mistrust.

If assessments are rushed, children might withhold what they need to say and assessment can miss the point if they fail to disclose their worst experiences and fears (Jones 2003). Children sometimes describe harmful experiences in ways that differ from how abuse and victimisation are understood by researchers and professionals (Cawson *et al.* 2000). When children tell their troubles to an adult they trust, the adult should avoid interrogating or making assumptions but listen carefully and make a verbatim record in case what they say needs forensic investigation. The most important thing in these circumstances is to show children that you are interested, concerned and will be able to cope, so that they know that they can be heard and understood safely:

> They kept talking longer than small, so I couldn't keep up with it, and they kept talking a question then a different question before I answered…put the questions a bit smaller!

> (Advice of a six-year-old to professionals, quoted by Westcott and Davies 1996, p.465)

Whenever it is suspected that children have been victim of, or witness to, a criminal offence, they may be formally interviewed by specially trained police officers and social workers following procedures set out in *Achieving Best Evidence* (Ministry of Justice 2011). The threshold for determining children's capacity to give evidence in criminal proceedings requires only that the child should be able to understand questions put to them and to give answers to them which can be understood. This means that children as young as three can record their evidence.

It can be difficult, and sometimes traumatic, for children to articulate their experiences in these interviews. If there is sufficient evidence to go to a criminal trial, children can be offered therapeutic support but should not be encouraged to talk about the offences until after the trial. *Achieving Best Evidence* is based on psychological research (Holliday and Marche 2012) but workers without the specialist training sometimes feel uncertain about how and when children can recall and report events accurately enough to provide good evidence. Workers also worry that they might inadvertently mess up children's forensic evidence. Five main threads in the psychological literature inform *Achieving Best Evidence*:

1. social and linguistic rules

2. suggestibility to leading and misleading questions

3. memory

4. language development.

Deception and lies. An understanding of the forensic research evidence is helpful not just for those conducting formal investigative interviews but for any worker who wants to enable children to explain their experiences authentically and clearly.

Child development

Various assessment frameworks set out the progress children usually make as they grow up. These are useful but need to be applied with caution because the differences between individual children are as important as the similarities you might expect at each stage of development (Davis 1998). Most research on child development is conducted in Western Europe or North America and is based on those growing up in white, middle-class families of European origin (Lightfoot *et al.* 2008). This knowledge may have little relevance to children raised in families where parents' behaviour and expectations generate different developmental patterns.

Robinson's discussion of how different child-rearing practices and norms affect attachment strategies, cognition, communication, socialisation and identity formation provides a helpful starting point for assessing individual children's developmental needs (Robinson 2007). The danger is that, without a cross-cultural perspective, family assessments will scrutinise deficits rather than identifying strengths when they assess children who do not fit universal/biological 'norms' determined by studies of atypical groups.

The shockwave from Victoria Climbié's tragic death highlighted how the importance of sensitive and flexible approaches to assessing children's development should not eclipse professional focus on children's health and development (Laming 2003). Cultural relativism, whereby poor parenting and compromised child health or development are attributed to cultural factors, is a seductive but dangerous trap. Social work still struggles to resolve the problem of cultural relativism. Given continuing evidence of endemic racism in British institutions, social work's journey from indifference to liberal celebration of diversity/multi-culturalism is deeply problematic. The USA's experience of forging its 'rainbow' identity out of the civil rights conflict, South Africa's struggle towards 'Peace and Reconciliation' and the Northern Irish experience of building non-sectarian communities still have little impact on how social work in the UK frames anti-racist practice in the complex communities we serve. The law is explicit that harm and its significance should be measured against the norm of most children's experience. We cannot afford to drop our expectations on behalf of children who face adverse circumstances.

Points to consider

Is it 'normal' for:

- working-class boys to be encouraged to model themselves on men who abuse women?

- a blind 16-year-old to be dressed in hand-made clothes?

- the needs of a boy with autism to be met in a purpose-built annexe of the family home by a 24-hour rota of paid carers?

- a 13-year-old Muslim girl to be beaten with a belt when she comes home late?

What examples of cultural relativism have you encountered?

Family law defines 'development' broadly to embrace physical, intellectual, emotional, social and behavioural development, incorporating both physical and mental health. Children should be active, changing, developing and growing, influencing and being influenced by the environment they live in (Aldgate *et al.* 2006). Other professionals such as nursery nurses and health visitors, school nurses, teachers, whose training focuses them on developmental issues, contribute invaluable knowledge to whole family assessments where there are concerns about a child's progress (SCIE 2008b). When children experience poor parenting, their development can be compromised from conception right through into adolescence and in ways that can last throughout their adult lives. Understanding how adult difficulties can impact on children's emotional and psychological development is crucial to whole family assessment. The significance of attuned sensitive care-giving is discussed further in Chapter 6 (Brandon *et al.* 2012; Cleaver *et al.* 2011; King and Trowell 1992; O'Hagan 2006).

Because adolescence is a period of fundamental and sometimes rapid physical, psychological and intellectual change in preparation for adulthood. It is also a period of enormous vulnerability (Stein, Ward and Courtney 2011, cited by Brown and Ward 2012, p.68). Development throughout adolescence builds on milestones achieved earlier and maturational changes in brain structure partly depend on having achieved earlier developmental steps. Early exposure to stress and adversity can lead to increased risk-taking in adolescence, and to unhealthy lifestyle choices: using drugs, alcohol and cigarettes, poor eating habits and early sexual activity.

There is little discussion or consensus about the kind of care adolescents need within families and from the state. It is easy to neglect the experience and needs of adolescents living with parents who face difficulties, especially if they actively distance themselves from efforts to involve them. Continuing stress and adversity interfere with adolescents' ability to form positive relationships, putting them at greater risk of educational failure, gang membership, unemployment, poverty, homelessness, domestic abuse, criminal activity and violent crime, imprisonment, and early single parenthood (Brown and Ward 2012, pp.68–69; Shonkoff and Garner 2012). The fact that teenagers are second only to babies in suffering untoward death is testament to their continuing vulnerability (Brandon, Bailey and Belderson 2010).

Disabled children

Disabled children are easily marginalised in the assessment process. Workers need to create opportunities for disabled children to have their own say:

> James communicates through body language and facial expression. His sister describes him well. She says that he 'beams all over' when is happy and 'screams all over' when he is upset. I think that sums him up really. Perhaps I would add that there are many shades of grey between the beam and the scream.

> (Parent quoted by Murray 2006, cited by Marchant 2008, p.153)

Working from the assumption that all children can, and will want to, express their experience, needs, wishes and feelings, the responsibility for finding ways of communicating rests with the social worker. Sometimes this will mean being especially assertive with carers or seeking the help of independent interpreters (Marchant 2008). Several helpful resources are available to support communication with disabled children listed in Appendix 3:

> The enhanced vulnerability of disabled children is becoming well recognised and was a feature in 12 per cent of these serious case reviews. The risk of harm went unrecognised in these cases, sometimes where the family presented as loving and cooperative… For disabled children of all ages there was a tendency to see the disability more clearly than the child. This could mean accepting a different and lower standard of parenting for a disabled child than

would be tolerated for a non-disabled child – for example keeping a child shut in a bedroom for long periods of 'safety'.

(Brandon *et al.* 2012, p.4)

Approximately 3 per cent of children in the UK are disabled and they are over-represented in the population of Looked After Children (DoH 2000b). Disabled children are less likely to receive services they need. Even though they are more likely to be harmed (both in families and in care settings) the abuse of disabled children is often unrecognised, overlooked, ignored, and even tolerated (Cross, Kaye and Ratnofsky 1993; Stuart and Baines 2004; Sullivan and Knutson 2000). Altered mood, injury or difficult behaviour that might be interpreted as indicators of abuse in other children are sometimes mistakenly attributed to the child's impairment. Any social worker involved with a family that includes a disabled child needs to ensure that assessment identifies their specific needs and any risk of harm and is underpinned by an understanding of their developmental trajectory (Ofsted 2011). This will often mean seeking out different perspectives on the child from several sources because we cannot assume that a disabled child has the ability to conceptualise or articulate their experiences of harm or abuse (Oosterhoorn and Kendrick 2001).

The impact of adult difficulties on children

The link between adult life difficulties experienced by parents and harm to their children is well-established (Brandon *et al.* 2012; Cleaver *et al.* 2011). High service thresholds for intervention, and respect for family life, should not distract from the imperative to improve children's lives so that the essential question becomes not 'Is this a child protection case?' but 'What does this child need?' (Munro 2002). The National Assessment Framework's focus on needs is helpful in that it draws attention to the developmental journeys children make towards reaching their full potential.

EXERCISE

Think back about the children in your class in your first year at secondary school.

- How did you find out about any problems they had at home?

- What did you notice about the behaviour of children who had problems at home?

- Did the children who had problems at home have any difficulties with people in the class?

Children's experience of parents' emotional/mental distress

I used to feel guilty leaving a Lucozade bottle around 'cos she'd use that to slice herself…

(Carly, aged 21, a mother of baby twins, reflecting on her own childhood experience in Royal College of Psychiatrists 2004)

EXERCISE
The film *About a Boy* is a romantic comedy directed by Chris and Paul Weitz in 2002, and based on a novel by Nick Hornby. It tells the story of Marcus, a boy who teaches Will, a cynical and selfish young man, about caring for others and taking responsibility.

- How is Marcus affected by Fiona's emotional/mental distress?

- What stressors contribute to its impact on Marcus?

- What does Marcus need?

- What would happen if Marcus reaches adulthood with his needs still unmet?

Over two million dependent children in the UK, at least seven in every primary school class, live in families affected by emotional/mental distress (Layard 2005; Morris and Wates 2006). These children will not necessarily be known to children's services but may be seen by adult mental health practitioners who need to think about how parents' mental distress can compromise family life and/or pose a risk of harm to children (CSIP/Barnardo's 2007; SCIE 2009). Barnardo's resource pack *Keeping the Family in Mind* is designed to raise workers' awareness of the issues parents, their children and families may face (Wardale 2007).

Children of parents experiencing emotional/mental distress make up about a quarter of all new referrals to children's social services, are more likely to be subject to child protection processes, and indeed are more likely to be looked after by the local authority than other children referred (Tunnard 2004).

Most children in families where an adult is emotionally/mentally distressed have good childhoods. For example, a child living with a parent affected by a severe and enduring psychiatric illness such as schizophrenia need experience no harm if the family enjoys good professional care and informal support. However, emotional/mental distress can seriously affect people's ability to function as parents (Cleaver *et al.* 2011).

Distressed parents may not even be diagnosed with psychiatric illness or receive treatment but, nevertheless, subject a child to profoundly damaging experiences. Services provided for parents in emotional/mental distress may not match up with what they need (Schizophrenia Commission 2012; Wells 1997).

Case study

Angela first experienced anxiety as a teenager and found that this returned when she was 31 after the birth of her son. Angela separated from her partner two years ago, Oliver is now six and Angela suffers from agoraphobia that sometimes leaves her unable to leave the house for days at a time.

- What impact might Angela's agoraphobia have on Oliver's day-to-day life?

- What difficulties might Oliver face when he is 12 years old if nothing changes?

- What support does this family need to meet Oliver's needs?

- What support does Angela need in order to fulfil her role as a parent?

- What support does Angela need in her own right?

Children can face three distinct types of adversity:

1. Parental mental distress can affect the child's opportunities to form a secure attachment, and consequently impact on their development, and damage their own mental health. Up to two-thirds of children whose parents are psychiatrically ill also experience mental health difficulties. The significance of attachment experiences within families is explored further in Chapter 6.

2. Parental emotional/mental distress is often a contributory factor in cases of abuse and neglect. Its contribution has been identified in at least one in three child deaths and, indeed, recent reports (Brandon *et al.* 2012) found that emotional/mental distress featured in a majority of cases. Parents who self-harm or are suicidal should be taken very seriously. Risks to their children always need to be assessed, since these situations sometimes culminate in the parent killing their children as well as themselves (Brandon *et al.* 2009, 2012; Falkov 1996; Reder and Duncan 1999).

3. Thirty per cent of the UK's 150,000 young carers are helping parents in mental distress (Blewitt *et al.* 2011). They are the group least likely to be offered a carers' assessment. These children are three times more likely than others to experience distress themselves, and are often affected by stigma or bullying. Because emotional/mental distress can give rise to unpredictable crises, young carers need strategies for dealing with difficult times. Chapter 6 contains further discussion of the implications for children of being a carer.

Some children are also affected by practical and social consequences of their parents' distress such as disproportionately conflict-ridden relationships, disruption and discontinuity (Falkov 1996, 2012; Green 2002).

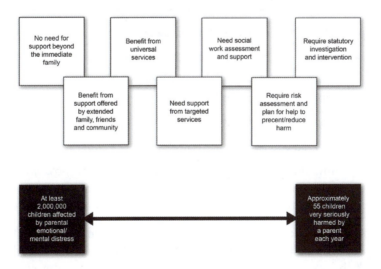

Figure 5.2 The continuum of well-being, need and risk (adapted from Falkov et al. 1998)

Well-being, need and risk form a continuum (Figure 5.2) (Falcov *et al.* 1998). At the troubled end of this continuum children can be profoundly affected by parents who, for example are:

- experiencing delusions and hallucinations
- feel preoccupied with a private world
- feel unable to carry out everyday activities while feeling depressed
- are emotionally blunted by medication and unavailable
- are prone to unpredictable behaviour.

Assessing whether children growing up alongside a parent's emotional/ mental distress experience harm or danger always requires careful analysis. Family relationships must be understood from both children's and parents' perspectives. Co-ordinated assessment between a child-focused expert and an adult-focused expert is usually the best way forward and should include an analysis of any psychological conflicts underlying the parent's mental distress (Reder and Duncan 2003a).

The impact of compulsive behaviour, dependency and addiction

Points to consider

- How do you define problem drug use?
- How do you define problem alcohol use?
- Have you lived or worked alongside someone affected by a dependency or addiction?
- What was the impact on you?
- How did you cope?
- How does your personal experience influence how you approach assessment in families where dependencies or addictions may impact on family well-being?

Children may know more about their parents' dependencies than parents realise. They can feel stigma and shame, and fear that they might be taken away from home. Some parents struggle to meet their children's basic needs, stay emotionally available and keep the family safe because of erratic mood or impaired concentration and memory. Dependency and addiction are often involved in the most severe cases of abuse, particularly neglect, and feature in up to two-thirds of all care proceedings. The heartbreak of losing the care of their children often contributes to vicious circles of dependency and addiction driven by overwhelming distress and further undermines people's motivation for change.

Alcohol/drug use is the problem most frequently worked with by children's social workers, accounting for 34 per cent of families known to children's services in London and 40 per cent in Scotland (Harwin, Ruan and Tunnard 2011, cited by Munro 2011b). Both adult and children's services often now work with families where dependencies affect three generations (Bancroft *et al.* 2004). Social workers receive limited training about problem alcohol/drug use, even though it is an increasing focus of caseloads both in adult and children's services. They are often ill-equipped to estimate the risks it poses to children (Adamson and Templeton 2012).

EXERCISE
Conduct an informal audit of your workload over the past 12 months.

- What part did compulsive behaviour, dependency and addiction play in the lives of the families you encountered?

- What are your professional development needs in relation to these phenomena?

- Draw up an action plan to enhance your knowledge/ understanding and discuss this with your supervisor.

Problem drug use
The Advisory Council on the Misuse of Drugs (2003) estimated that 250,000–350,000 children in the UK have a parent who is a problem drug user. This represents 2–3 per cent of all children in England and Wales. There is a higher incidence of 4–6 per cent in Scotland (Scottish Executive 2003). Parents with serious drug problems and the most chaotic lives are less likely to live with their children.

Assessment and treatment programmes are largely based on research conducted in the USA, but three aspects of drug use that are specific to the UK are particularly significant for whole family assessment:

1. Most problem drug users use several drugs. Depending on what is available, they typically combine heroin with benzodiazepines or cocaine, as well as other substances. Most problem drug users also make heavy use of alcohol, tobacco and cannabis. This pattern means that users experience, and their children are exposed to, unpredictable effects.

2. Many problem users inject their drugs because this enables them to experience maximum impact at minimum cash outlay. However, injecting risks several unintended detrimental consequences, for example overdose, unconsciousness, death while unconscious, and exposure to blood-borne viruses. Knowing this, their children may live in a state of heightened anxiety and persistent dread.

3. Parental problem drug use is part of a wider pattern where several factors such as the parent's own difficult childhood experiences, poor education, emotional/mental distress and living in disadvantaged communities compromise effective and safe parenting and impact negatively on outcomes for children.

A wide range of disadvantages and risks are associated with any sort of problem drug use during pregnancy. These include low birth weight, premature delivery, perinatal mortality and cot death. Women who inject drugs during pregnancy risk passing HIV or viral hepatitis to the baby. Using drugs, especially cocaine, can affect the growth and development of the baby from conception. Because drugs can result in structural brain damage in the first 12 weeks, harm sometimes occurs before the pregnancy is even confirmed. Using heroin and other opiates, cocaine and benzodiazepines in the second and third trimesters can all cause the baby to be born dependent, suffer withdrawal symptoms and need treatment in hospital.

As children grow up, they can be exposed to further damaging experiences including: unnecessary poverty; physical and emotional abuse or neglect; dangerously inadequate supervision; occasional or permanent separations; poor housing; frequent moves; harmful substances and paraphernalia in the home; interrupted education; restricted social contacts; exposure to inappropriate adult behaviour; and involvement in criminal activity (Advisory Council on the Misuse of Drugs 2003).

The adverse consequences for children are typically multiple and cumulative and will vary according to the child's stage of development... These can range greatly in severity and may often be subtle and difficult to detect.

(Advisory Council on the Misuse of Drugs 2003, Chapter 2, p.10)

Indicators of the impact of parents' problem drug use on children can include:

- failure to thrive

- blood-borne virus infection

- incomplete immunisation and inadequate health care

- a wide range of emotional, cognitive, behavioural and psychological problems

- early problem drug/alcohol use

- offending behaviour

- poor educational attainment.

Problem drinking

Estimates of the prevalence of problem drinking within families vary because there is limited research evidence and no agreed definition of what constitutes a problem. Government estimates suggest that around 1.3 to 2 million children in the UK live alongside alcohol misuse (Cabinet Office 2004). However, meta-analyses of UK household surveys provide significantly higher figures (Manning *et al.* 2009). These indicate that just under three-and-a-half million children (30%) live with an adult binge-drinker and 22 per cent with a hazardous drinker. The same research found that around half a million children (4%) live with an adult defined as a problem drinker with a mental health problem, and some 12,000 children (1%) have witnessed domestic violence in the context of alcohol use. Parental alcohol misuse featured in 22 per cent of child death reviews (Brandon *et al.* 2010).

It is not necessarily alcohol-dependent parents that cause children most harm. Alcohol is implicated in one-third of all domestic abuse assaults. Children often suffer not so much from the drinking itself but because of the conflict and disharmony it generates, its link with domestic oppression, and the parenting styles associated with it (Finney 2004).

Children affected by a parent's problem alcohol use tend to come to the attention of services later than children living with problem drug use. Boys growing up alongside problem alcohol use are less likely than girls to seek help but are more likely to be assessed because of their presenting behaviour, for example in Youth Offending Services (Adamson and Templeton 2012).

Women who use alcohol very heavily during pregnancy are more likely to miscarry. Drinking alcohol during pregnancy can cause Foetal Alcohol Spectrum Disorders (FASD). This syndrome describes a pattern of behavioural, physical and intellectual difficulties with a range of symptoms that includes: poor growth; a distinct pattern of facial features and physical characteristics; and problems with the central nervous system (Cleaver *et al.* 2011). We do not know how many children are affected by FASD but growing evidence from America and Canada suggests that it may affect many children who come into contact with social workers (Adamson and Templeton 2012). FASD should be considered during assessments when children present with undiagnosed developmental delays. Children can continue to experience harm resulting from parents' problem drinking throughout childhood, resulting in physical, psychological and behavioural problems (Tunnard 2002b).

Problem gambling

Problem gambling is associated with both unemployment and bad health, and can fracture families. Historically, gambling has mostly been a problem for men, affecting only 0.6 per cent of the adult UK population, but changing patterns point to an increase in female problem gamblers (Gambling Commission 2011; Shaw *et al.* 2007). The impact of growing up with a compulsive gambler is rarely researched but is thought to put children at risk of problem alcohol/drug misuse, psychosocial problems, education difficulties, self-harm, suicide, and of becoming gamblers themselves (Jacobs *et al.* 1989). Qualitative studies have reported children's overwhelmingly negative emotions including anger, sadness, depression, confusion, shame, helplessness and sense of pervasive loss (Darbyshire, Oster and Carrig 2001; Lesieur and Rothschild 1989).

Internet addiction

The Fifth Edition of the Diagnostic and Statistical Manual of Mental Disorders (DSM-V) now recognises internet addiction as a psychiatric disorder, but there is little research about its impact on family life. Anecdotally, it seems that workers in both adult and children's services work often meet people whose internet use interferes with relationships, sleep patterns and attention to everyday responsibilities such as shopping, cooking and cleaning. These experiences suggest that the psychosocial impact on children where a parent is compulsively drawn into on-line activity could be comparable with the effects of problem alcohol/drug use (Lyn McLean, Senior Social Work Manager, personal communication, May 2011).

Case study continued

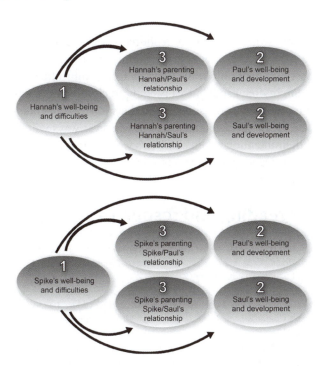

Figure 5.3 Assessing the impact of Hannah and Spike's difficulties on Paul and Saul (adapted from Falkov, 2012)

- How has Hannah's vulnerability affected Paul and Saul?
- Can you hypothesise about the significance of other adults in their lives?
- What are Paul's immediate needs?
- How can Saul's long-term needs be assessed?

Conclusion

...having the confidence to get to know and work with the child requires a sound knowledge of child development... *The anxiety that surrounds working with children and families, point up the emotional toll that working with children from any discipline and especially social work, takes on the practitioner.*

(Brandon *et al.* 2012, p.7)

Whether you work in adult or children's services it is easy to be distracted from paying attention to children. Sometimes a practitioner in adult services working with a parent facing difficulties is the only person their children can talk to. Listening to children does not demand specialist training but it does require workers to convey genuine interest in them, be prepared to communicate in whatever ways will work best, and hold their intention to put children's welfare first. After all, these are the things we expect good parents to do.

Further reading and resources

Berg, I.K. and Steiner, T. (2003). *Children's Solution Work.* New York: Norton.

Cleaver, H., Unell, I. and Aldgate, J. (2011) *Children's Needs – Parenting Capacity. Child Abuse: Parental Mental Illness, Learning Disability, Substance Misuse and Domestic Violence* (Second edition). London: The Stationery Office.

Cossar, J., Brandon, M. and Jordan, P. (2011) *'Don't make assumptions.' Children's and Young People's Views of the Child Protection System and Messages for Change.* London: Office of the Children's Commissioner. Available at www.childrenscommissioner.gov.uk, accessed on 19 July 2013.

Dalzell, R. and Chamberlain, C. (2006) *Communicating with Children: A Two-Way Process.* London: National Children's Bureau. Available at www.ncb.org.uk, accessed on 19 July 2013.

Falcov, A., Mayes, K. and Diggins, M. (eds) (1998) *Crossing Bridges: Training Resources for Working with Mentally Ill Parents and their Children.* Brighton: Pavilion.

Falcov, A. (2002) 'Addressing Family Needs when a Parent is Mentally Ill' in H. Ward and W. Rose (eds) *Approaches to Needs Assessment in Children's Services*. London: Jessica Kingsley Publishers.

Falcov, A. (2012) *The Family Model Handbook. An Integrated Approach to Supporting Mentally Ill Parents and their Children*. Brighton: Pavilion. www.thefamilymodel.com.

Holliday, R. and Marche, T. (2012) *Child Forensic Psychology. Victim and Eyewitness Memory*. London: Palgrave Macmillan.

Hutton, A. and Partridge, K. (2006) *'Say It Your Own Way'. Children's Participation in Assessment: A Guide and Resources*. Barkingside: Barnardo's/Department for Education and Skills.

Lefevre, M. (2010) *Communicating with Children and Young People. Making a Difference*. Bristol: Policy Press.

Lightfoot, C., Cole, M. and Cole, S. (2008) *The Development of Children* (Sixth edition). New York: Worth.

Ofsted (2011) *The Voice of the Child: Learning Lessons from Serious Case Reviews. A Thematic Report of Ofsted's Evaluation of Serious Case Reviews from 1 April to 30 September 2010*. Available at www.ofsted.gov.uk/resources/voice-of-the-child-learning-lessons-serious-case-reviews.

Phillips, R. (ed.) (2004) *Children Exposed to Parental Substance Misuse. Implications for Family Placement*. London: BAAF.

Reder, P. and Duncan, S. (2003) 'How Much Should Children's Views Count?' In P. Reder, S. Duncan and C. Lucey (eds) *Studies in the Assessment of Parenting*. London: Routledge.

Robinson, L. (2007) *Cross-Cultural Child Development for Social Workers*. London: Palgrave Macmillan.

Ward, H., Brown, R. and Westlake, D. (2012) *Safeguarding Babies and Very Young Children from Abuse and Neglect*. London: Jessica Kingsley Publishers.

Weld, N. (2009) *Making Sure Children Get 'HELD'. Ideas and Resources to Help Workers Place Hope, Empathy, Love and Dignity at the Heart of Child Protection and Support*. Lyme Regis: Russell House Publishing.

CHAPTER 6

Making Sense of Family Relationships

Key messages

- Engaging with the whole family enables assessors to reach a systemic understanding of individual needs.

- Well-informed application of neuroscience enables assessors to understand the significance of attachment and relationships for individual well-being.

- Supporting the contribution to family well-being made by kin and friendship networks and by young carers often depends upon good collaboration between adult and children's services.

- The enactment of power and control is the link between domestic abuse, physical harm to children and sexual violence.

Case study continued

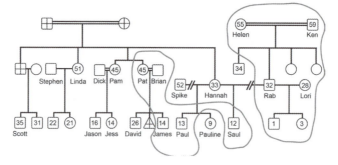

Figure 6.1 Paul and Saul's family tree nine years later

Paul and Saul have lived with Pat and Brian since they offered to look after the boys soon after care proceedings were initiated nine years ago. Hannah's sisters, Linda, Pat and Pam, have always kept contact with Hannah. The whole family was relieved when children's social care intervened and it was agreed that Pat and Brian represented the best option for Paul and Saul. Dick and Pam offered to care for the new baby Pauline, but she remained with Hannah, initially in a mother and baby unit while Hannah underwent an intensive detoxification programme.

Pat and Brian are supported by the whole family and everyone has given their all to welcoming the two boys into the extended family. Pat and Brian have made many changes to their lives to meet Paul and Saul's needs, for example building into the roof to create separate bedrooms. They harbour the hope that Hannah will 'grow up' and be reconciled with the family but this has not yet happened.

Paul and Saul are much harder to care for than the family anticipated and they have not had any support from children's services. Paul and Saul have an intensely close relationship and do not allow Pat or Brian to get as close to them as they are to each other. This did not worry the family unduly at first, but as they enter into adolescence the boys have frighteningly fierce fallings out, and often cause each other real physical harm. The boys immediately ally themselves against any adult who tries to intervene. Hours of distress and drama usually ensue. The boys openly masturbate each other and are often lewd in public. At home they have a number of strange habits that have proved impossible to explain or eliminate. Paul picks at his skin and at wallpaper; Saul defecates in cupboards and sometimes smears faeces. They both fill their rooms with tiny shreds of torn paper and they 'snot' people when they are angry. They have sometimes set small fires together. Both now go to an excellent special school for moderate learning disability because of development delays and behavioural problems. Saul is very small and slight. He presents as timid, careworn, and feels that he is to blame for anything that might go wrong. Paul has been in trouble for bullying, is impulsive and has problems with physical co-ordination and a speech impediment.

Brian is in hospital having had a stroke last week. Pat is beside herself with worry and cannot cope without him. Having always been 'highly-strung' she is now unable to function normally.

Pam is happy to look after James, and says that Saul could stay with her family too. She does not want to see the two brothers separated but feels that they will not be able to manage Paul. Scott feels really strongly that Paul should stay within the family and together they approach children's social services.

Paul and Saul's case was closed soon after they were placed with Pam and Brian. Arziki, a children's social worker who has previously worked in the field of adult mental health, visits Pam and Pat. Arziki is concerned to hear from Pam and Pat that the boys have presented such a challenge. Arziki learns that the family now realises that Paul is Spike's son. Pam and Pat express fears that he has inherited some of his father's character traits. They have come to think of Paul as a sexual risk to other children.

Soon after she meets with Pam and Pat, Arziki receives an email from Helen, Rab's mother. It turns out that Rab first met Hannah through his older brother who still works with Scott, Hannah's nephew. Rab's family have been aware of Saul's progress through the years and now offer him a home with them. Rab, Lori and their two children already live with Ken and Helen because they both have intellectual impairments. They deeply regret that they didn't offer Saul a home until now.

- What are the questions for assessment?
- What were Pam's needs nine years ago?
- What kind of parenting relationship does Paul need now?
- What kind of parenting relationship does Saul now need?
- What are the pros and cons of Paul and Saul living apart?
- What support does the family need?

Families as relationship systems

When people talk about protecting children they talk about the need to understand the child (Laming 2009) but they tend not to talk about what drives the perpetrators of abuse or neglect, and therefore the heart of the matter is missed: the relationship between the child and those charged with the child's care. This is an infuriating systemic failure for me.

(Gopfert *et al.* 2010, p.40)

Children are shaped by their different experiences of family life (Whiting and Whiting 1975, cited by Lightfoot *et al.* 2008, p.424). Family is the biggest thing in most children's lives, even as they grow older and even if they no longer live with their families (Morgan 2011).

Families can be understood as systems in which each member plays a part. Expectations evolve determining how people will respond to each other: patterns develop. Each member's behaviour influences, and is influenced by, others' in predictable ways.

> Human development is facilitated through interaction with persons who occupy a variety of roles and through participation in an ever broadening role repertoire.
>
> (Bronfenbrenner 1979, p.104)

Although family members' insights, reflections and unique perspectives are valuable, relying on what people say is not enough. People do not always do what they say or even what they believe. Children may withhold information out of loyalty, secrecy or denial (Taylor and Kroll 2004, p.1126). Spending time with family members together offers opportunities to observe, and listen to their interactions. This is crucial for assessing attachment in babies and very young children. Watching children's relationships with parents and siblings still provides useful information as they grow up. For example, how do they interact? Do children use parents as a 'secure base' and look to them for comfort/reassurance? What are relationships between the siblings like? (Lefevre 2010, p.161)

Assessors' thinking can sometimes be skewed by the social work relationship, either because families are likeable and friendly, or angry and hostile. This pitfall is avoided when workers consciously refocus on relationships within the family (Juffer, Bakermas-Kranenburg and van Ijzendoorn 2007). Direct observation can also be a powerful antidote to deception when families have reason to lie or withhold information (Fauth *et al.* 2010, p.11).

Case study continued

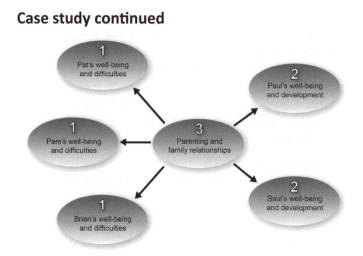

Figure 6.2 Identifying the impact of parenting and family relationships on Pat, Pam, Brian, Saul and Paul (adapted from Falkov, 2012)

- How has the relationship between Paul and Saul impacted on Brian?

- How has Pam and Pat's relationship influenced Pam's parenting?

- How does Paul's role in the family impact on Saul?

Thinking and talking about relationships

When you sit down and ask them questions about their relatonships, and how the family works as a system, people may feel inhibited, not quite knowing how to talk about such matters, or even where to start. Everyday processes are often played out outside of conscious awareness.

EXERCISE

Think about your closest colleagues.

- What different ways do they each have of communicating with you?

- Where are you most likely to confide in each other?

- Do some of your colleagues communicate differently with each other from how they do with you?
- Which of your colleagues explain anything particularly complicated by:
  - drawing a diagram, map or picture?
  - acting it out?
  - using metaphors and stories?
  - giving you a long carefully worded description?
- Do you know your colleagues' preferred learning styles?

Go on-line to www.vark-learn.com and complete the questionnaire to find out your own preferred learning style.

People who enjoy reading and writing can be encouraged to notice and describe family interactions and experiences by keeping a diary for a few days or weeks. These can be completed together or individually. Some parents or children might prefer to share the content with the worker confidentially; others might feel able to compare their entries and discuss any areas of disagreement or difference (Lyn McLean, Senior Social Work Manager, personal communication, June 2013). People who are happiest reading and writing will want to make sure that they generate a detailed account of everything there is to say. Notice who assumes the role of story-teller.

Using pens and large bits of paper to create diagrams and images can be a very helpful way of enabling families to communicate with you about these out-of-awareness processes. You can ask them to draw family trees, eco-maps, floor-plans of their home, portraits and self-portraits, time lines or cartoon stories to explain their experiences. Some families find creating mind maps particularly helpful (www.thinkbuzan.com). You can ask families to work with the various tools used in this book, especially the discrepancy matrix introduced in Chapter 3 (Figure 3.9), to help them unfold their complex life stories. Visual learners are likely to think and describe their experience differently or more fully as images emerge on the page. Kinaesthetic learners will emphasise their ideas by pointing, tapping the page, and may even take the pen out of your hand and take over! These processes will produce something useful and interesting that you can look at together, but their real purpose is to get people talking about how they interact with each other. Family therapists and drama therapists have a long tradition of also using more

198 Mastering Whole Family Assessment in Social Work

physical approaches such as family sculpts, or using objects that people can move around to represent relationships at home.

Some people only really feel comfortable to talk freely when the focus is on something else. Most social workers are familiar with the phenomenon that children and young people often tell you most about themselves and their experiences when you are driving. With parents, it can be helpful to roll up your sleeves and get on with something alongside them, for example washing up while they dry, to enable them to think more deeply and communicate what they know about family relationships. Or you could work with the whole family to spring-clean a room.

Attachment and the parent–child relationship

> The development of the self is tantamount to the aggregation of experiences of the self in relationships.
>
> (Fonagy *et al.* 2002, p.40)

The literature on attachment, family relationships and neurobiology is likely to be uppermost in the mind of children's workers but may not routinely feature in the thinking of practitioners in adult services.

Adults often bring the attachment strategies developed in childhood into subsequent relationships but can also adapt and change the way they relate to others. This emphasis on attachment patterns as working strategies emphasises that although some parents reproduce troubled relationships when they have their own families, others are able to break the cycle (Baim and Morrison 2011; Main and George 1985; Ricks 1985):

> Young children experience their world as an environment of relationships, and these relationships affect virtually all aspects of their development – intellectual, social, emotional, physical, behavioural and moral.
>
> (National Scientific Council on the Developing Child 2004)

Children's progress and family happiness depend on healthy attachment relationships (National Scientific Council on the Developing Child 2004). Where children benefit from secure attachment they grow up with:

- a love of learning

- a comfortable sense of themselves

- positive social skills

- the ability to form and understand human relationships

- an understanding of emotions, commitment, morality.

In the parent–child relationship the adult's job is to be preoccupied with the child and have the child in mind at all times; the child's job is to express its needs and create this preoccupied state of mind in the adult (Bowlby 1999; Hill 2004).

Brain development in infancy depends upon positive interaction between the baby and its parents (Gerhardt 2004). This means that parents have enormous influence over a child's emotional brain development, especially during the critical early years when it is growing fast (Brown and Ward 2012):

> Parents are not magicians. They can't guarantee their children happiness in later life, or protect them from loss and rejection. But they can dramatically influence systems in their children's brains that are key to the potential for a deeply fulfilling life…
>
> (Sunderland 2006, p.15)

There are different models for understanding attachment. Most social workers are familiar with characterising four attachment patterns: secure, avoidant, ambivalent and disorganised (Howe 2005). Children develop these strategies to stay connected with parents whenever they face stress:

- *Secure*: Around 55 per cent of the population experience sensitive parenting that is responsive and attuned. They develop internal working models in which they expect others to be available, experiencing themselves as loved and loveable.

- *Avoidant*: Around 23 per cent of the population have parents who are, to some degree, hostile, rejecting or controlling. These children learn to regulate their emotions by themselves, making few demands, so that they do not drive their parent further away by seeming weak, demanding or needy.

- *Ambivalent*: Around 8 per cent of the population have parents preoccupied with their own emotional needs, whose responses are inconsistent. These children learn to exaggerate attachment behaviours to ensure they get noticed.

- *Disorganised*: Around 15 per cent of the population are parented by adults who are sometimes fearful and/or do frightening things. When children realise that they cannot predict their parents' erratic behaviour, they become afraid to approach them. With their needs unmet, these children do not learn how to regulate their emotions and may in turn behave unpredictably. Disorganised attachment strategies are found in around 80 per cent of children who experience neglect or abuse.

Understanding attachment is fundamental to whole family assessment but should be approached with some caution:

- There are several different tools in use for assessing attachment (see Appendix 2). Some of these were developed for research purposes rather than in clinical settings and have limited value in assessment practice (Solomon and George 1999).

- Attachment is one important aspect of relationship but they are not synonymous. It is not always easy to distinguish between attachment behaviours and general parenting activity/care. Attachment cannot be assessed in isolation from the parent–child relationship (O'Hagan 2006).

- Where children experience harm it will rarely prove possible or helpful to establish whether any problems they manifest result from disrupted attachment or distress/trauma (Allen 2001).

- Children actively adapt to their experience and environment by discovering, inventing and reinventing attachment strategies moment by moment, (Crittenden and Landini 2011).

- In troubled families, relationships between parents and children may be so impoverished that siblings attempt to meet each other's attachment needs.

- Each child's experience within a family is unique. Parents' care may be compromised in the early years of some but not all of their children. Each child's temperament and needs differ. A child may benefit from their parents' attention at one stage of their development but not at another.

Where family dynamics prove difficult to understand Crittenden and Landini (Crittenden 2008; Crittenden and Landini 2011) suggest that commissioning an Adult Attachment Assessment by an expert with training in the protocol can shed light on intractable problems.

EXERCISE

Think about a family you have recently assessed.

- Could the parents give a coherent account of their childhood experiences and development?

- How did you explore this with them?

- Were they able to reflect on the impact of their childhood?

- Was there evidence that unresolved issues from childhood interfere with their ability to function as parents?

Neuroscience and biochemistry

We now understand much more about how and why very early experiences influence brain development. Emotional life has its origins in the limbic system, the unconscious, primitive core of the brain. The human brain develops in response to all experiences, whether good or bad, and the relationship between baby and parent is the most powerful environmental influence on brain development. Emotional attunement and positive early interactions with their parents enable children to create stress-regulating systems that will serve them throughout childhood and into adult life. Adverse experiences, especially during sensitive 'critical periods', shape the architecture of the brain and influence well-being in the very long term. For example, unborn babies are particularly vulnerable if the mother's stress hormones are high during the brain-growth spurt in the third trimester.

Poorly-attuned parenting affects several different, interlinked aspects of brain growth: the generation of synapses and development of the higher regions of the brain, the hypothalamic–pituitary–adrenal axis (which determines physical responses to stress), and neural processes. There are short windows of opportunity that depend on specific types of experiences at different stages of childhood for optimum developmental progress. The impact of parents' care-giving on children's well-being is both cumulative and long-term: practitioners need to take account of each child's developmental trajectory when working with parents who are struggling to cope (Brown and Ward 2012). Fortunately, it is never too late to remedy early harm. There are several important windows of opportunity for intervention that offer children new ways of relating to others during adolescence and early adulthood. Where emotional abuse and neglect have been allowed to drift, whole family assessment should consider the needs of older children as well as younger ones.

If a parent is poorly attuned or unresponsive, their baby's learning about how to regulate stress can be affected. Depression, preoccupation with their need for drugs/alcohol or the demands of an oppressive partner can compromise mothers' attunement. Because much of the research in this field has focused on post-natal depression we know little about how children fare when their father is unwell, or when either parent's emotional/mental well-being fluctuates (Marryat and Martin 2010).

Assessing emotional harm and neglect

Assessing emotional and psychological well-being is notoriously nebulous and challenging. Where there are concerns about emotional harm or neglect, social workers in either service may struggle to define or identify them and decide when or how to assess and intervene (Davies and Ward 2012, cited by Brown and Ward 2012, p.55) because:

- emotional harm and neglect cover such a wide and diverse range of issues

- patterns in families developed slowly over months and years sometimes mean workers come to accept poor parenting and expect little change

- acts of commission are easier to identify than acts of omission – workers often wait for a specific incident to trigger intervention

- it is often hard to identify when low-level care crosses the line into emotional harm and neglect since definitions of good parenting are subjective. Different workers involved with the same family may disagree with each other!

Understanding the impact of emotionally harmful and neglectful parenting helps us to make sense of the complex ways in which parents' well-being, children's development, parenting and family relationships all affect each other.

EXERCISE

Jeannette Winterson published her first novel, *Oranges are not the Only Fruit*, a roman-à-clef, in 1985. Twenty-seven years later she published her autobiography, *Why Be Happy When You Could Be Normal?* They give a fictional and non-fictional account of the deeply troubled relationships and the trauma she grew up with.

- Read *Why Be Happy When You Could Be Normal?*

- What is the impact of her adoptive mother's behaviour on Jeannette?

- Does her adoptive father's benign presence in any way mitigate Jeannette's harmful experiences?

- What are the sources of resilience in Jeannette's childhood?

- Do you agree with Jeannette's perspectives on the development of identity?

Emotional abuse and neglect compromise every aspect of children's development, and manifest in cognitive, emotional, social and behavioural problems at each stage of their growing up (Iwaniec 2006; Taylor and Daniel 2005). Referrals for assessment are likely to arise differently as children grow up. The most commonly seen problems at each stage (MacMillan and Wathan 2009) are:

- affect regulation, attachment, growth and developmental delays in babies and very young children

- anxiety disorder, mood disorders, disruptive behaviour, academic failure and poor peer relations during mid-childhood

- conduct disorder, alcohol abuse, drug abuse, other risk-taking behaviours and recurrent victimisation in adolescence.

Howe (2005) provides a framework that integrates insights into parental attachment patterns. His typology groups characteristics found in the background of families where there is emotional harm and neglect, and indicates how these different patterns can affect children at each stage of development.

Everything points to the importance of early evidence-gathering and legal intervention in situations of emotional abuse and neglect and a more inquisitorial approach within family justice (Davies and Ward 2012). Reforms to the Family Justice system mean that care applications should now more readily reach the threshold of significant harm.

Where a critical incident such as a non-accidental injury or an allegation of sexual abuse subsequently arises, findings of fact should run alongside any pre-existing application already in progress because of emotional harm or neglect. The opportunity for solicitors to advise parents at early stages of legal planning means they can support parents to recognise the need for change and avert proceedings. This places an onus on social workers assessing families to co-operate with parents' solicitors so that they can offer parents helpful, realistic legal guidance.

Assessing the impact of emotional harm

O'Hagan (2006) emphasises that assessment should include an exploration of both the psychological and emotional life of the child and provides a framework for observing and identifying these at each stage of development and suggest that professionals' analysis of emotional harm can be flawed:

- The umbrella term 'emotional abuse' subsumes and conflates emotional and cognitive aspects of harm. Although these often co-exist, the impact of emotional harm is distinct from the impact of psychological harm. Whereas the quality of emotional attunement provided by primary carers in infancy is crucial to emotional development, relationships with other adults and siblings can contribute to psychological development throughout childhood.

- The common usage of terms such as 'harm', 'abuse', 'ill-treatment' and 'maltreatment' as if they were interchangeable is unhelpful.

- Our working definitions of emotional abuse are difficult to apply to babies – and yet it is in early infancy that children are most damaged by emotional harm.

The version of *Working Together* published in 2010 (DCSF 2010) helpfully stressed that:

> Some level of emotional abuse is involved in all types of maltreatment of a child, though it may occur alone.

Physical and/or sexual abuse usually indicates serious problems within family relationships since they are most likely to arise when care and trust are already compromised. Investigation of physical injuries often reveals developmental and behavioural problems associated with emotional abuse. Pre-exisitng evidence of emotional harm or neglect are often found alongside the childhood problems particularly associated with sexual harm. Behavioural problems indicative of sexual harm include sleep disorders, bed-wetting or soiling, problems with school work or missing school, risk-taking behaviour during adolescence, emotional/mental distress, problem alcohol/drug use, becoming sexually active at a young age and entering into multiple sexual relationships.

The impact of neglectful parenting

When the needs of neglected children are left unmet, they are exposed to the 'trauma of absence' (Golding and Hughes 2012). Neglect has an immediate impact, particularly evidenced in early language delays. It is associated with extremely damaging long-term consequences for children: severe cognitive and academic problems; social withdrawal and difficulties with peers; and internalising problems (Hildyard and Wolfe 2002, cited by Brown and Ward 2012). When children experience extremely severe neglect this can even stunt the physical growth of the brain.

Reviews of child deaths often expose neglect as a significant background feature in the children's lives. Sadly, Brandon's overviews (Brandon *et al.* 2008, 2012) suggest that many of their mothers were themselves affected by:

- emotional and/or physical neglect in childhood
- parented by adults who were physically ill and/or in mental distress but failed to seek and accept or did not receive effective help
- periods of care away from parents
- sexual abuse or sexual exploitation
- leaving home when young
- being sexually active when young
- multiple pregnancies with many losses.

Networks of kinship and friendship

> An excessive focus on what services do, rather than an understanding of the source of protective influences that lie within individuals, families or communities, may devalue and diminish the naturally occurring buffers against childhood risk.
>
> (Newman and Blackburn 2002)

Sometimes change is best achieved with minimal intervention. A light professional touch that mobilises informal support sometimes enables more naturalistic, organic and sustainable change. The maintenance of key existing relationships contributes to children's capacity for resilience (Gilligan 2007).

In 2007 some 7000 children looked after by local authorities in England were in kinship care with relatives or friends. The Family Rights Group estimates that a further 300,000 households offer informal care arrangements to children. Forty-five per cent of informal carers are grandparents (Hadley Centre 2008). Most children of problem drug users living away from both birth parents are cared for by relatives, and only 5 per cent enter the care system (Advisory Council on the Misuse of Drugs 2003, 2007; SCIE 2004).

Kinship carers may have other caring responsibilities and often have to manage volatile and complex family dynamics (Barnard 2003; Pitcher 1999). Compared with other foster carers, relatives and friends are more likely to live in overcrowded conditions, to have a disability or chronic illness, to be lone carers and to be in financial hardship (Farmer and Moyers 2008). They describe feeling isolated and would generally welcome more financial and social work support (Broad, Hayes and Rushforth 2001). The use of formal placements with kinship carers varies from one local authority to the next and it is a bitter irony that they and the children they parent usually receive less advice and practical support than foster carers and children in care. Their situations require careful assessment of both adults' and children's needs, especially as informal kinship care arrangements are often entered into in moments of crisis and people may need help to anticipate the longer-term challenges (Lindsay Hill, Senior Lecturer in Social Work, personal communication, April 2013).

Case study continued

- How has taking responsibility for Paul and Saul affected the relationship between Pat and Pam?

- What are the questions for assessment in relation to family members' continuing commitment to Paul?

- What support will Rob's parents need if they take care of Saul?

Young carers

Caregiver: That word should weigh more than others on a page, sag it down a bit and wrinkle it, because the simple-sounding job frazzles as it consumes and depletes. Not that it's only gloomy. Caregiving offers many fringe benefits, including the sheer sensory delight of nourishing and grooming, sharing and playing. There's something uniquely fulfilling about being a lodestar, feeling so deeply needed, and it's fun finding ways to gladden a loved one's life. But caregiving does buttonhole you: you're stitched in one place.

(Ackerman 2011, p.135)

Points to consider

- Do you think the burden of responsibility for parents who need care should rest entirely with the state?

- What household responsibilities should a child have at five years old?

- Do you think it is OK for a 15-year-old girl to help her father with intimate care such as bathing or toileting?

- Do you think it is OK for an eight-year-old boy to monitor his mother's medication?

Conceptualising children as carers needs careful attention. We do not know exactly how many children provide care for family members but it is estimated that there are at least 150,000 young carers in the UK (Blewitt *et al.* 2011). Around 15 per cent of these are from ethnic minorities and 30 per cent care for a family member with emotional/

mental distress (Dearden and Becker 2004; SCIE 2005a). The economic value of the care offered by children is impossible to calculate but it is likely to be significant since the value of informal carers' contribution in the UK has been quantified as over £119 billion – four times the combined annual cost of adult and children's social care services and more than the entire annual NHS budget (Buckner and Yeandle 2011). The impact of caring responsibility is typically greater for girls because mothers are more likely to suffer mental distress than fathers, girls are more likely to provide emotional and domestic care than boys, especially for their mothers (Dearden and Becker 2000, 2004; Roberts *et al.* 2008). Young carers cannot be considered as a single group. Their experiences vary completely.

Points to consider

- What role(s) do you fulfil within your own family or friendship group?
- Who can you rely on?
- What tasks do you undertake for others?
- Do you care for anyone?
- Do you define yourself as a carer?

(Adapted from Wallace and Davies 2009, p.15)

Young carers' experiences are not always and inevitably negative. In the context of a loving relationship, and with appropriate support, children need not experience the caring role as burdensome. Caring can bring fulfilment and respect. Far from feeling damaged by role reversal, some children experience authentic pride in their responsibilities (Aldridge and Becker 2003; Cooklin 2006; Newman 2002; SCIE 2005a; Warren 2007). Many report that caring gives them a sense of belonging and closeness and that they are happy to perform this role (SCIE 2005a). Caring responsibilities can offer children opportunities to develop and mature positively, gaining confidence, practical life skills, organisational abilities and authority within the family and can lead to very good outcomes in adult life (Barnett and Parker 1998; Dearden and Becker 2000).

Young carers deserve well-informed, focused assessment that takes into account the emotional support, practical help and intimate care they provide (Cossar *et al.* 2011; SCIE 2005a). Social workers need time to get to know them and their specific needs as carers should be assessed even if they are not the only person offering support. Allocating them a separate worker can be helpful if there are particularly difficult family dynamics (Cossar *et al.* 2011).

Workers in adult services are best positioned to provide information about a parent's condition, about support services available, to use the Carers (Recognition and Services) Act 1995 to assess any needs that arise from the child taking responsibility in the household, and to assess the parent's need for specific support in relation to parenting using Section 8 of the Disabled Persons (Services, Consultation and Representation) Act 1986. The Princess Royal Trust for Carers published the *Manual for Measures of Caring Activities and Outcomes for Children and Young People* (Joseph, Becker and Becker 2009), which can be used as a one-off for assessment or before, during and after an intervention to explore the impact of support.

Assessment by workers in children's services can focus in on young carers' developmental well-being with a view to providing support for a 'child in need'. It is not unusual for children's needs to be overlooked by family, friends and professionals alike. When a parent experiences emotional/mental crisis all eyes are drawn to the more pressing issue of managing their distress (Hetherington *et al.* 2003; Weir 2003). Young carers' needs can go unnoticed because teachers sometimes misconstrue lateness, absences, tiredness and missed deadlines as misbehaviour and lose opportunities to intervene and initiate family assessment (Butler and Astbury 2005; Eley 2004).

Young carers help out with a very wide range of responsibilities (Mental Health Foundation and Princess Royal Trust for Carers, 2010) including: sibling care, daily personal care such as dressing, collecting prescriptions, administering medication, lifting, interpreting, translating, emotional support, intimate nursing care such as toileting and bathing, general household work such as cooking, cleaning and shopping, and taking parents to medical appointments. These caring responsibilities can impact adversely on physical and mental health, psychological well-being, education and social development (Aldridge and Becker 2003; Blewitt *et al.* 2011; Finkelstein *et al.* 2005; Gorin 2004). For example, caring can affect children's education, result in isolation, bullying and limited social development, and increase the likelihood of unemployment, poverty and isolation when children grow up.

The Mental Health Foundation and Princess Royal Trust for Carers (2010) provide telling information that young carers of parents in mental distress describe feeling:

- isolated – because they don't go out as a family
- lonely – because they don't like to ask friends round
- upset because of inconsistency
- upset because they cannot understand why parents' mood/behaviour changes
- guilty if they go out and leave the parent alone
- no time for play and friends
- lonely because stigma makes it difficult to find friends
- compliant – not wanting to upset the parent
- worried about living away from home when the parent has to go into hospital
- upset when the parent is in hospital under compulsion
- worried that they will be taken into care
- frightened to tell anyone about the problems at home because of the consequences
- bullied
- worried about getting behind with schoolwork because of responsibilities
- unable to concentrate at school when feeling worried or tired
- worried that professionals may not understand if a young carer has a good relationship with parent, feels mature, loves their parent and wants to help them
- unable to refuse taking on too much
- worried about compromising their education and future.

Barnardo's (2007) makes a series of recommendations about the needs of children caring for parents in mental distress and these readily extend to the assessment of all families with complex needs:

> Adult mental health workers should recognise the role that a young carer plays in their family and should take time to inform and involve them.

Young carers whose parents have mental health problems should be able to access good quality age appropriate information about mental health problems.

Young carers whose parents have mental health problems should have access to support that values their family, while giving them the space to talk openly and get the help that they need.

Adult mental health services should support parents in their parenting role by providing them with specialist services and by helping them to make contact with their local parenting support projects.

Adult mental health services should collect information on the numbers of parents accessing their services in order to inform service development.

(Barnardo's 2007, pp.8–9)

Toxic networks, abuse and exploitation

Workers in adult services report growing concerns about 'mate crime', where people living independently, with minimal professional support, are open to abuse and exploitation by malicious 'befrienders'. This is not a new phenomenon. Edgerton's ethnographic studies of people with intellectual impairment demonstrate how that 'hidden majority' may choose more able friends or partners. These relationships allow them to live independently, to achieve a 'cloak of competence', but leave them vulnerable to friends or partners who can abuse their authority through financial or sexual exploitation, physical or sexual violence, harassment or bullying (Edgerton 1967, 1993, 2001).

Despite the recent rapid development of policies and procedures for protecting adults who are at risk of harm or exploitation, social workers have no legal powers to intervene without the individual's consent unless their capacity to secure the help they need is demonstrably compromised. Abusive adults who target parents to gain opportunities to harm or exploit them and their children can actively isolate and alienate the family from friends, neighbours and professional contacts (Children's Commissioner 2010, p.29). Sometimes mothers are directly implicated in abusing their children under the detrimental influence of a more powerful partner (Gannon and Cortini 2010).

Domestic abuse

On first encountering domestic abuse it can be hard for inexperienced practitioners to understand why anyone would stay in an abusive relationship. The complex dynamics within families where there is domestic abuse only make sense when we begin to understand how victims might (as in 'Stockholm Syndrome') become caught up in complex triangulated relationships, internalise their oppression, or act upon unconscious defence mechanisms to form a traumatic bond with their abuser. The power and control wheel, developed by the Domestic Abuse Intervention Programme in Duluth, Minnesota (www. theduluthmodel.org), helps assessors to understand the overall pattern of behaviours abusers typically employ to establish and maintain control (Figure 6.3).

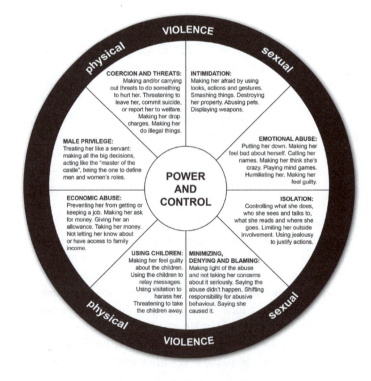

Figure 6.3 The power and control wheel: the Duluth model

Assessments miss the point if they fail to look under the surface to understand what drives abusive behaviour, and consider the underlying issues that trigger or sustain abuse. We cannot afford to make assumptions about how violence is played out or what it means in a relationship (Fiona Lewis, Independent Reviewing officer, personal communication, February 2013). Remember: both men and women experience incidents of interpersonal violence and in all kinds of relationships. Lesbians and men (whether heterosexual, bisexual or gay) often find it difficult to access appropriate help.

Case studies

1. Ryan, aged 21, and Aaminah, aged 19, are living in bed and breakfast accommodation with their four-year-old daughter, Wareesha. Aaminah has diabetes and expects a son in two months' time. Ryan used to work in a warehouse but lost his job a year ago and feels no hope of working locally again. Having previously got on well, they have had more and more rows over the last six months. Neighbours call the police having witnessed Ryan simultaneously grab Wareesha's hand and push Aaminah down the stairs.

2. Within weeks of Aaron moving in with her, Stephanie, aged 39, takes her 16-year-old daughter Chelsea to the GP surgery for 'something to help keep her calm'. When casually asked about some cuts visible on her own face Stephanie tells the receptionist that Aaron has hit her and reveals further bruises about a week old on her back and arms. Aaron is well known to local police for getting into fights, for violent crime, and for domestic abuse.

3. Debbie, aged 56, recently took early retirement from a career in pharmacy having lived with multiple sclerosis for several years. She recently met and has entered into a relationship with Sophie, aged 29. Debbie's only son, Pranav, aged 14, tells his school counsellor that last night he heard his mum shouting and ran downstairs to find Sophie burning Debbie's arm with a cigarette. Pranav grappled with Sophie to protect his mum and forced Sophie to leave the house.

4. Crystal has three children aged 4, 6 and 12. Crystal has a long history of problem alcohol use and self-harm. Both community mental health services and family support

workers have been involved with the family for many years. Each of the children has different fathers and everyone knows that all these relationships featured violence. Over the years, workers have been concerned that Crystal seems to thrive on the drama of these troubled relationships. A new man moved in last week.

Consider each of these scenarios and compare them.

- What is driving the abuse?
- What are the questions for assessment?
- What will you need to take into account when planning this assessment?
- Who in the immediate family, the wider family and the professional network needs to be involved in this assessment?

Domestic abuse is most commonly inflicted by men towards women. In the UK, misogyny is increasingly common among younger adults, and women aged 16 to 24 are now the most likely to experience abuse. Abused women are more likely to suffer associated mental and physical health problems, and are more likely to experience repeated, severe forms of physical violence (DoH 2002). Patriarchal practices and traditions exist in all cultures and women experience domestic oppression across the whole of society. Attitudes that minimise or justify violence against women are widely held.

EXERCISE

Watch Eminem and Rihanna's *Love the way you lie*.

- What messages does the imagery convey about the relationship portrayed?
- What messages do the lyrics convey about the relationship described?
- What beliefs underpin these messages?

Media representations often echo the ambiguity in contemporary attitudes towards domestic abuse, sometimes condemning but at other times glamorising it. Assessors therefore must try to understand each family member's attitudes and expectations in relation to individual identity, gender roles, parenting style, family relationships and partnership and take account of any particular cultural influences.

Despite significant changes in police practice, and in both criminal and civil law, the legal framework remains fragmented, confusing and often inadequate to protect families affected by domestic abuse (Musgrove and Groves 2007, cited by Braye and Preston-Shoot 2010, p.40).

Workers in adult settings, and especially those in targeted domestic abuse services, can make a crucial contribution to supporting victims of domestic abuse in their role as parents. Domestic abuse can undermine parents' self-esteem and damage confidence in parenting especially if one parent is belittled and undermined by the other (Davies and Ward 2012). Children's services responses to domestic abuse are fragmented: very few families are fully assessed, fewer still receive a service and there remains a tendency to minimise domestic abuse, misattribute responsibility for it and disregard its implications for children's safety and well-being (Family Rights Group 2011).

Including the oppressor as well as the victim of abuse in assessment, planning and intervention takes confidence and skill (Stanley *et al.* 2009). The assessment process must be carefully judged because it inevitably alters the dynamic of abuse within a family. Assessment can make matters worse: sometimes exploring and naming the problem intensifies abusers' behaviour. However, ignoring the problem or colluding with the silence can reinforce the pattern of abuse. The toolkit for practitioners *Improving Safety, Reducing Harm* provides practitioners with practical information and guidance (DoH 2009).

EXERCISE

To get a sense of the complex dynamics at work in situations of domestic abuse watch *Once Were Warriors*. Directed by Lee Tamahori in 1994, and based on a novel by Alan Duff, it tells the story of a family struggling with urban poverty, problem alcohol use, and what it means to be Maori. It vividly portrays abuse perpetrated by Jake, the complex dynamic between Jake and his partner Beth, the impact of Jake's behaviour on the children and the dangers this exposes them to.

- In what sense might some hold Beth responsible for Jake's behaviour?

- In what ways does Jake's violence towards Beth contribute to Grace's tragedy?

- What is the significance of Nig tattooing the Moko on only one side of his face?

- What part does the strength of the sexual relationship between Jake and Beth play in her decision-making?

Approximately one in three children lives with some form of domestic abuse (Mullender, Hague and Imam 2002). Both universal services such as the police and targeted services such as refuges are now required to notify children's social services of any violent incident where children are involved.

It is now recognised that the trauma of 'seeing or hearing the ill-treatment of another' can damage children's physical health, behaviour, emotional well-being and cognitive development (Stanley 2009). The impact of abuse and how children cope with stress varies from child to child, and depends on children's age and stage of development (Shonkoff and Garner 2012). Unborn babies can be injured during physical assaults on their mother and are affected by stress she experiences, especially since women sometimes find that domestic abuse begins or escalates when they are pregnant. Some children exhibit externalising behaviours so that they are more aggressive, non-compliant, destructive and anti-social than other children. Others internalise their distress, presenting therefore as over-controlled, anxious, inhibited, sad and withdrawn with low self-esteem and depressive symptoms (Onyskiw 2003). Whole family assessment should not only identify the harm abuse has caused, stop it and ensure future safety, but also address its consequences and its impact on children's future well-being and development (Cleaver *et al.* 2011).

Domestic abuse often occurs alongside child abuse and there is a strong connection between domestic and sexual violence (DoH 1995, 2009). Tellingly, domestic abuse is a factor in two-thirds of cases where children are killed or seriously injured (Brandon *et al.* 2009). These links should come as no surprise since many perpetrators of abuse are driven to exercise power destructively towards others and/or use violence because they have poor self-regulation and impulse control. Although we have longstanding evidence of this pattern, it has taken a long time for the links between men abusing their partners and also abusing their children to be taken into account in the legal system (Shipway 2004).

Unfortunately, assessments tend to be left half completed and support withdrawn when victimised parents leave abusive partners even though domestic abuse continues after 50 per cent of separations. Social media have added a new dimension to abusive behaviour when parents break up. Brandon *et al.* (2012) emphasise the potential adverse effects on children linked with parental separation, especially where separation is associated with continuing threats or controlling behaviour. Acrimonious separations can present direct risks to children's safety including risks of homicide. Children suffer emotional harm, are used by parents to get at each other and can be caught in the middle of conflict. Incidents are especially prone to arise during contact (Stanley *et al.* 2009). The Children and Family Court Advisory and Support Service (CAFCASS) estimates that allegations of domestic abuse are involved in about 60 per cent of the families dealt with in the court and yet contact is refused in less than 1 per cent of cases (Coy *et al.* 2012).

Even in the absence of an abusive history, separation/divorce is recognised as one of the most stressful life events for adults, and can trigger or exacerbate the individual difficulties parents face. Most parents do not set out to harm their children when they separate, but disruptions, life changes and acrimony are probably the most common source of distress to children, and family breakdown generates profound short- and long-term disadvantages for children (Fawcett 1998; Pryor and Rodgers 2001). It has been suggested that the rising divorce rate contributes to the parallel rise in depression and suicide during adolescence (Evans, Hawton and Rodham 2005).

Relationship contexts of physical and sexual harm

Every year around 55 children die in England as a direct result of violence or neglect. Physical assaults on children are best understood as acts of aggression. In most instances of physical abuse the parent felt anger, has not contained it and has not been inhibited from acting on it. Physical abuse usually arises in the context of a relationship that is already troubled (Frude 2003, p.195).

Babies under a year old are the most vulnerable to physical harm: they are nearly three times more likely to be subject to a child protection plan than at any other age and they face around eight times the average risk of being murdered. Babies account for 45 per cent of untoward child deaths (Cuthbert, Rayns and Stanley 2011, cited by Brown and Ward 2012, p.50). The long-term consequences of physical abuse are far-reaching. Adolescents and adults who have been physically abused in childhood are particularly likely to experience depression, anxiety and post-traumatic stress disorder; develop poorly both physically and intellectually; have problems with social relationships; show more difficult, aggressive behaviour; and be more frequently arrested for crimes of violence (Creighton 2002; Gibbons *et al.* 1995; both cited by Brown and Ward 2012).

The single most useful predictor that a child is likely to be injured is that a parent has already caused them injury previously. Where physical assaults have led to serious injury or death, both mothers and fathers often had a history of living with and witnessing domestic abuse during childhood. Mothers who physically abused were often young and described as 'immature' with 'poor temper control' and fathers had a history of 'behavioural problems' (Brandon *et al.* 2008). Parents who experienced abandonment, neglect or rejection during their childhood can be over-reliant on others and fear being left.

These pressures mean that some parents seem highly dependent on others. Meanwhile some steer clear of anyone who might be able to support them. Some adults who felt helpless in childhood and faced neglect, sexual abuse, physical assaults, coercion and aggression can grow up feeling a need to be violent and dominant and in control. When these people's parenting comes under scrutiny, they may feel unable to control their own behaviour at the same time as feeling that others are unduly controlling, resulting in unresolved 'care and control conflicts' (Reder and Duncan 1999, 2003c).

Gathering information about a violent parent's developmental and relationship history, hearing parents' stories, examining what they say, how they say it, and the impact of their experience on how they behave, builds a foundation for understanding how they are likely to react and cope under stress (Howe 2005). Social work assessments that focus exclusively on the incident itself are unhelpful. How and why a child is at risk of harm can only be understood by exploring underlying patterns, attitudes and beliefs.

Assessments of physical harm are sometimes complicated by ambiguity about corporal punishment within UK law. In 1998, the Court of Human Rights ruled that corporal punishment represents inhuman and degrading treatment (*A* v. *UK* [1998]). It is no longer tolerated in public settings such as schools, but in all three UK jurisdictions the use of reasonable punishment/justifiable assault/reasonable chastisement is a matter for individual parents to decide even though this is inconsistent with the UN Convention on the Rights of the Child (1989).

Far more children experience physical abuse than are reported to child protection agencies. GPs are unlikely to report injuries unless they consider children 'likely or very likely' to have been abused and are seriously hurt. Social workers in both children's and adult services need to be confident that they know enough to enable them to identify when medical assessment is needed. This means understanding whether the pattern of injuries fits with the child's stage of development, knowing the usual patterns of injuries that accidentally arise as children play, and enough basic anatomical knowledge to know whether the injury matches the explanation given (Brandon *et al.* 2010a, 2012). The research evidence about non-accidental injuries is not as comprehensive and conclusive as most people expect it to be!

There are three useful sources of information available on-line:

- The Child Accident Prevention Trust (2009) provides helpful guidelines about keeping children safe (www.capt.org.uk).

- NICE have published guidelines for about when to suspect child maltreatment (www.nice.org.uk/Guidance/CG/wave12/11).

- The NSPCC and Welsh CPSR group have produced some key information about bruising, burns and scalds, fractures, bites and oral injuries, and head and spinal injuries (www.core-info.cardiff. ac.uk).

When concerns about a child's safety require paediatric assessment, paediatricians should be included in strategy discussions. It is helpful to provide the paediatrician with clear, specific information about the concerns and as much context as possible before they meet with the child. Children and parents need to be prepared for the detailed medical assessments the paediatrician will undertake. Paediatric assessments are holistic so children and parents need to understand that they involve:

- taking a structured paediatric history using some open and some direct questions

- reviewing a chronology of health issues where these are complex and longstanding

- observation of the child's behaviour and manner, the parent–child interaction, and the child's response to medical examination

- physical examination.

The physical examination will involve observing and recording:

- injuries using a body map

- height/weight/head circumference and assessment of growth

- general appearance and hygiene
- general physical examination
- mouth and dental hygiene
- ears
- scalp/hairline
- genitalia/perineum – depending on the child's age and the presenting concerns
- toes/fingers/nails.

Paediatric assessment can achieve much more than simply providing an opinion about an injury. Assesments frequently identify unmet health needs or developmental/behavioural difficulties, and sometimes diagnose medical problems that will benefit from treatment. Paediatricians can help clarify whether bruises/fractures/failure to thrive/developmental problems have a legitimate medical cause. However, paediatric assessment cannot be expected to age bruises, age fractures accurately, or confirm sexual abuse or exclude it. It cannot always explain an injury or distinguish between accidental and abusive injuries (Dr Sian Bennett, Clinical Director, Brighton and Hove Children's Services, personal communication, February/May 2013).

Working with families where you suspect or know about sexual abuse is especially challenging because it is only human to feel disgusted, anxious, angry, contaminated. Some practitioners identify very closely with the child victim and others empathise with the parent who has proved unable to protect their children. Some may also feel sympathy for the abuser. Harnessing emotional intelligence to recognise and manage the family's and your own feelings demands honesty, integrity, self-awareness and the ability to stay respectfully engaged with everybody involved.

Points to consider

- What, in your experience, are the challenges of identifying physical harm to children?
- How confident do you feel about identifying child sexual abuse?

- What professional skills and personal qualities are key to working with the victims of physical or sexual harm?

- Draw up an action plan to enhance your knowledge/ understanding on these issues and discuss this with your supervisor.

Although some mothers do abuse their children, most child sex offences are committed by men already known to their victims. However, social workers only see the tip of the iceberg. It is currently thought that around 21 per cent of girls and 11 per cent of boys experience sexual abuse at some point during childhood. The least resilient children are more likely to be seriously and repeatedly abused and to experience lasting harm.

Thirty-one per cent of sexually abused children reach adulthood without telling anyone. Only about 10 per cent of child sexual abuse is reported to the police and consequently it represents only 1 per cent of recorded crime. Only one in ten of the child sexual abuse incidents reported to the police are actually put before criminal courts, where most abusers are acquitted of the charges brought against them. The least resilient children are more likely to be very seriously and repeatedly abused and to experience lasting harm.

Once the risk of a parent sexually abusing children in a family has been identified, assessment focuses on what can be done to keep the whole family safe in future. Key interventions are:

- empowering the safe/protective parent, the victim and the protective network around them

- reinforcing the abuser's internal and external inhibitors if s/he is to live with children in the future

- actively monitoring family functioning. This monitoring has to be sustained, co-ordinated and involve all the agencies engaged with family members.

Conclusion

Social work has long been criticised for concentrating on high threshold evidence of harm (Howe 1996; Munro 2011a, b). High thresholds for intervention have led us into looking for what can be proved when we should be trying to understand. Many of the problems parents and children live with are rooted in troubled relationships. Assessment needs to focus not just on incidents or events but on relationships and what they convey about attitude, beliefs and patterns within families. To access what is really going on within families, social workers need to stop 'doing', listen, and make a genuine human connection with people. Formulas and procedures provide a necessary framework for whole family assessment, but to understand families we have to try and join with them so that they will take us underneath the surface of the difficulties they face. Determining whether family relationships can be supported, healed or must be ended is often at the heart of assessments where families' problems are complex.

Further reading and resources

Baim, C. and Morrison, T. (2011) *Attachment Based Practice with Adults. Understanding Strategies and Promoting Positive Change. A new practice model and interactive resource for assessment, intervention and supervision.* Brighton: Pavilion Publishing.

Brown, R. and Ward, H. (2012) *Decision-making Within a Child's Timeframe. An Overview of Current Research Evidence for Family Justice Professionals Concerning Child Development and the Impact of Maltreatment.* Working Paper 16. London: Childhood Wellbeing Research Centre.

DoH (Department of Health) (2009) *Improving Safety, Reducing Harm. Children, Young People and Domestic Violence. A Practical Toolkit for Front-Line Practitioners.* London: HMSO.

Gerhardt, S. (2004) *Why Love Matters: How Affection Shapes a Baby's Brain.* Hove: Brunner-Routledge.

Howe, D. (2005) *Child Abuse and Neglect: Attachment, Development and Intervention.* Basingstoke: Palgrave Macmillan.

Iwaniec, D. (2006) *The Emotionally Abused and Neglected Child. Identification, Assessment and Intervention. A Practice Handbook.* London: Wiley.

O'Hagan, K. (2006) *Identifying Emotional and Psychological Abuse. A Guide for Childcare Professionals.* Maidenhead: Open University Press.

Satir, V. (1988) *The New Peoplemaking.* Palo Alto, CA: Science and Behaviour Books.

CHAPTER 7

Postscript

Points to consider

Consider these questions either on your own or with colleagues.

- How should local authorities set up adult and children's services so that we can work together to assess whole families' needs AND be alert to the risk of harm to children, and midful of some adults' needs for protection?

- How can individual social workers manage the competing demands of discourses such as respect for the voice of experts through experience, inter-agency working, community-based prevention, early intervention, family support, child and adult protection, risk-management, personalisation and permanence-planning?

- How can we ensure our assessments lead to SMART (specific, measurable, achievable, realistic and timely) plans for interventions that promote better outcomes for both children AND their parents?

- How can public sector services ensure that integrating different disciplines within adult and children's teams does not compromise collaboration between social workers who are engaged with families who need both services?

- What support do you need to fulfil your responsibilities in whole family assessment?

This book started out by describing assessment as a process with the purpose of guiding action. Yet the chapters that followed have emphasised being, watching and listening. Settling alongside parents, children and your social work colleagues in other services, to quietly understand their different perspectives, reflect, and make sense of the whole, allows you to know the situation in some depth and make properly informed judgements. This means engaging with the past, the present and indeed the future so that social work interventions made now take into account what the family has already experienced and projects them all forward into the best possible future they could hope for.

Chapters 1–6 have explored different aspects of the complexity and uncertainty that is inevitable when you are working with families where parents' problems have implications for family life and for children's well-being. Social workers conducting assessments with parents and their families face a series of very fundamental challenges including:

- being open-minded, non-judgemental and optimistic whilst thinking the unthinkable, identifying and challenging abuse

- recognising the uniqueness of each individual and family whilst drawing on the evidence-base for achieving good outcomes

- prioritising children's well-being whilst managing the parents' different and competing needs

- the inconsistent political agenda about risk-taking and risk-aversive practice

- exercising authority whilst ensuring that professional powers are never used arbitrarily or abusively.

These and the specific dilemmas families raise cannot be resolved simply by locating the correct place to stand on a continuum. Social workers often have to manage ways of thinking about their practice that are fundamentally opposed and incompatible (Cooper *et al.* 2003). This can sometimes leave us feeling very confused!

> Social work's predominant location in Local Authorities has always meant the negotiation of multiple accountabilities – between employers, professional values, professional self, service users and the public. The challenge has always been to hold the dynamic tension that this involves, rather than to succumb to bureaucracy… in policy and practice…and practice unquestioningly.

> (Braye and Preston-Shoot 2002)

To add to these complexities, three aspects of each social worker's being sit alongside and mirror these multiple accountabilities. We all have to accommodate our sense of self, identity and role. In order to offer authentic relationships with colleagues and with members of the families we work with, we each have to find a way of managing the dissonance between these three aspects of ourselves and integrate them (Figure 7.1).

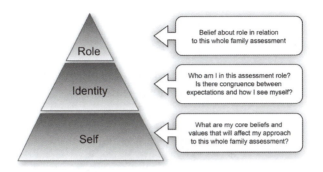

Figure 7.1 Role, identity and self (Wonnacott 2012)

EXERCISE

Imagine that an announcement has been made: the world is about to come to a cataclysmic end in just 30 minutes. All the existing records and information systems in the world will be destroyed but a handful of people will survive. Every individual in the world is invited to contribute a written message to a knowledge base that will be passed on to future generations.

- Take 15 minutes now to record your own knowledge and experience so that those helping troubled families of the future can draw on the practice wisdom you have achieved.

(Adapted from Dolan 1998)

Relationship-based practice is widely advocated and relies on the creative use of self. Use of self is a difficult concept to articulate and involves walking an ill-defined tightrope of 'appropriate professional behaviour' (Figure 7.2). The integration of self, identity and role means that as a social worker you must be:

- warm and friendly…but not over-familiar

- strong and assertive…but not bossy

- relaxed…but not unconcerned

- concerned…but not nosey

- cheerful…but not flippant

- helpful…but not paternalistic

- open minded…and able to form judgements
- down to earth…but not patronising
- honest…but not brutal or rude.

Munro (2008) identified the range of knowledge and skills social workers must use in order to reflect and reason.

Figure 7.2 Knowledge and skills at the interface between adult and children's services (Munro 2008)

The premise throughout this book is that good social work assessments rely on building relationships. This rests on ideas about co-construction. Integrating families' own insights with professional perspectives is crucial to reaching sound judgements that will guide purposeful intervention. Assessment encounters demand that each family member and assessor involved takes down their guard enough to open a channel through which to communicate their own, and hear the other's, worldview, knowledge and experience. Multiple realities are created whenever we engage with whole families and collaborate with counterparts in other services. It is the social worker's responsibility to make sense of the story these multiple realities tell (Figure 7.3).

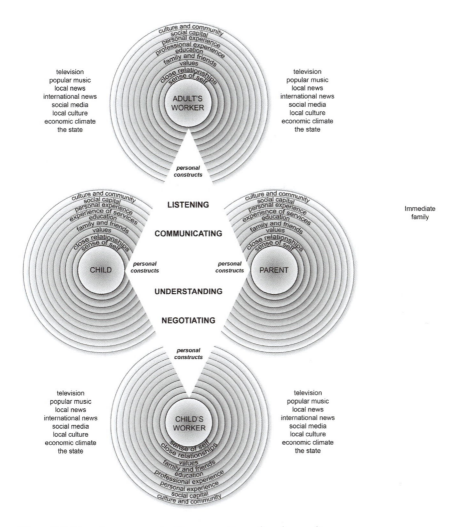

Figure 7.3 Listening, communicating, engaging and understanding

Each chapter has framed social work as a moral-relational undertaking, fraught with the many dilemmas that arise in practice. Ethical problems often arise out of uncertainty about how to balance competing values. Enacting ethical social work in everyday practice therefore demands a highly developed sense of morality. Kohlberg (1969) provides a model for understanding how our capacity for moral reasoning develops through six stages. This process starts at a simple level of 'I do it because I will be punished if I do not' and progresses to a level of reasoning that demonstrates internalised norms and values, owned personally but linked to overriding principles. The level of moral reasoning required of social work practitioners reflects the most sophisticated of Kohlberg's six stages where:

> What is right or wrong is based upon self-chosen, ethical principles which we arrive at through individual reflection… The principles are abstract and universal such as justice, equality…and respect for the dignity of human beings as individuals, and only by acting on them do we ultimately attain full responsibility for our actions.

> (Gross 1996)

This is what professional accountability and defensible practice are all about.

APPENDIX 1
ACRONYMS AND ABBREVIATIONS USED IN WHOLE FAMILY ASSESSMENT

Acronym	Meaning
ABE	Achieving Best Evidence
ADHD	Attention Deficit Hyperactivity Disorder
AHP	Allied Health Professionals
AMHP	Approved Mental Health Professional
AOT	Assertive Outreach Team
ASBO	Anti-Social Behaviour Order
BPD	Borderline Personality Disorder
BPI	Basic Personal Information
CAADA	Co-ordinated Action Against Domestic Abuse
CAFCASS	Children and Family Court Advisory and Support Service
CAMHS	Child and Adolescent Mental Health Services
CBT	Cognitive Behavioural Therapy
CCPAS	Churches' Child Protection Advisory Service
CDRP	Crime and Disorder Reduction Partnerships
CMHT	Community Mental Health Team
CPA	Care Programme Approach

cont.

Acronym	Meaning
CPN	Community Psychiatric Nurse
CPS	Crown Prosecution Service
CQC	Care Quality Commission
CRB	Criminal Records Bureau
CRT	Crisis Resolution Team
CSCI	Commission for Social Care Inspection
CST	Care Standards Tribunal
DAAT	Drug and Alcohol Action Team
DBT	Dialectical Behaviour Therapy
DCSF	Department for Children, Schools and Families
DoH	Department of Health
DoLS	Deprivation of Liberty Safeguards
DRR	Drug Rehabilitation Requirement
DSM-V	Diagnostic and Statistical Manual of Mental Disorders – 5th edition
DTTO	Drug Treatment and Testing Order
ECHR	European Convention on Human Rights and Fundamental Freedoms
ECM	Every Child Matters
EHRC	Equality and Human Rights Commission
FACS	Fair Access to Care Services
FGM	Female Genital Mutilation
FIP	Family Intervention Project
FMA	Family Mediation Association
FMU	Forced Marriage Unit
ICS	Integrated Children's System
IMCA	Independent Mental Health Advocate

IRO	Independent Reviewing Officer
ISA	Independent Safeguarding Authority
LAA	Local Area Agreement
LEA	Local Education Authority
LGBT	Lesbian, Gay, Bisexual and Trans
LSCB	Local Safeguarding Children's Board
LSP	Local Strategic Partnership
MAPPA	Multi-Agency Public Protection Arrangements
MARAC	Multi-Agency Risk Assessment Conference
MASH	Multi-Agency Safeguarding Hubs
MHA	Mental Health Act
MHAC	Mental Health Act Commission
MHRT	Mental Health Review Tribunal
NASS	National Asylum Support Service
NHS	National Health Service
NIs	National Indicators
NOMS	National Offender Management Service
NR	Nearest Relative
NSF	National Service Framework
NTA	National Treatment Agency
PBR	Payment by Results
PCG	Primary Care Group
PCO	Primary Care Organisation
PCP	Person-Centred Planning
PCT	Primary Care Trust
PHCT	Primary Health Care Team
PTSD	Post-Traumatic Stress Disorder
SAP	Single Assessment Process

cont.

Acronym	Meaning
SARCs	Sexual Assault Referral Centres
SCAN	Specialist Clinical Addiction Network (disbanded April 2011)
SCT	Supervised Community Treatment
SEN	Special Educational Needs
SENCO	Special Educational Needs Co-ordinator
SHA	Strategic Health Authority
SMMGP	Substance Misuse Management in General Practice
SSD	Social Services Department
SWP	Social Work Practices
TAC	Team Around the Child
TAF	Team Around the Family
UNCRC	United Nations Convention on the Rights of the Child
WAG	Welsh Assembly Government

CLINICAL TOOLS AND MEASURES MOST FREQUENTLY USED TO INFORM ASSESSMENT IN ADULT AND CHILDREN'S SERVICES

Achieving Best Evidence (Ministry of Justice 2011)	Provides detailed statutory guidance for the conduct of forensic interviews with vulnerable adults, children and intimidated witnesses who are victims or witnesses of crime. Structured interviews conducted by police officers and social workers trained to use the protocol.
Adolescent Well-Being Scale (Birleson 1980)	An 18-item self-report questionnaire for use with children aged 11–16 to identify indicators of childhood depression.
Adult Attachment Inventory (Main 1990)	Intended for adults and young people aged 16-plus. Identifies adult attachment strategies.
Adult Well-Being Scale (Snaith *et al.* 1978)	An 18-item self-report questionnaire for use with parents used to identify indicators of irritability and depression.
Adult-Adolescent Parent Inventory (Bavelock 1984)	Self-report questionnaire for use with parents to identify expectations of the child, sensitivity to the child's needs, and attitudes towards corporal punishment and parent–child roles.
Alcohol Scale (Piccinelli *et al.* 1997)	Self-report questionnaire for use with adults to indicate the impact of alcohol consumption.
Alcohol Use Disorders Identification Test: AUDIT (Babor *et al.* 1992)	Brief self-report questionnaire for use with adults, completed and coded by clinician in interview. Developed by the World Health Organization as a simple screening tool to pick up early indicators of hazardous and harmful drinking and to identify mild dependence.
Alcohol Use Questionnaire (Bentovim and Cox 2000)	A 5-item self-report questionnaire used in children's services as a tool to help raise the subject of problem alcohol use with parents.
Assessment of Family Competence, Strengths and Difficulties (Bentovim and Bingley Miller 2001)	Consists of various modules that explore family and professional views of the current situation, the adaptability to the child's needs, and quality of parenting, various aspects of family relationships and the impact of history. Provides a standardised evidence-based approach to current family strengths and difficulties which have played a role in the significant harm of the child, and also in assessing the capacity for change, resources in the family to achieve a safe context for the child, and the reversal of family factors which may have played a role in significant harm, and aiding the recovery and future health of the child.

Assessment of Mental Capacity Audit Tool: AMCAT (Mental Health Foundation and SCIE 2010)	An on-line questionnaire that helps staff in adult health and social care reflect, evaluate, audit and learn about an assessment of mental capacity they have made.
ASSET (Youth Justice Board 2006)	Provides a common structured framework for assessment of all young offenders who come into contact with the criminal justice system. It identifies factors or circumstances that may have contributed to the offending behaviour. It includes a serious harm risk-assessment and a self-report questionnaire to capture the child's account.
ASSIST	A self-report questionnaire for use with victims of domestic abuse to assess risk of future harm.
Beck Depression Inventory-II: BDI-II (Beck, Steer and Brown 1996)	A 21 question multiple-choice, self-report inventory for adults and children over 13. Used by health professionals, the test is scored with each answer assigned a score of 0 to 3 to determine the depression's severity.
Bene-Anthony Family Relations Test (Bene and Anthony 1957; Bene 1985)	Used by psychologists to assess the emotional aspects of family relationships from the child's perspective using a scoring system.
Bethlem Mother-Infant Interaction Scale (Kumar and Hipwell 1996)	An observation schedule used in psychiatric mother and baby settings. Seven subscales describe eye contact, physical contact, vocal contact, mood, general routine, physical risks to baby, and baby's contribution to the interaction.
CAGE questionnaire (Kitchens 1994)	A questionnaire used by GPs and alcohol services to screen adults for alcoholism using four simple questions. Two 'yes' responses indicate the need to investigate further.
Checklist for Living Environments to Assess Neglect: CLEAN (Watson-Perczel et al. 1988)	Checklist assesses the cleanliness of the home environment to produce a composite percentage score reflecting home conditions along three dimensions: clean/dirty, clothes/linens, and items not belonging.

cont.

Chemical Use, Abuse and Dependence Scale: CUAD (Appleby *et al.* 1996)	A semi-structured interview format used in psychiatric hospitals to screen for substance use in adults with severe psychiatric disorder.
Child Abuse Potential Inventory: CAP (Milner 1986)	A 160-item questionnaire conducted by a psychologist screens for parents' potential to inflict physical abuse. Used to inform and support clinical assessment.
Child Well-Being Scale: CLL (Gaudin, Plansky and Kilpaqtrick 1992)	A 43-item scale conducted by a family practitioner to assess dimensions of care related to the physical, psychological and social needs of children.
Childhood Level of Living Scale (Polansky *et al.* 1981)	A 99-item scale completed by a professional working with a family on the basis of observation of parent assesses the quality of parental childcare to identify neglect.
Conflict Tactics Scale: CTS (Straus *et al.* 1996)	A 20-item self-report scale relating to parental discipline strategies.
Common Assessment Framework: (DoH 2005)	A standardised approach used by practitioners across all children's services to assess children's needs and identify children whose needs are not met by universal services.
Co-ordinated Action Against Domestic Abuse: CAADA (www.caada.org.uk)	A risk assessment tool used by Independent Domestic Violence Advisers to identify adult victims at high or medium risk from domestic violence and to co-ordinate safety interventions.
CRAAFT (Knight *et al.* 1999)	A 2-item brief screening instrument for adolescents to assess need for treatment for problem drug or alcohol use.
Dartmouth Assessment of Lifestyle Instrument: DALI (Rosenberg *et al.* 1998)	An 18-item interviewer-administered self-report scale used in psychiatric settings to screen for substance misuse in adults with severe psychiatric disorder.
Domestic Abuse, Stalking and 'Honour-based' Violence Risk Identification, Assessment and Management Model: DASH (Richards 2009)	Checklist intended for multi-agency use to identify risk to adult victims of abuse and inform the mobilisation of resources.

Domestic Violence Risk Assessment Model (Bell 2007)	Developed by Barnardo's to assess the severity of risk posed by domestic violence within families with children. It aims to help practitioners make decisions about the risks presented for children and to plan effective interventions for the family. It has nine assessment areas to assist social workers and other childcare professionals reach decisions about when a child is 'in need' or is 'in need of protection'.
Drug Disorders Identification Test: DUDIT (Berman et al. 2005)	An 11-item self-report questionnaire intended for use with adults completed and coded by a clinician in interview, intended to be used alongside AUDIT.
Drug Abuse Screening Instrument: DAST-10 (Skinner 1982)	A 28-item self-report scale screens for the abuse of drugs other than alcohol and measures the severity of drug dependence.
Edinburgh Post-Natal Depression Scale: EPDS (Cox, Holden and Sagovsky 1987)	A10-item self-report questionnaire screens women for symptoms of clinical depression after childbirth, frequently used by GPs and Health Visitors.
Eyberg Child Behaviour Inventory: ECBI (Eyberg and Pincus 1999)	A 36-item self-report scale indicating parents' evaluation of the frequency of their child's problem behaviour.
Family Activity Scales (Bentovim and Cox 2000)	A self-report questionnaire derived from a Child Centredness Scale (Smith 1985)[AQ] identifies the extent of joint, child-centred family activity and independent/autonomous child activity. There are two versions for children aged 2–6 and 7–12.
Form F1 (BAAF 2000)	Provides fostering and adoption agencies with a standard way of collecting, analysing and presenting information about prospective foster carers, adoptive parents, and other carers.
Framework for the Assessment of Children in Need and their Families: NAF (DoH et al. 2000a)	Provides an ecological paradigm for assessment in children's social services.

Functional Assessment of Mental Health and Addiction: FAMHA (Anderson and Bellsfield 1999)	A 44-item scale administered by clinical staff trained in the protocol assesses current bio-psychosocial functioning in patients with a dual diagnosis. Tailored to assess the needs of severely distressed patients and to identify appropriate therapeutic interventions.
Graded Care Profile: GCP (Polnay and Srivastava 1997)	A descriptive tool to indicate the quality of parental care and identify neglect on a scale graded by childcare/family workers.
G-Map Assessment (Print *et al.* 2007)	A therapeutic assessment model used with young people who have exhibited sexually abusive behaviours.
Historical-Clinical-Risk Management-20: HCR-20 (Webster *et al.* 1997)	A 20-item structured professional judgement risk assessment used in prisons and forensic psychiatric settings to assess the probability of violence and management strategies for potentially violent offenders with psychiatric illness.
Home Accident Prevention Inventory: HAPI (Tertinger, Green and Lutzker 1984)	A checklist to assess the safety of children's home environment including five categories of safety hazards: home-fire and electrical; mechanical-suffocation; ingested object suffocation; firearms; and solid/liquid poisons.
Home Conditions Assessment Scale (Davie *et al.* 1984)	Applies eleven indicators of household cleanliness as an initial screening about basic childcare.
Home Inventory (Caldwell and Bradley 2003)	A structured observation/interview instrument to assess the quality of the child-rearing home environment covering parental interactions and activity with the child, the safety and quality of the physical home environment and the discipline and emotional nurturing of the child.
Initial Deviance Assessment: IDA (Thornton 2002)	A psychometric measure using four key domains to assess the risk posed by imprisoned sex offenders (in England and Wales). Integrates static risk assessment (STATIC-99), stable dynamic risk assessment, evaluation of progress based on response to treatment, and management of risk.

Mini-Mental State Examination: MMSE (Folstein, Folstein and McHugh 1975)	A brief quantitative instrument to measure cognitive status of adults in psychiatric settings and screen for cognitive impairment.
Multi-dimensional Assessment of Caring Activities: MACA-YC18 (Joseph, Becker and Becker 2009)	An 18-item self-report measure providing an index of the caring activity undertaken by a young person that differentiates between domestic tasks, household management, personal care, emotional care, sibling care and financial/practical care.
Multi-dimensional Assessment of Caring Activities-Young Carers: MACA-YC42 (Joseph *et al.* 2009)	A 42-item self-report measure providint a detailed account of the nature and extent of caring activity undertaken by a young person.
Offender Assessment System: OASys	Provides a common structured framework for assessment of adult offenders who come into contact with the criminal justice system.
Parent Assessment Manual: PAM (McGaw *et al.* 1998)	A structured assessment and screening tool based on the parental Knowledge-Skills-Practice Model used to assess parents with intellectual impairments covering areas such as childcare and development, independent living skills, safety and hygiene, parents' health, relationships and support.
Parent Behaviour Checklist (Fox 1994)	A 100-item self-report scale assessing the strengths and weakness of parents raising children aged 1–5 using three sub-scales: expectations; discipline; and nurturing.
Parent-Child Relationship Inventory: PCRI (Gerard 1994)	A 78-item self-report inventory that assesses how parents of 5–15-year-olds view the task of parenting and how they view their children using seven distinct scales: parental support; satisfaction with parenting; involvement; communication; limit-setting; autonomy; and role orientation.

cont.

Parent Development Interview: PDI (Aber *et al.* 1985; Slade 2005)	A 45-item semi-structured clinical interview examining parents' representations of their children, themselves as parents and their relationships with their children. There is an infancy version, a toddler version and a brief version.
Parent Opinion Questionnaire: POQ (Azar *et al.* 1984)	An 80-item self-report questionnaire designed to assess parental expectations of child behaviour at various development stages using six subscales: self-care; family responsibility and care of siblings; help and affection to parents; leaving children alone; proper behaviour and feelings; and punishment.
Parental Anger Inventory (Hansen and Sedlar 1998)	A 50-item self-report inventory that assesses parents' feelings of anger by exploring their response to a series of child-related scenarios.
Parenting Daily Hassles Scale (Crnic and Greenberg 1990)	A self-report questionnaire that assesses the frequency, impact and intensity of 20 parenting stresses.
Parenting Locus of Control Scale: PLOC-SF (Campis, Lyman and Prentice-Dunn 1986)	A 25-item self-report questionnaire measuring the degree to which parents feel in control of their child's behaviour.
Parenting Risk Scale (Mrazek, Mrazek and Klinnert 1995)	Semi-structured interview with parent assessing stress and coping by exploring five key dimensions of parenting: emotional availability (degree of emotional warmth); control (degree of flexibility and facilitation); psychiatric disturbance (presence, type, severity); knowledge base (understanding basic childcare and development); commitment (adequate prioritising of childcare responsibilities).
Parenting Stress Index – Short Form: PSI-SF (Abidin 1995)	A 36-item self-report psychometric instrument that measures stress directly associated with the parenting role using three factors: parent/child dysfunctional interactions; parent distress; and difficult child.

Person-Centred Risk Assessment and Management System (Titterton 2005)	A systemic/collaborative approach to assessing, managing and taking risk to vulnerable adults in the community and in long-stay settings with a view to enhancing quality of life.
Positive and Negative Outcomes of Caring: PANOC-YC20 (Joseph et al. 2009)	A 20-item self-report measure indexing positive and negative outcomes experienced by young carers.
Post-Intervention Self-Assessment: PISA-CR2 (Joseph et al. 2009)	A self-report questionnaire eliciting young carers' views of the interventions received and their impact.
Psychiatric Research Interview for Substance and Mental Disorders: PRISM (Hasin et al. 1996)	A semi-structured diagnostic interview developed for research purposes to identify co-morbidity of substance abuse and psychiatric illness.
Rapid Risk Assessment of Sexual Re-offending: RRASOR (Hanson 1997)	A four-item static actuarial scale identifying risk of reoffending by known sex offenders. Used in forensic settings.
Recent Life Events Questionnaire (Brugha et al. 1985)	A 21-item self-report questionnaire eliciting information about the significance of recent negative life events.
Sex Offender Treatment Evaluation Project: STEP (Beech et al. 2002)	Psychometric measure used by probation services in England and Wales to assess stable–dynamic factors in the risk posed by adult child-sex offenders.
Sexual Violence Risk-20: SVR-20 (Boer et al. 1997)	A 20-item checklist of risk factors to assess risk of future violence by convicted sex offenders in forensic mental health settings It uses three main categories of known risk factors: psychosocial adjustment; history of sexual offences; and future plans.

cont.

Sheridan Charts (Sheridan 1960)	Charts mostly used by health visitors to describe key stages of child development between 0–5 years using information based on parents' report, professional observation and interaction. Includes the development of motor, perception, play communication and independence skills and development of attention and self-regulation.
Sheridan Charts (Sheridan 1960)	Charts mostly used by health visitors to describe key stages of child development between 0–5 years using information based on parents' report, professional observation and interaction. Includes the development of motor, perception, play communication and independence skills and development of attention and self-regulation.
STATIC-99 & Static-2002R (www.static.org)	A 10-item actuarial measurement tool for use with adult male sex offenders when they are released from prison.
Statutory Assessment of Special Educational Needs (DoE)	An assessment conducted by local authorities setting out a statement in six parts describing a child's special educational needs and the help they should receive.
STELLA Project Toolkit 2007 (www. avaproject.org.uk)	A toolkit and guidance to provide practitioners in the field of domestic abuse and substance misuse to respond safely and appropriately to concerns.
Strange Situation Test (Ainsworth *et al.* 1978)	A procedure formulated to observe attachment relationships between a caregiver and child aged 9–18 months.
Strengths and Difficulties Questionnaires (Goodman 1997)	25-item self-report questionnaires elicit information from parents about their children's emotional and behavioural development. Three different versions are designed to assess children aged 3–4, 4–11 and 11–16.

Substance Abuse Treatment Scale: SATS (McHugo *et al.* 1995)	A scale used to assess the stage of substance abuse treatment in people with severe mental illness using an eight-stage model of the recovery process.
Symptom Checklist-90-Revised SCL-90-R (Derogatis 1983)	A 90-item self-report psychometric inventory designed to assess patterns of current psychological symptoms.
The Family Pack of Questionnaires and Scales (Bentovim and Cox 2000)	A collection of eight questionnaires and scales published alongside the Framework for the Assessment of Children in Need and their Families:
	Strengths and Difficulties Questionnaires
	Parenting Daily Hassle Scale
	Home Conditions Scale
	Adult Well-being Scale
	The Adolescent Well-being Scale
	The Recent Life Events Questionnaire
	The Family Activity Scale
	The Alcohol Scale.
UK90 Chart (RCPCH)	Percentile chart used by health visitors to monitor the growth of babies.

SOME PRACTICAL TOOLS AND RESOURCES FOR WORK WITH CHILDREN AND PARENTS

Name of resource	Source	Intended for	Description
Boardmaker software	www.mayer-johnson. co.uk		Boardmaker creates printed symbol-based communication materials. The software features over 4000 picture communication symbols and more than 40 languages.
Communi-CRATE	Inclusive Solutions in partnership with Niki Lyne	Children	A resource designed for use in social care teams to enhance listening to children and enable workers to take children's views into account. It contains tools and resources to enable effective participation and each box is specifically designed to best meet the needs of the ages or abilities of your service.
Draw on Your Emotions	Margot Sunderland and Philip Engleheart	Children	Creative ways to explore, express and understand important feelings.
HELD	Nicki Weld	Children and families	A resource book containing ideas for work that promotes hope, empathy, love and dignity with a focus on the personal/interpersonal.
How It Is: an image vocabulary for children about feelings, rights and safety, personal care and sexuality	NSPCC and Triangle	Disabled children	Provides 389 images that can be used as a vocabulary to help children communicate about a range of important issues.
I'll Go First	Children's Society	Disabled children	A pack containing a good practice guide and a toolkit with stickers and illustrated boards to help children communicate their views.

cont.

Name of resource	Source	Intended for	Description
In My Shoes	www.childandfamilytraining.org.uk	Children and vulnerable adults	A computer package that supports communication about experiences including potentially distressing events or relationships.
Listening to Young Children	Penny Lancaster and Vanessa Broadbent	Young children	A pack containing a conceptual framework for listening to young children. It includes a professional development handbook, 'listening and looking', and comes with a CDROM, audio-visual material and a booklet of case studies.
The Mosaic Approach	Clark and Moss (2001); Clark and Statham (2005)	Very young children	A methodology that brings together verbal and visual tools and uses participatory activities to elicit very young children's perspectives on important details of their lives.
Parenting Toolkit	London Network of Parents with Learning Difficulties, Elfrida Society and Valuing People Team	Parents	Created by parents in London with learning impairments on the basis of their experiences of what their families need.
Preventing Breakdown	Mark Hamer	Families	Guidebook with tools and ideas for solution-focused crisis interventions.
'Say it your own way'	Hutton and Partridge (2006)	Children and Young People	A toolkit containing a guide and CDROM of practical resources encouraging children to participate in assessment processes.

Title	Author/Source	Target Group	Description
Secrets	National Deaf Children's Society	Deaf Children	Aims to encourage deaf children to think carefully, helps them make choices in potentially harmful situations, and encourages them to seek help quickly from a responsible adult.
Talking Mats	Joan Murphy and Lois Cameron, University of Stirling	Adults and children with a range of communication difficulties	A communication tool which uses a mat with symbols attached as a basis for communication. It is designed to help people with communication difficulties to think about issues discussed with them, and provide them with a way to effectively express themselves in a visual way that can be easily recorded. It helps people to understand, consider and express their views and can be used with people with different abilities, from different cultures and living in different situations.
The Parent–Child Game	Jenner and McCarthy (1995)	Parent and child	A treatment method that trains the parent to use positive child-centred strategies to influence their child's behaviour through live skills training.
The Therapist's Toolbox	Susan Carrell	All service users	A manual full of techniques for enhancing therapeutic interventions.
The Wise Mouse	Virginia Ironside	Children aged 5–11	A children's book that aims to help them understand what is happening to a family member who may be experiencing a mental illness.

REFERENCES

Aber, L., Slade, A., Berger, B., Bresgi, I. and Kaplan, M. (1985) 'The Parent Development Interview.' Unpublished manuscript, Barnard College, Columbia University, NY.

Abidin, R.R. (1995) *Parenting Stress Index – Manual* (Third edition). Odessa, FL: Psychological Assessment Resources.

Ackerman, D. (2011) *One Hundred Names for Love: A Stroke, a Marriage and the Language of Healing.* New York: Norton.

Adams, T. (2001) 'The social construction of risk by community psychiatric nurses and family carers for people with dementia.' *Health, Risk and Society 3,* 3, 307–319.

Adamson, J, and Templeton, L. (2012) *Silent Voices. Supporting Children and Young People Affected By Parental Alcohol Misuse.* London: Children's Commissioner. Available at www. childrenscommissioner.gov.uk, accessed on 19 July 2013.

ADCS (Association of Directors of Children's Services) (2012) *Safeguarding Pressures. Phase Three.* Available at www.adcs.org.uk, accessed on 19 July 2013.

Advisory Council on the Misuse of Drugs (2003) *Hidden Harm. Responding to the Needs of Children of Problem Drug Users.* London: Home Office. Available at www.gov.uk/ government/uploads/system/uploads/attachment_data/file/120620/hidden-harm-full.pdf, accessed on 19 July 2013.

Advisory Council on the Misuse of Drugs (2007) *Hidden Harm Report Three Years On: Realities, Challenges and Opportunities.* London: Home Office. Available at www.gov.uk/ government/publications/hidden-harm-report-three-years-on-realities-challenges-and-opportunities, accessed on 19 July 2013.

Ainsworth, M.D.S., Bleher, M.C., Waters, E. and Wall, S. (1978) *Patterns of Attachment.* Hillsbaum, NJ: Erlbaum.

Aldgate, J., Jones, D.P.H., Rose, W. and Jeffrey, D. (2006) *The Developing World of the Child.* London: Jessica Kingsley Publishers.

Aldridge, J. (2006) 'The experiences of children living with and caring for parents with mental illness.' *Child Abuse Review 15,* 2, 79–88.

Aldridge, J. and Becker, S. (2003) *Children Caring for Parents with Mental Illness. Perspectives of Young Carers, Parents and Professionals.* Bristol: Policy Press.

Allen, J.G. (2001) *Traumatic Relationships and Serious Mental Disorders.* Chichester: Wiley.

Anderson, A.J. and Bellsfield, H. (1999) 'Functional assessment of mental health and addiction.' *International Journal of Psychosocial Rehabilitation 4,* 39–45.

Appleby, L. (2000) 'Safer services: Conclusions from the Report of the Confidential Inquiry.' *Advances in Psychiatric Treatment 6,* 5–15.

Appleby, L., Dyson, V., Altman, E., McGovern, M.P. and Luchins, D.J. (1996) 'Utility of the Chemical Use, Abuse and Dependence Scale in screening patients with severe mental illness.' *Psychiatric Services 47,* 647–649.

Archard, D. and Skivenes, M. (2009) 'Hearing the child.' *Child and Family Social Work 14,* 4, 391–399.

Arksey, H., O'Malley, L., Baldwin, S., Harris, J., Mason, A. and Golder, S. (2002) *Services to Support Carers of People With Mental Health Problems.* London: National Co-ordinating Centre for NHS Service Delivery and Organisation R & D.

Armstrong, C. (2002) 'Behind closed doors: Living with a parent's mental illness.' *Young Minds Magazine 61*, 28–30.

Asmussen, K. and Weizel, K. (2009) *Evaluating the Evidence: What Works in Supporting Parents Who Misuse Drugs and Alcohol.* London: National Academy for Parenting Practitioners. Available at www.pupprogram.net.au/media/8998/napp_briefing_substance_misuse. pdf, accessed on 19 July 2013.

Azar, S.T., Robinson, D.R., Hekimian, E. and Twentyman, C.T. (1984) 'Unrealistic expectations and problem-solving ability in maltreating and comparison mothers.' *Journal of Counselling and Clinical Psychology 52*, 687–691.

Babor, T.F., de la Fuente, J.R., Saunders, J. and Grant, M. (1992) *AUDIT: The Alcohol Use Disorders Identification Test. Guidelines for Use in Primary Health Care.* Geneva: World Health Organization.

Baim, C. and Morrison, T. (2011) *Attachment Based Practice with Adults. Understanding Strategies and Promoting Positive Change. A New Practice Model and Interactive Resource for Assessment, Intervention and Supervision.* Brighton: Pavilion Publishing.

Bancroft, A., Wilson, S., Cunningham-Burley, S., Becket-Milburn, K. and Masters, H. (2004) *Parental Drug and Alcohol Misuse: Resilience and Transition Among Young People.* York: Joseph Rowntree Foundation. Available at www.jrf.org.uk, accessed on 19 July 2013.

Banerjee, S., Clancy, C. and Crome, I. (2002) *Co-existing Problems of Mental Disorder and Substance Misuse (Dual Diagnosis).* London: Royal College of Psychiatrists Research Unit. Available at http://handbooks.homeless.org.uk/hostels/individuals/multipleneeds/ rcpsydd.pdf, accessed on 19 July 2013.

Banks, S. (2006) *Ethics and Values in Social Work* (Third edition). Basingstoke: Palgrave.

Bannister, D. and Fransella, F. (1980) *Inquiring Man. The Psychology of Personal Constructs* (Second edition). London: Penguin.

Barker, I. and Pack, E. (1996) 'User involvement. A decade of experience.' *Mental Health Review 1*, 4, 5–13.

Barlow, J. and Scott, J. (2010) *Safeguarding in the 21st Century: Where to Now?* Dartington: Research in Practice.

Barnard, M. (2003) 'Between a rock and a hard place: the role of relatives in protecting children from the effects of parental drug problems.' *Child and Family Social Work 8*, 291–299.

Barnardo's (2007) *Keeping the Family in Mind: A Briefing on Young Carers Whose Parents Have Mental Health Problems.* Barkingside: Barnardo's. Available at www.barnardos.org.uk, accessed on 17 July 2013.

Barnardo's (2008) *Homes Fit for Children? The Housing Crisis for Large Low Income Households in the South West.* Bristol: Barnardo's.

Barnes, M., Chanfreau, J. and Tomaszewski, W. (2010) *Growing up in Scotland: The Circumstances of Persistently Poor Children.* Edinburgh: The Scottish Government.

Barnett, B. and Parker, G. (1998) 'The parentified child: early competence or childhood depriation?' *Clinical Child Psychiatry and Psychology 3*, 4, 146–155.

Bavelock, S.J. (1984) *Adult-Adolescent Parenting Inventory.* Eau Claire, WI: Family Development Resources.

Beck, A.T., Steer, R.A. and Brown, G.K. (1996) *Manual for the Beck Depression Inventory II.* San Antonio, TX: Psychological Corporation.

Beech, A., Friendship, C., Erikson, M., et al. (2002) 'The relationship between static and dynamic risk factors and reconviction in a sample of UK child abusers.' *Sexual Abuse: A Journal of Research and Treatment 14*, 155–167.

Bell, M. (2002) 'Promoting children's rights through the use of relationship.' *Child and Family Social Work 7*, 1–11.

Bell, M. (2007) *Domestic Violence Risk Assessment Model.* Barkingside: Barnardo's.

Belsky, J. and Vondra, J. (1989) 'Lessons from Child Abuse: the Determinants of Parenting.' In D. Cicchetti and V. Carlson (eds) *Child Maltreatment: Theory and Causes and Consequences of Child Abuse and Neglect.* Cambridge: Cambridge University Press.

Bene, E. (1985) *Manual for the Family Relations Test* (Second edition). Windsor: NFER-Nelson.

Bene, E. and Anthony, E.J. (1957) *Manual for the Family Relations Test.* Windsor: NFER-Nelson.

Bentovim, A. (2010) 'Safeguarding and Promotion of the Welfare of Children Who Have Been Sexually Abused. The Assessment Challenges.' In J. Horwath (ed.) *The Child's World. The Comprehensive Guide to Assessing Children* (Second edition). London: Jessica Kingsley Publishers.

Bentovim, A. and Cox, A. (2000) *The Family Pack of Questionnaires and Scales.* London: Department of Health.

Bentovim, A. and Bingley Miller, L. (2001) *The Family Assessment: Assessment of Family Competence, Strength and Difficulties.* London: Child and Family Training.

Beresford, P. (2007) *The Changing Roles and Tasks of Social Work from Service Users' Perspectives: A Literature Informed Discussion Paper.* London: Shaping Our Lives.

Berman, A.H., Bergman, H., Palmstierna, T., et al. (2005) 'Evaluation of the Drug Use Disorders Identification Test (DUDIT) in criminal justice and detoxification settings and in a Swedish population sample.' *European Addiction Research 11*, 22–31.

Bernstein, B. (1964) 'Social class, speech systems and psychotherapy.' *British Journal of Sociology 15*, 54–64.

Biesteck, F.P. (1961) *The Casework Relationship.* London: George Allen & Unwin.

Birleson, P. (1980) 'The validity of depressive disorder in childhood and the development of self-rating scales.' *Journal of Child Psychology and Psychiatry 22*, 73–88.

Birmingham SCB (Safeguarding Children Board) and Radford, J. (2010) *Serious Case Review in Respect of the Death of a Child. Case Number 14.* Available at www.lscbbirmingham.org.uk/downloads/Case+14.pdf, accessed on 6 November 2013.

Blewitt, J., Noble, J. and Tunstill, J. (2011) *Improving Children's Outcomes by Supporting Parental Physical and Mental Health.* London: Centre for Excellence and Outcomes in Children and Young People's Services (C4EO). Available at www.c4eo.org.uk, accessed on 19 July 2013.

Boer, D.P., Hart, S.D., Kropp, P.R. and Webster, C.D. (1997) *Manual for the Sexual Violence Risk-20 (SVR-20): Professional Guidelines for Assessing Risk of Sexual Violence.* Vancouver, Canada: British Columbia Institute Against Family Violence.

Bogenschneider, K., Small, S. and Tsay, J. (1997) 'Child, parents and contextual influences on perceived parenting competence among parents of adolescents.' *Journal of Marriage and the Family 59*, 345–362.

Bond, C.F.J. and DePaulo, B.M. (2006) 'Accuracy of deception judgements.' *Personality and Social Psychology Review 10*, 3, 214–234.

Bostock, L., Bairstow, S., Fish, S. and Macleod, F. (2005) *Managing Risk and Minimising Mistakes in Services to Children and Families.* Children and Families Services Report 6. London: Social Care Institute for Excellence. Available at http://socialworkpdf2.tripod.com/scierisk.pdf, accessed on 19 July 2013.

Bourdieu, P. (1991) *Language and Symbolic Power.* Cambridge: Polity Press.

Boushel, M. (1994) 'The protective environment of children: towards a framework for anti-oppressive, cross-cultural and cross-national understanding.' *British Journal of Social Work 21*, 2, 173–190.

Bowlby, J. (1988) *A Secure Base: Parent–Child Attachment and Healthy Human Development.* New York: Basic Books.

Bowlby, J. (1998) *Attachment: Attachment and Loss* (Volume 1) (Second edition). New York: Basic Books.

Bowlby, J. (1999) *Attachment and Loss, Volume 1* (Second edition). New York: Basic Books.

Bradshaw, J. (2002) 'Child poverty and child outcomes.' *Children and Society 16*, 131–140.

Bradshaw, J., Finch, N., Mayhew, E., Ritakallio, V. and Skinner, C. (2006) *Child Poverty in Large Families.* Bristol and York: Policy Press and Joseph Rowntree Foundation.

Brandon, M., Schofield, G. and Trinder, L. (1998) *Social Work with Children.* Basingstoke: Macmillan.

Brandon, M., Belderson, P., Warren, C., Howe, D., Gardner, R., Dodsworth, J. and Black, J. (2008) *Analysing Child Deaths and Serious Injury through Abuse and Neglect: What Can We Learn? A Biennial Analysis of Serious Case Reviews, 2003–2005.* London: Department for Children, Schools and Families.

Brandon, M., Bailey, S., Belderson, P., Gardner, R., *et al.* (2009) *Understanding Serious Case Reviews and their Impact – A Biennial Analysis of Serious Case Reviews 2005–2007.* London: Department for Children, Schools and Families. Available at www.education.gov.uk/publications/standard/publicationdetail/page1/DCSF-RR129, accessed on 19 July 2013.

Brandon, M., Bailey, S. and Belderson, P. (2010) *Building on the Learning from Serious Case Reviews: A Two Year Analysis of Child Protection Database Notifications 2007–2009.* London: Department for Education.

Brandon, M., Sidebotham, P., Ellis, C., Bailey, S. and Belderson, P. (2010a) *Child and Family Practitioners' Understanding of Child Development: Lessons Learnt from a Small Sample of Serious Case Reviews.* London: Department for Education.

Brandon, M., Sidebotham, S., Bailey, S. Belderson, P. Hawley, C., Ellis, C., and Megson, M. (2012) *New Learning from Serious Case Reviews.* Research Report DFE-RR226. London: Department for Education.

Brawn, E., Bush, M., Hawkings, C. and Trotter, R. (2013) *The Other Care Crisis. Making Social Care Funding Work for Disabled Adults in England.* The National Autistic Society, Mencap, Leonard Cheshire Disability, Services for Deaf-blind People and Scope. Available at www.scope.org.uk, accessed on 19 July 2013.

Braye, S. and Preston-Shoot, M. (2010) *Practising Social Work Law* (Third edition). Basingstoke: Palgrave Macmillan.

Braye, S. and Preston-Shoot, M. (2002) 'Social Work and the Law.' In R. Adams, L. Dominelli and M. Payne, *Social Work Themes, Issues and Critical Debates* (Second edition). Basingstoke: Palgrave.

Brayne, H. and Carr, H. (2010) *Law for Social Workers* (Eleventh edition). Oxford: University Press.

Breakwell, G.M. (1993) 'Psychological and Social Characteristics of Teenagers Who Have Children.' In A. Lawson and D.L. Rhode (eds) *The Politics of Pregnancy: Adolescent Sexuality and Public Policy.* New Haven, CT: Yale University Press.

Brearley, C.P. (1982) *Risk in Social Work.* London: Routledge & Kegan Paul.

Brewer, M., Dickerson, A., Gambin, L., Green, A., Joyce, R. and Wilson, D. (2012) *Poverty and Inequality in 2020. Impact of Changes in the Structure of Employment.* York: Joseph Rowntree Foundation. Available at www.jrf.org.uk, accessed on 19 July 2013.

British Association of Social Workers (2012) *The Code of Ethics for Social Work. Statement of Principles.* Available at www.cdn.basw.co.uk, accessed on 16 December 2013.

British Medical Association (2001) *Consent, Rights and Choices in Health Care for Children and Young People.* London: BMJ Books.

Broad, B., Hayes, R. and Rushforth, C. (2001) *Kith and Kin: Kinship Care for Vulnerable Young People.* London: National Children's Bureau.

Bronfenbrenner, U. (1979) *The Ecology of Human Development: Experiments by Nature and Design.* Cambridge, MA: Harvard University Press.

Brophy, J. (2008) 'Child maltreatment in diverse households: challenges to law, theory, and practice.' *Journal of Law and Society 35,* 1, 75–94.

Brown, G.W. and Harris, T. (1978) *Social Origins of Depression.* London: Tavistock.

Brown, R. and Ward, H. (2012) *Decision-making Within a Child's Timeframe. An Overview of Current Research Evidence for Family Justice Professionals Concerning Child Development and the Impact of Maltreatment.* Working Paper 16. London: Childhood Wellbeing Research Centre.

Browne, K.D., Beech, A.R. and Craig, L.A. (2010) *Assessments in Forensic Practice. A Handbook.* Chichester: Wiley.

Brugha, T., Bebington, P., Tennant, C. and Hurry, J. (1985) 'The list of threatening experiences: a subset of 12 life-event categories with considerable long-term contextual threat.' *Psychological Medicine 15,* 189–194.

Buckner, L. and Yeandle, S. (2011) *Valuing Carers: Calculating the Value of Carer's Support.* London: Carers UK.

Butler, A.H. and Astbury, G. (2005) 'The caring child: an evaluative case study of the Cornwall Young Carers project.' *Children and Society 19,* 4, 292–303.

Butler, I. and Roberts, G. (2004) *Social Work with Children and Families: Getting into Practice.* London: Jessica Kingsley Publishers.

Butler, I. and Williamson, H. (1994) *Children Speak: Children, Trauma and Social Work.* Harlow: Longman/NSPCC.

Butler-Sloss, B. (1988) *Report of the Inquiry into Child Abuse in Cleveland, 1987.* Cmnd 412. London: HMSO.

Byng-Hall, J. (1995) *Rewriting Family Scripts.* London: Guilford Press.

Cabinet Office (2004) *Alcohol Harm Reduction Strategy for England.* London: Prime Minister's Strategy Unit. Available at http://webarchive.nationalarchives.gov.uk/20100407195200/http://www.cabinetoffice.gov.uk/media/cabinetoffice/strategy/assets/alcohol_ria.pdf, accessed on 19 July 2013.

Cabinet Office (2005) *The Multidimensional Analysis of Social Exclusion Bibliography.* London: Cabinet Office. Available at www.bris.ac.uk/poverty/downloads/socialexclusion/multidimensional.pdf, accessed on 19 July 2013.

Calder, M.C. and Hackett, S. (2003) *Assessment in Child Care. Using and Developing Frameworks for Practice.* Lyme Regis: Russell House Publishing.

Caldwell, B.M. and Bradley, R.H. (2003) *Home Observation for Measurement of the Environment: Administration Manual.* Tempe, AZ: Family and Human Dynamics Research Institute, Arizona State University.

Cameron, G. and Coady, N. (2007) *Moving Toward Positive Systems of Child and Family Welfare.* Waterloo, Ontario: Wilfred Laurier University Press.

Campis, L.K., Lyman, R.D. and Prentice-Dunn, S. (1986) 'The parental locus of control scale: development and validation.' *Journal of Clinical Child Psychology 15,* 260–267.

Cassell, D. and Coleman, R. (1995) 'Parents with psychiatric problems.' In P. Reder and C. Lucey (eds) *Assessment of Parenting: Psychiatric and psychological contributions.* London: Routledge.

Cawson, P., Wattam, C., Brooker, S. and Kelly, G. (2000) *Child Maltreatment in the United Kingdom: A Study of the Prevalence of Abuse and Neglect.* London: NSPCC.

Child Accident Prevention Trust (2009) *Accidents and Child Development.* Available at www.capt.org.uk, accessed on 19 July 2013.

ChildLine (2003) *Boys Allowed.* London: NSPCC.

Children's Workforce Development Council (CWDC) (2009) *NQSW Guide for Supervisors.* Available at www.cwdcouncil.org.uk, accessed 9 December 2013.

Children's Commissioner (2010) *Family Perspectives on Safeguarding and on Relationships with Children's Services.* London: The Office of the Children's Commissioner.

Clark, A. and Moss, P. (2001) *Listening to Young Children: The Mosaic Approach.* London: NCB.

Clark, A. and Statham, J. (2005) 'Listening to young children. Experts in their own lives.' *Adoption and Fostering 29*, 1, 45–56.

Clark, B., and Davis. A. (1997) 'When money's too tight to mention.' *Professional Social Work*, March, 12–13.

Clarke, C.L. (2000) 'Risk: Constructing care and care environments in dementia.' *Health, Risk and Society 2*, 1, 83–93.

Cleaver, E. (1969) *Post Prison Writing and Speeches.* (Ed. R. Scheer). London: Cape.

Cleaver, H. and Nicholson, D. (2008) *Parental Learning Disability and Children's Needs. Family Experiences and Effective Practice.* London: Jessica Kingsley Publishers.

Cleaver, H. and Walker, S. (2004) 'From policy to practice: The implementation of a new framework for social work assessment of children and families.' *Child and Family Social Work 9*, 81–90.

Cleaver, H., Unell, I. and Aldgate, J. (1999) *Children's Needs – Parenting Capacity: The Impact of Parental Mental Illness, Problem Alcohol and Drugs Use, and Domestic Violence on the Development of Children.* London: HMSO.

Cleaver, H., Unell, I. and Aldgate, J. (2011) *Children's Needs – Parenting Capacity. Child Abuse: Parental Mental Illness, Learning Disability, Substance Misuse and Domestic Violence* (Second edition). London: The Stationery Office.

Cleaver, H., Nicholson, D., Tarr, S. and Cleaver, D. (2008) *Child Protection, Domestic Violence and Parental Substance Misuse: Family Experiences and Effective practice.* London: Department for Children, Schools and Families.

Colmer, E. (2010) 'Addressing mental health legacies: Learning from research.' *Context 108*, 9–13.

Cooklin, A. (2006) 'Children as carers of parents with mental illness.' *Psychiatry 5*, 1, 32–35.

Cooklin, A. Bishop, P., Francis, D., Fagin, L., and Asen, E. (2012) *Kidstime Workshops: A Multi-Family Social Intervention for the Effects of Parental Mental Illness.* London: Wisepress.

Cooper, A., Hetherington, R. and Katz, I. (2003) *The Risk Factor. Making the Child Protection System Work for Children.* London: Demos.

Cooperrider, D.L. and Whitney, D. (1999) *Appreciative Inquiry.* San Francisco, CA: Berrett-Koehler.

Copeland, M.E. and Mead, S. (2000) *What Recovery Means for Us.* New York: Plenum Press.

Core Info (2013) Cardiff Child Protection Systematic Reviews. Available at www.core-info.cardiff.ac.uk, accessed on 19 July 2013.

Cornell, S. and Hartmann, D. (1998) *Ethnicity and Race – Making Identities in a Changing World.* London: Sage.

Cossar, J., Brandon, M. and Jordan, P. (2011) *'Don't make assumptions.' Children's and Young People's Views of the Child Protection System and Messages for Change.* London: Office of the Children's Commissioner. Available at www.childrenscommissioner.gov.uk, accessed on 19 July 2013.

Cossar, J. and Long, C. (2008) *Children and Young People's Involvement in the Child Protection Process in Cambridgeshire.* Submitted to the Children's Workforce Development Council, February.

Coy, M., Perks, K., Scott, E. and Tweedale, R. (2012) *Picking up the Pieces. Domestic Violence and Child Contact.* London: Rights of Women and CWASU. Available at www.rightsofwomen. org.uk/pdfs/Policy/Picking_Up_the_Pieces_Report_final.pdf, accessed on 19 July 2013.

Cox, J.L., Holden, J.M. and Sagovsky, R. (1987) 'Detection of post-natal depression: development of the 10 item Edinburgh Post-Natal Depression Scale.' *British Journal of Psychiatry 150,* 782–786.

CPAG (Child Poverty Action Group) (2012) *Child Poverty Facts and Figures.* Available at www. cpag.org.uk/child-poverty-facts-and-figures, accessed on 19 July 2013.

Craig, G. (2005) 'Poverty Among Black and Minority Ethnic Children.' In CPAG (Child Poverty Action Group), *At Greatest Risk: The Children Most Likely to be Poor.* London: CPAG.

Crawshaw, M. and Wates, M. (2005) 'Mind the gap: A case study for changing organisational responses to disabled parents and their families using evidence based practice.' *Research, Policy and Practice 23,* 2, 111.

Cree, V.E. (2003) 'Worries and problems of young carers: issues for mental health.' *Child and Family Social Work 8,* 4, 301.

Creighton, S. (2002) *Physical Abuse.* London: NSPCC. Available at www.nspcc.org.uk/Inform/ research/briefings/physicalabuse_wda48220.html, accessed on 19 July 2013.

Crittenden, P. (2008) *Raising Parents: Attachment, Parenting and Child Safety.* Milton: Willan.

Crittenden, P.M. and Landini, A. (2011) *Assessing Adult Attachment. A Dynamic-Maturational Approach to Discourse Analysis.* New York: Norton.

Crnic, K.A. and Greenberg, M.T. (1990) 'Minor parenting stresses with young children.' *Child Development 61,* 1628–1637.

Cross, S.B., Kaye, E. and Ratnofsky, A.C. (1993) *A Report on the Maltreatment of Children with Disabilities.* Washington, DC: National Centre on Child Abuse and Neglect.

CSCI (Commission for Social Care Inspection) (2005) *Every Child Matters: Messages from Inspections of Children's Social Services.* London: CSCI.

CSIP/Barnardo's (2007) *Keeping the Family in Mind* (Second edition). Available at www. barnardos.org.uk/keeping_the_family_in_mind.pdf, accessed on 19 July 2013.

Cuthbert, C., Rayns, G. and Stanley, K. (2011) *All Babies Count: Prevention and Protection for Vulnerable Babies.* London: NSPCC.

CWDC (Children's Workforce Development Council) (2009) *NQSW Guide for Supervisors.* Available at www.cwdcouncil.org.uk, accessed on 19 July 2013.

Dale, P. (2004) 'Like a fish in a bowl: parents' perceptions of child protection services.' *Child Abuse Review 13,* 137–157.

Dale, P., Davies, M., Morrison, T. and Waters, J. (1986) *Dangerous Families: Assessment and Treatment of Child Abuse.* London: Tavistock.

Daniel, B., Taylor, J. and Scott, J. (2010) 'Recognition of neglect and early response. Overview of a systematic review of the literature.' *Child and Family Social Work 15,* 2, 248–257.

Darbyshire, P., Oster, C., and Carrig, H. (2001) 'Children of parents who have a gambling problem; a review of the literature and commentary on research approaches.' *Health & Social Care in the Community 9,* 185–193.

Davidson, L. (2005) 'Recovery, self management and the expert patient – Changing the culture of mental health from a UK perspective.' *Journal of Mental Health 14,* 1, 25–35.

Davie, C.E., Hutt, S.J., Vincent, E. and Mason, M. (1984) *The Young Child at Home.* Windsor: NFER-Nelson.

Davies, C. and Ward, H. (2012) *Safeguarding Children Across Services: Messages from Research on Identifying and Responding to Child Maltreatment.* London: Jessica Kingsley Publishers.

Davis, J.M. (1998) 'Understanding the meanings of children: a reflexive process.' *Children and Society 12,* 5, 325–335.

DCSF (Department for Children, Schools and Families) (2010) *Working Together to Safeguard Children.* Nottingham: DCSF Publications.

Dearden, C. and Aldridge. J. (2010) 'Young Carers: Needs, Rights and Assessment.' In J. Howarth (ed.) *The Child's World: The Comprehensive Guide to Assessing Children in Need* (pp.214–228) (Second edition). London: Jessica Kingsley Publishers.

Dearden, C. and Becker, S. (2000) *Growing Up Caring: Vulnerability and Transition to Adulthood – Young Carers' Experience.* York: Youth Work Press.

Dearden, C. and Becker, S. (2004) *Young Carers in the UK: The 2004 Report.* London: Carers UK and the Children's Society.

Derogatis, L.R. (1983) SCL-90-R: Administration, Scoring and Procedures Manual II. Towson, MD: Clinical Psychometric Research.

DfE (Department for Education) (2008) *Safeguarding Children in whom Illness is Fabricated or Induced.* London: HMSO.

DfES (Department for Education and Skills) (2005) *What to do if you're Worried a Child is being Abused.* London: HMSO.

DfES (2006) *Information Sharing: Practitioners' Guide.* London: HMSO. London: Office for National Statistics.

de Shazer, S. (1985) *Keys to Solutions in Brief Therapy.* New York: Norton.

de Shazer, S. (1994) *Words Were Originally Magic.* New York: W.W. Norton.

Dickenson, D., Johnson, M. and Samson Katz, J. (1993) *Death, Dying and Bereavement.* London: Sage.

Dingwall, R., Eekelaar, J. and Murray, T. (1983) *The Protection of Children: State Intervention and Family Life.* Oxford: Blackwell.

Dixon, L., Browne, K.D. and Hamilton-Giacritsis, C. (2005) 'Risk factors of parents abused as children national analysis of the interagency continuity of child maltreatment (part 1).' *Journal of Psychology and Psychiatry 46,* 47–57.

DoH (Department of Health) (1995) *Child Protection. Messages from Research.* London: HMSO.

DoH (2000a) *No Secrets: Guidance on Developing and Implementing Multi-Agency Policies and Procedures to Protect Vulnerable Adults from Abuse.* London: HMSO.

DoH (2000b) *Quality Protects: Disabled Children Numbers and Categories and Families.* London: HMSO.

DoH (2001) *Valuing People. A New Strategy for Learning Disability for the 21st Century.* London: HMSO.

DoH (2002) *Women's Mental Health: Into the Mainstream.* London: HMSO.

DoH (2005) *Common Assessment Framework for Children and Young People.* London: DoH.

DoH (2007). *Our Health, Our Care, Our Say.* London: HMSO.

DoH (2009) *Improving Safety, Reducing Harm. Children, Young People and Domestic Violence. A Practical Toolkit for Front-Line Practitioners.* London: HMSO.

DoH, DfEE (Department for Education and Employment), and Home Office (2000a) *Framework for the Assessment of Children in Need and Their Families.* London: HMSO.

DoH, DfEE, and Home Office (2000b) *Framework for the Assessment of Children in Need and Their Families. Practice Guidance.* London: HMSO.

Dolan, Y.M. (1998) *One Small Step. Moving Beyond Trauma and Therapy to a Life of Joy.* Watsonville, CA: Papier-maché Press.

Dulwich Centre (2008) 'Children, parents and mental health.' *The International Journal of Narrative Therapy and Community Work 4*, 3–14.

Dumbrill, G.C. (2006) 'Parental experience of child protection intervention: a qualitative study.' *Child Abuse and Neglect 30*, 27–37.

DWP (Department for Work and Pensions) (2005) *Households Below Average Income 2004.*

Edgerton, R.B. (1967) *The Cloak of Competence. Stigma in the Lives of the Mentally Retarded.* Berkeley, CA: University of California Press.

Edgerton, R.B. (1993) *The Cloak of Competence* (Revised and updated). Berkeley, CA: University of California Press.

Edgerton, R.B. (2001) 'The Hidden Majority of Individuals with Mental Retardation and Developmental Disabilities.' In A.J. Tymchuck, C.K. Lakin and R. Luckasson (eds), *The Forgotten Generation: The Status and Challenges of Adults with Mild Cognitive Limitations.* Baltimore, MD: Paul H. Brookes.

Egan, G. (2002) *The Skilled Helper. A Problem-Management and Opportunity-Development Approach to Helping* (Seventh edition). Belmont, CA: Thomson.

Eley, S. (2004) 'If they don't recognise it, you've got to deal with it yourself: gender, young caring and educational support.' *Gender and Education 16*, 1, 65–75.

Eminson, D.M. and Postlethwaite, R.J. (1992) 'Factitious Illness: recognition and management.' *Archives of Disease in Childhood 67*, 12, 1510–1516.

Erickson, M. (1959/1980) 'Further Clinical Techniques of Hypnosis: Utilization Techniques.' In E. Rossi (ed.) *The Collected Papers of Milton H. Erickson on Hypnosis. 1. The Nature of Hypnosis and Suggestion.* New York: Irvington.

Essex, S., Gumbleton, J. and Luger, C. (1996) 'Resolutions: working with families where responsibility for abuse is denied.' *Child Abuse Review 5*, 191–201.

Evans, E., Hawton, K. and Rodham, K. (2005) 'Suicidal phenomena and abuse in adolescents: A review of epidemiological studies.' *Child Abuse and Neglect 29*, 1, 45–58.

Eyberg, S.M. and Pincus, D. (1999) *Eyberg Child Behaviour Inventory and Sutter-Eyberg Student Behaviour Inventory, Revised: Professional Manual.* Odessa, FL: Psychological Assessment Resources.

Falkov, A. (1996) *A Study of Working Together Part 8 Reports. Fatal Child Abuse and Parental Psychiatric Disorder: An Analysis of 100 Area Child Protection Committee Case Reviews Conducted under the Terms of Part 8 of Working Together under the Children Act 1989.* London: Department of Health.

Falkov, A. (2012) *The Family Model Handbook. An Integrated Approach to Supporting Mentally Ill Parents and their Children.* Hove: Pavilion. www.thefamilymodel.com.

Falkov, A., Mayes, K. and Diggins, M. (eds) (1998) *Crossing Bridges: Training Resources for Working with Mentally Ill Parents and their Children.* Brighton: Pavilion.

Family Policy Alliance (2005) *Response to Draft Consultation on Guidance and Working Together to Safeguard Children.* London: Family Rights Group.

Family Rights Group (2011) *Working with Risky Fathers.* London: Family Rights Group.

Farmer, E. and Moyers, S. (2008) *Fostering Effective Family and Friends Placements.* London: Jessica Kingsley Publishers.

Farmer, E. and Owen, M. (1995) *Child Protection Practice: Private Risks and Public Remedies.* London: HMSO.

Farnfield, S. (2008) 'A theoretical model for the comprehensive assessment of parenting.' *British Journal of Social Work 38*, 1076–1099.

Fauth, R., Helicic, J., Hart, D., Burton, S. and Shemmings, D. (2010) *Effective Practice to Protect Children Living in 'Highly Resistant' Families.* London: C4EO. Available at www.c4eo.org.uk, accessed on 19 July 2013.

Fawcett, M. (1998) *What Hurts? What Helps: A Study of Needs and Services for Young People Whose Parents Separate and Divorce.* Belfast: RELATE.

Fawcett, M. (2009) *Learning through Child Observation* (Second edition). London: Jessica Kingsley Publishers.

Featherstone, B. and Evans, H. (2004) *Children Experiencing Maltreatment: Who Do They Turn To?* London: NSPCC.

Ferguson, H. (2011) *Child Protection Practice.* Basingstoke: Macmillan.

Finkelstein, N., Rechsberger, E., Russell, L., VanDeMark, N., *et al.* (2005) 'Building resilience in children of mothers who have co-occurring disorders and histories of violence: intervention model and implementation issues.' *Behavioural Health Services and Research 32*, 2, 141–154.

Finney, A. (2004) *Alcohol and Intimate Partner Violence: Key Findings from the Research.* Home Office Findings No. 216. Available at www.ncjrs.gov/App/publications/abstract.aspx?ID=205274, accessed on 19 July 2013.

Fish, S., Munro, E. and Bairstow, S. (2008) Report 19. *Learning Together to Safeguard Children: Developing a Multi-Agency Systems Approach for Case Reviews.* London: SCIE. Availble at www.scie.org.uk, accessed on 16 December 2013.

Folstein, M.F., Folstein, S. and McHugh, P.R. (1975) 'Mini-mental state. A practical method for grading the cognitive state of patients for the clinician.' *Journal of Psychiatric Research 12*, 3, 189–198.

Fonagy, P. and Target, M. (1997) 'Attachment and reflective function: their role in self-organisation.' *Development and Psychopathology 9*, 679–700.

Fonagy, P., Gergely, G., Jurist, E. and Target, M. (2002) *Affect Regulation, Mentalisation and the Development of Self.* New York: Other Press.

Fonagy, P., Steele, H., Higgitt, A. and Target, M. (1994) 'The Emmanuel Miller Memorial Lecture 1992: "The theory and practice of resilience".' *Journal of Child Psychology and Psychiatry 35*, 2, 231–257.

Forrester, D., Kershaw, S., Moss, H. and Hughes, L. (2008a) 'Communication skills in child protection: how do social workers talk to parents?' *Child and Family Social Work 13*, 1, 41–51.

Forrester, D., McCambridge, J., Waissbein, C. and Rollnick, S. (2008b) 'How do child and family social workers talk to parents about child welfare concerns?' *Child Abuse Review 17*, 1, 23–35.

Fox, R.A. (1994) *Parent-Behaviour Checklist.* Brandon, VT: Clinical Psychology.

Franey, C., and Quirk, A. (1996) 'Dual diagnosis: Executive summary.' *The Centre for Research on Drugs and Health Behaviour 51*, 1–4.

Frankl, V. E. (1984) *Man's Search for Meaning.* New York: Washington Square Press.

Freake, H., Barley, V. and Kent, G. (2007) 'Adolescents' views of helping professionals: a review of the literature.' *Journal of Adolescence 30*, 639–653.

Frude, N. (2003) 'A Framework for Assessing the Physical Abuse of Children.' In M. Calder and S. Hackett (eds) *Assessment in Child Care. Using and Developing Frameworks for Practice.* Lyme Regis: Russell House.

Gallagher, E. (2008) *Children's Violence Towards Parents.* Melbourne: Monash University.

Gambling Commission (2011) *British Gambling Prevalence Survey 2010.* Available at www.gamblingcommission.gov.uk, accessed on 19 July 2013.

Gambrill, E. and Shlonsky, A. (2000) 'Risk assessment in context.' *Children and Youth Services Review 22*, 11–12, 813–837.

Gannon, T. A. and Cortoni, F. (2010) *Female Sexual Offenders: Theory, Assessment and Treatment.* Oxford: Wiley-Blackwell Press.

Gast, L. and Patmore, A. (2012) *Mastering Approaches to Diversity in Social Work.* London: Jessica Kingsley Publishers.

Gaudin, J.M., Polansky, N.A. and Kilpaqtrick, A.C. (1992) 'The Child Well Being Scales: A field trial.' *Child Welfare 6,* 319–328.

Gerard, A.B. (1994) *Parent-Child Relationship Inventory (PCRI): Manual.* Los Angeles, CA: Western.

Gerhardt, S. (2004) *Why Love Matters: How Affection Shapes a Baby's Brain.* Hove: Brunner-Routledge.

Ghate, D. and Hazel, N. (2002) *Parenting in Poor Environments: Stress, Support, and Coping.* London: Jessica Kingsley Publishers.

Gibb, M. (2009) *Facing Up to the Task: The Interim Report of the Social Work Task Force, July 2009.* Nottingham: Department for Children, Schools and Families.

Gibbons, J., Gallagher, B., Bell, C. and Gordon, D. (1995) *Development after Physical Abuse in Early Childhood.* London: HMSO.

Gilligan, R. (2007) 'Adversity, resilience and the educational progress of young people in public care.' *Emotional and Behavioural Difficulties 12,* 2, 135–145.

Goddard, C.R., Saunders, B.J., Stanley, J. and Tucci, J. (1999) 'Structured risk assessment procedures: instruments of abuse?' *Child Abuse Review 8,* 251–263.

Golding, K.S. and Hughes, D.A. (2012) *Creating Loving Attachments. Parenting with PACE to nurture confidence and security in the troubled child.* London: Jessica Kingsley Publishers.

Goleman, D. (1996) *Emotional Intelligence.* London: Bloomsbury.

Goodinge, S. (2000) *A Jigsaw of Services. Inspection of Services to Support Disabled Adults in their Parenting Role.* London: Department of Health.

Goodman, R. (1997) 'The Strengths and Difficulties Questionnaire: a research note.' *Journal of Child Psychology and Psychiatry 38,* 581–586.

Gopfert, M., McClelland, N., and Wilson, J. (2010) 'Parental mental ill health: What informs good practice?' *Context 108,* 40–42.

Gorin, S. (2004) *Understanding What Children Say About Living With Domestic Violence, Parental Substance Misuse or Parental Health Problems.* York: Joseph Rowntree Foundation.

Gottlieb, L.N., Feeley, N. and Dalton, C. (2006) *The Collaborative Partnership Approach to Care. A Delicate Balance.* Toronto: Moby Elsevier Canada.

Graham, M., and Bruce, E. (2006) '"Seen and not heard" – sociological approaches to childhood: black children, agency and implications for child welfare.' *Journal of Sociology and Social Welfare 34,* 4, 31–48.

Green, R. (2002) *Mentally Ill Parents and Children's Welfare.* London: NSPCC.

Griffin, J. and Tyrrell, I. (2003) *Human Givens: A New Approach to Emotional Health and Clear Thinking.* Chalvington: HG Publishing.

Gross, R. (1996) *Psychology: The Science of Mind and Behaviour.* London: Hodder & Stoughton.

Grotberg, E. (1997) *A Guide to Promoting Resilience in Children: Strengthening the Human Spirit.* The Hague, Holland: Bernard Van Leer Foundation.

Gurney, A. (2004) *Models of Assessment.* Birmingham: Open Learning Partnership, University of Central England and RNIB.

Habermas, J. (1973) *Theory and Practice.* Cambridge: Polity Press.

Habermas, J. (1984) *The Theory of Communicative Action. Volume One: Reason and the Rationalisation of Society.* Boston, MA: Beacon Press.

Hadley Centre (2008) *Care Provided by Family and Friends – Briefing.* Bristol: The Hadley Centre, University of Bristol.

Hallett, C. and Birchall, E. (1992) *Co-ordination and Child Protection: A Review of the Literature.* Edinburgh: HMSO.

Hansen, D.J. and Sedlar, G. (1998) *The Parental Anger Inventory: A Guide for Practitioners and Researchers.* Lincoln, NE: Clinical Psychology Training Programme.

Hanson, R.K. (1997) *The Development of a Brief Actuarial Scale for Sexual Offense Recidivism.* Ottawa, Ontario: Public Works and Government Services of Canada.

Harwin, J., Ruan, M. and Tunnard, J. (2011) *The Family Drug and Alcohol Court (FDAC) Evaluation Project Final Report.* Available at www.brunel.ac.uk/fdacresearch, accessed on 19 July 2013.

Hasin, D.S., Trautman, K.D., Miele, G.M., Samet, S., Smith, M. and Endicott, J. (1996) 'Psychiatric research interview for substance and mental disorders: Reliability for substance abusers.' *American Journal of Psychiatry 153,* 9, 1195–1201.

Hayes, D. and Spratt, T. (2009) 'Child welfare interventions: Patterns of social work practice.' *British Journal of Social Work 39,* 8, 1575–1597.

Hayes, D., and Spratt, T. (2012) 'Child welfare as child protection then and now: What social workers did and continue to do.' *British Journal of Social Work,* 1–21.

Health and Care Professions Council (2012) *Your duties as a registrant. Standards of conduct, performance and ethics.* London: HCPC. Available at www.hpc-uk.org, accessed on 16 December 2013.

Healy, K. (2005) *Social Work Theories in Context. Creating Frameworks for Practice.* Basingstoke: Palgrave Macmillan.

Henricson, C. (2003) *Government and Parenting: Is there a Case for a Policy Review and a Parent's Code?* York: Joseph Rowntree Foundation.

Henwood, M. (2008) 'Self directed support: grounds for optimism.' *Community Care,* 15 May, 34–35.

Herrenkohl, E.C., Herrenkohl, R.C., Egolf, B.P. and Russo, M.J. (1998) 'The relationship between early maltreatment and teenage parenthood.' *Journal of Adolescence 21,* 291–303.

Hetherington, R., Baistow, K., Katz, K., Mesie, J. and Trowell, J. (2003) *The Welfare of Children with Mentally Ill Parents: Learning from Inter-Country Comparisons.* Chichester: Wiley.

Hildyard, K.L. and Wolfe, D.A. (2002) 'Child neglect: developmental issues and outcomes.' *Child Abuse and Neglect 26,* 679–695.

Hill, J. (2004) 'Parental Psychiatric Disorder and the Attachment Relationship.' In M. Gopfert, J. Webster and M. Seeman (eds) *Parental Psychiatric Disorder* (Second edition). Cambridge: Cambridge University Press.

HM Government (2008) *Information Sharing. Guidance for Practitioners and Managers.* London: HMSO.

HM Government (2013) *Working Together. A Guide to Inter-Agency Working to Safeguard and Promote the Welfare of Children.* London: HMSO.

Hobson, R.P. (1985) 'Piaget: On the Ways of Knowing in Childhood.' In M. Rutter and L. Hersov (eds) *Child and Adolescent Psychiatry, Modern Approaches* (Second edition). Oxford: Blackwell.

Hoghughi, M. (1997) 'Parenting at the Margins: Some Consequences of Inequality.' In K.N. Dwivedi (ed.) *Enhancing Parenting Skills. A Guide for Professionals Working with Parents.* Chichester: Wiley.

Hoghughi, M. and Long, N. (2004) *Handbook of Parenting: Theory and Research for Practice.* London: Sage Publications.

Holland, S. (2000) 'The assessment relationship: interactions between social workers and parents.' *British Journal of Social Work 30,* 149–163.

Holland, S. (2004) *Child and Family Assessment in Social Work Practice.* London: Sage.

Holland, S. and Scourfield, J. (2004) 'Liberty and respect in child protection.' *British Journal of Social Work 34,* 17–32.

Holliday, R. and Marche, T. (2012) *Child Forensic Psychology. Victim and Eyewitness Memory.* London: Palgrave Macmillan.

Hollingsworth, K. (2007) 'Responsibility and rights: children and their parents in the youth justice system.' *International Journal of Law, Policy and the Family 21*, 190–219.

Holt, A. (2012) 'Adolescent-to-Parent Abuse and Frontline Service Responses: Does Munro Matter?' In M. Blyth and E. Solomon (eds) *Effective Safeguarding for Children and Young People. What Next After Munro?* Bristol: Policy Press.

Hopkins, C. and Niemiec, S. (2007) 'Mental health crisis at home: Service user perspectives on what helps and what hinders.' *Journal of Psychiatric and Mental Health Nursing 14*, 310–318.

Horwath, J. (ed.) (2010) *The Child's World. The Comprehensive Guide to Assessing Children* (Second edition). London: Jessica Kingsley Publishers.

Horwath, J. and Morrison, T. (2001) 'Assessment of Parental Motivation to Change.' In J. Horwath (ed.) *The Child's World. Assessing Children in Need and Their Families* (pp.19–28). London: Department of Health, NSPCC and University of Sheffield.

Howe, D. (1996) 'Surface and Depth in Social Work Practice.' In N. Parton (ed.) *Social Theory, Social Change and Social Work.* London: Routledge.

Howe, D. (2005). *Child Abuse and Neglect: Attachment, Development and Intervention.* Basingstoke: Palgrave Macmillan.

Howe, D. (2008) *The Emotionally Intelligent Social Worker.* Basingstoke: Palgrave Macmillan.

Hugman, R. and Phillips, N. (1992) '"Like bees round the honeypot". Social work responses to parents with mental health needs.' *Practice 6*, 3, 193–205.

Hutton, A. and Partridge, K. (2006) '*Say It Your Own Way'. Children's Participation in Assessment: A Guide and Resources.* Barkingside: Barnardo's/Department for Education and Skills.

IASSW (International Association of Schools of Social Work) and the IFSW (International Federation of Social Workers) (2005). *Ethics in Social Work, Statement of Principles.* Available at http://ifsw.org/policies/statement-of-ethical-principles, accessed on 19 July 2013.

Independent Police Complaints Commission (2011) *Report re Fiona Pilkington.* Available at www.ipcc.gov.uk/Documents/investigation_commissioner_reports/pilkington_report_2_040511.pdf, accessed on 19 July 2013.

Iveson, C., George, E. and Ratner, H. (2012) *Brief Coaching. A Solution Focused Approach.* London: Routledge.

Iwaniec, D. (2006) *The Emotionally Abused and Neglected Child. Identification, Assessment and Intervention. A Practice Handbook.* London: Wiley.

Jack, G. (2006) 'The area and community components of children's well-being.' *Children and Society 20*, 5, 334–347.

Jack, G. and Gill, O. (2003) *The Missing Side of the Triangle: Assessing the Importance of Family and Environmental Factors in the Lives of Children.* Barkingside: Barnardo's.

Jack, G. and Gill, O. (2010) 'The Impact of Economic Factors on Parents or Caregivers and Children.' In J. Horwath (ed.) *The Child's World. The Comprehensive Guide to Assessing Children* (Second edition). London: Jessica Kingsley Publishers.

Jackson, D., Firtko, A. and Edenborough, M. (2007) 'Personal resilience as a strategy for surviving and thriving in the fact of workplace adversity: a literature review.' *Journal of Advanced Nursing 60*, 1, 1–9.

Jacobs, D.F., Marston, A.R., Singer, R.D., Widsman, K., Little, T. and Veizades, J. (1989) 'Children of problem gamblers.' *Journal of Gambling Behaviour 5*, 261–268.

James, H. (2004) 'Promoting effective working with parents with learning disabilities.' *Child Abuse Review 13*, 31–41.

Jenkins, A. (1990) *Invitations to Responsibility.* Adelaide: Dulwich Centre Publications.

Jenner, S. and McCarthy, G. (1995) 'Quantitative measures of parenting: a clinical–developmental perspective.' In P. Reder and C. Lucey (eds) *Assessment of Parenting: Psychiatric and Psychological Contributions.* London: Routledge.

Jones, D.P.H. (1997) 'Treatment of the Child and the Family where Child Abuse or Neglect has Occurred.' In M.E. Heffer, R.S. Kempe and R.D. Krugman (eds) *The Battered Child* (Fifth edition). London: University of Chicago Press.

Jones, D. (2001) 'The Assessment of Parental Capacity.' In J. Horwath (ed.) *The Child's World. The Comprehensive Guide to Assessing Children* (Second edition). London: Jessica Kingsley Publishers.

Jones, D. (2003) *Communicating with Vulnerable Children: A Guide for Practitioners.* London: Gaskell.

Jones, D., Hindley, N. and Ramchandani, P. (2006) 'Making Plans: Assessment, Intervention and Evaluating Outcomes.' In J. Aldgate, D. Jones and C. Jeffery (eds) *The Developing World of the Child.* London: Jessica Kingsley Publishers.

Jones, S. (2004) *Toying with their Future: The Hidden Costs of the Housing Crisis.* London: Shelter.

Joseph, S., Becker, F. and Becker, S. (2009) *Manual for Measures of Caring Activities and Outcomes for Children and Young People.* London: The Princess Royal Trust for Carers.

Juffer, F., Bakermas-Kranenburg, M.J. and van IJzendoorn, M.M. (eds) (2007) *Promoting Positive Parenting: An Attachment Based Intervention.* Monographs in Parenting series. Abingdon: Lawrence Erlbaum Associates.

Kaptchuk, T. (1983). *Chinese Medicine. The Web that Has No Weaver.* London: Rider Books.

Katz, I., Corylon, J., La Placa, V., and Hunter, S. (2007) *The Relationship between Parenting and Poverty.* York: Joseph Rowntree Foundation.

Katz, M. (1997) *On Playing a Bad Hand Well. Insights from the Lives of those who Have Overcome Childhood Risks and Adversities.* New York: Norton Professional Books.

Kelly, G. (1996). 'Competence in Risk Analysis.' In K. O'Hagan (ed.) *Competence in Social Work Practice.* London: Jessica Kingsley Publishers.

Kemshall, H. and Pritchard, J. (2005) *Good Practice in Risk Assessment and Risk Management* (Ninth edition). London: Jessica Kingsley Publishers.

Kendall, S., Rodger, J. and Palmer, H. (2011) *The Use of Whole Family Assessment to Identify the Needs of Families with Multiple Problems.* Research Report DFE-RR045. London: Department for Education.

King, M. and Trowell, J. (1992) *Children's Welfare and the Law: The Limits of Legal Intervention.* London: Sage.

Kitchens, J.M. (1994) 'Does this patient have an alcohol problem?' *Journal of the American Medical Association 272,* 22, 1782–1787.

Klee, H. (1998) 'Drug-using parents: analysing the stereotypes.' *International Journal of Drug Policy 9,* 6, 437–448.

Knight, J.R., Shrier, L.A., Bravender, T.D., Farrel, L.M., Vander Bilt, J. and Shaffer, H.C. (1999) 'A new brief screen for adolescent substance abuse.' *Archives of Pediatric Adolescent Medicine 153,* 591–596.

Kohlberg, L. (1969) *Stages in the Development of Moral Thought and Action.* New York: Holt Rinehart and Winston.

Kumar, R.C. (1997). '"Anybody's child": Severe disorders of mother-to-infant bonding.' *British Journal of Psychiatry 171,* 175–181.

Kumar, R. and Hipwell, A.E. (1996) 'Development of a clinical rating scale to assess mother-infant interacyiton in a psychiatric mother and baby unit.' *British Journal of Psychiatry 169,* 18–26.

Laming, H. (2003) *The Victoria Climbié Inquiry.* Cmnd 5730. London: Department of Health and Home Office. Available at www.victoria-climbie-inquiry.org.uk, accessed on 19 July 2013.

Laming, H. (2009) *The Protection of Children in England: A Progress Report.* Available at http://webarchive.nationalarchives.gov.uk/20130401151715/https://www.education.gov.uk/publications/eOrderingDownload/HC-330.pdf, accessed on 19 July 2013.

Lapierre, S. (2010) 'Striving to be "good" mothers: Abused women's experiences of mothering.' *Child Abuse Review 19*, 342–357.

Lapper, A. (2005) *My Life in My Hands.* London: Simon & Schuster.

Laske, O.E. (2009) *Measuring Hidden Dimensions. The Art and Science of Fully Engaging Adults.* Gloucester, MA: IDM Press.

Layard, R. (2005) *Mental Health: Britain's Biggest Social Problem?* London: Centre for Economic Performance. Available at http://cep.lse.ac.uk/textonly/research/mentalhealth/RL414d.pdf, accessed on 19 July 2013.

Leeson, C. (2007) 'My life in care: experiences of non-participation in decision-making processes.' *Child and Family Social Work 12*, 268–277.

Lefevre, M. (2010) *Communicating with Children and Young People. Making a Difference.* Bristol: Policy Press.

Lesieur, H.R., and Rothschild, J. (1989) 'Children of Gamblers Anonymous members.' *Journal of Gambling Behaviour 5*, 269–281.

Lightfoot, C., Cole, M. and Cole, S. (2008) *The Development of Children* (Sixth edition). New York: Worth.

Luft, J. and Ingham, H. (1955) 'The Johari window. A graphic model of interpersonal awareness.' *Proceedings of the Western Training Laboratory in Group Development.* Los Angeles, CA: UCLA.

Lupton, R. (2003) *Poverty Street: The Dynamics of Neighbourhood Decline and Renewal.* Bristol: Policy Press.

Maccoby, E. (2000) 'Parenting and its effects on children: On reading and misreading behaviour genetics.' *Annual Review of Psychology 51*, 1–27.

Main, M. (1990) *A Typology of Human Attachment Organisation Assessed in Discourse, Drawings and Interviews.* New York: Cambridge University Press.

McConnell, D. and Llewellyn, G. (2002) 'Stereotypes, parents with intellectual disability and child protection.' *Journal of Social Welfare and Family Law 24*, 3, 297–317.

McHugo, G.J., Drake, R.E., Burton, H.L., et al. (1995) 'A scale for assessing the stage of substance abuse treatment in persons with severe mental illness.' *Journal of Nervous and Mental Disease 183*, 762–767.

MacMillan, H.L. and Wathan, C.N. (2009) 'Interventions to prevent child maltreatment and associated impairment.' *Lancet 373*, 9659, 250–266.

Main, M. and George, C. (1985) 'Responses of abused and disadvantaged toddlers to distress in agemates in the day care setting.' *Developmental Psychology 21*, 3, 407–412.

Manning, V., Best, D., Faulkner, N. and Titherington, E. (2009) 'New estimates of the number of children living with substance misusing parents: results from UK national household surveys.' *BMC Public Health 9*, 377.

Manthorpe, J. and Martineau, S. (2010) 'Serious case reviews in adult safeguarding in England: An analysis of a sample of reports.' *British Journal of Social Work 41*, 2, 224–241.

Manthorpe, J., Hindes, J., Martineau, S., Cornes, M., *et al.* (2011) *Self-Directed Support: A Review Of the Barriers and Facilitators.* Edinburgh: The Scottish Government. Available at www.kcl.ac.uk/sspp/kpi/scwru/pubs/2011/manthorpeetal2011selfdirected.pdf, accessed on 19 July 2013.

Marchant, R. (2008) 'Working with Disabled Children who Live Away from Home Some or All of the Time.' In B. Luckock and M. Lefevre (eds) *Direct work: Social Work with Children and Young People in Care.* London: BAAF.

Margolin, G. and Gordis, E.B. (2000) 'The effects of family and community violence on children.' *Annual Review of Psychology 51,* 445–479.

Marryat, L. and Martin, C. (2010) *Growing Up in Scotland. Maternal Mental Health and its Impact on Child Behaviour and Development.* Edinburgh: The Scottish Government.

Marsh, A., and Perry, J. (2003). 'Ethnic Minority Families: Poverty and Disadvantage.' In C. Kober (ed.) *Black and Ethnic Minority Children and Poverty: Exploring the Issues.* London: National Children's Bureau.

Masson, J., Pearce, J., Bader, K., Joyner, O., Marsden, J. and Westlake, D. (2008) *Care Profiling Study.* Research Series 4/08. London: Ministry of Justice. Available at www.bristol.ac.uk/law/research/researchpublications/2008/care-profiling-study-report.pdf, accessed on 19 July 2013.

Maslow, A.H. (1970) *Motivation and Personality* (Second edition). New York: Harper & Row.

Maxwell, N., Scourfield, J., Featherstone, B., Holland, S. and Tolman, R. (2012) 'Engaging fathers in child welfare services: a narrative review of recent research evidence.' *Child and Family Social Work 17,* 160–169.

McAuley, C., Pecora, P.J. and Rose, W. (2006) *Enhancing the Well-being of Children and Families through Effective Interventions. International Evidence for Practice.* London: Jessica Kingsley Publishers.

McCracken, D.G. (1988) *The Long Interview.* Beverley Hills, CA: Sage.

McGaw, S. (2000) *What Works for Parents with Learning Disabilities?* Barkingside: Barnardo's. Available at www.barnardos.org.uk/resources, accessed on 23 July 2013.

McGaw, S. and Newman, T. (2005) *What Works for Parents with Learning Disabilities?* Barkingside: Barnardo's. Available at www.barnardos.org.uk/resources, accessed on 23 July 2013.

McGaw, S., Beckley, K., Connolly, C. and Ball, K. (1998) *Parenting Assessment Manual.* Truro: Trecore NHS Trust. Available at www.cornwall.nhs.uk, accessed on 23 July 2013.

McKinnon, F. (2009) 'Child Observation and Professional Practice.' In G. Ruch (ed.) *Post-qualifying Child Care Social work.* London: Sage.

McLaughlin, H. (2009) 'What's in a name: "client", "patient", "customer", "expert by experience", "service user" – what's next?' *British Journal of Social Work 39,* 6, 1101–1117.

McPherson, L., Macnamara, N. and Hemsworth, C. (1997) 'A model for multi-disciplinary collaboration in child protection.' *Children Australia 22,* 1, 21–28.

Mental Health Foundation (1996) *Knowing Our Own Minds. A Survey of How People in Emotional Distress Take Control of Their Lives.* London: Mental Health Foundation.

Mental Health Foundation and Princess Royal Trust for Carers (2010) *MyCare. Caring for a Parent With a Mental Health Problem.* Available at www.mentalhealth.org.uk, accessed on 23 July 2013.

Mental Health Foundation and SCIE (Social Care Institute for Excellence) (2010) *Mental Capacity Assessment. The Assessment of Mental Capacity Tool.* Available at www.mentalhealth. org.uk, accessed on 6 November 2013.

Millar, M. and Corby, B. (2006) 'The framework for the assessment of children in need and their families. a basis for a "therapeutic" encounter?' *British Journal of Social Work 36,* 6, 887–899.

Miller, W.R and Rollnick, S. (1991) *Motivational Interviewing: Preparing People to Change Addictive Behaviour.* New York: Guilford Press.

Milner, J., and O'Byrne, P. (2009) *Assessment in Social Work.* Basingstoke: Palgrave Macmillan.

Milner, J.S. (1986) *The Potential Child Abuse Inventory: Manual* (Second edition). Webster, NC: Psytec.

Ministry of Justice (2011) *Achieving Best Evidence in Criminal Proceedings. Guidance on Interviewing Victims and Witnesses and Guidance on Using Special Measures.* London: Ministry of Justice. Available at www.cps.gov.uk, accessed on 23 July 2013.

Minuchin, S. and Fishman, C. (1981) *Family Therapy Techniques.* Cambridge, MA: Harvard University Press.

Moran, P., Ghate, D. and van der Merwe, A. (2004) *What Works in Parenting Support? A Review of the International Evidence.* London: Department for Education and Skills. Available at www.prb.org.uk/wwipaprenting/RR574, accessed on 23 July 2013.

Morgan, M. (2006) *About Social Workers. A Children's Views Report.* Newcastle upon Tyne: Commission for Social Care Inspection. Available at www.rights4me.org/~/media/Library%20Documents/Reports/Reports%202006/REPORT%20About%20Social%20Workers.pdf, accessed on 23 July 2013.

Morgan, R. (2010) *Children on Rights and Responsibilities. A Report of Children's Views by the Children's Rights Director for England.* London: Ofsted. Available at www.rights4me.org, accessed on 23 July 2013.

Morgan, R. (2011) *Younger Children's Views. A Report of Children's Views by the Children's Rights Director for England.* Available at www.rights4me.org, accessed on 23 July 2013.

Morris, J. and Wates, M. (2006) *Adults' Services Knowledge Review 11. Supporting Disabled Parents and Parents with Additional Support Needs.* London: SCIE. Available at www.scie.org.uk/publications/elearning.asp, accessed on 23 July 2013.

Morris, J. (2003) *The Right Support: Report of the Task Force on Supporting Disabled Adults in their Parenting Role.* York: Joseph Rowntree Foundation.

Morrison, T. (1991) 'Change, Control and the Legal Framework.' In M. Adcock, R. White and A. Hollows (eds) *Significant Harm: Its Management and Outcome* (pp.85–100). London: Significant Publications.

Morrison, T. (2006) 'Assessing Parental Motivation for Change.' In J. Horwath (ed.) *The Child's World. The Comprehensive Guide to Assessing Children in Need* (pp.305–322) (Second edition). London: Jessica Kingsley Publishers.

Moss, B. (2008) *Communication Skills for Health and Social Care.* London: Sage.

Mrazek, D.A., Mrazek, P. and Klinnert, M. (1995) 'Clinical assessment of parenting.' *Journal of the American Academy of Child and Adolescent Psychiatry 34*, 272–282.

Mullender, A. and Perrott, S. (2002) 'Social Work and Organisations.' In R. Adams, L. Dominelli and M. Payne (eds) *Social Work. Themes, Issues and Critical Debates* (Second edition). Basingstoke: Palgrave.

Mullender, A., Hague, G. and Imam, U. (2002) *Children's Perspectives on Domestic Violence.* London: Sage.

Munro, E. (2001) 'Empowering looked-after children.' *Child and Family Social Work 6*, 2, 129–137.

Munro, E. (2002) *Effective Child Protection.* London: Sage.

Munro, E. (2008) *Effective Child Protection* (Second edition). London: Sage.

Munro, E. (2011a) *Interim Report: The Child's Journey.* London: Department of Health.

Munro, E. (2011b) *The Munro Review of Child Protection: Final Report. A Child-centred System.* London: Department of Health.

Murray, P. (2006) *About ibk initiatives.* Available at www.ibkinitiatives.com, accessed on 6 November 2013.

Musgrove, A. and Groves, N. (2007) 'The Domestic Violence, Crime and Victims Act 2004: relevant or "removed" legislation?' *Journal of Social Welfare and Family Law 29*, 3–4, 233–244.

National Children's Bureau (2004) *What Young People Thought Would Be the World's Worst CAF Assessor.* Available at www.education.gov.uk/consultations/downloadableDocs/NCB%20CAF%20report.doc, accessed on 23 July 2013.

National Institute for Health and Care Excellence (NICE) (2009) *When to Suspect Child Maltreatment.* Available at www.nice.org.uk/Guidance/CG/Wave12/11, accessed on 23 July 2013.

National Scientific Council on the Developing Child (2004) *Young Children Develop in an Environment of Relationships.* Working Paper No. 1. Available at www.developingchild.net, accessed on 23 July 2013.

Newman, T. (2002) 'Young carers and disabled parents: time for a change of direction?' *Disability and Society 17*, 6, 613–625.

Newman, T. and Blackburn, S. (2002) *Interchange 78: Transitions in the Lives of Children and Young People: Resilience Factors.* Edinburgh: The Scottish Executive. Available at www.scotland.gov.uk, accessed on 23 July 2013.

Nietzche, F. (1992) *Basic Writings of Nietzche.* London: Random House.

Northway, R. (2005) 'Disabled Children.' In CPAG (Child Poverty Action Group), *At Greatest Risk: The Children Most Likely to be Poor.* London: CPAG.

Ofsted (2011) *The Voice of the Child: Learning Lessons from Serious Case Reviews. A Thematic Report of Ofsted's Evaluation of Serious Case Reviews from 1 April to 30 September 2010.* Available at www.ofsted.gov.uk/resources/voice-of-the-child-learning-lessons-serious-case-reviews, accessed on 23 July 2013.

O'Hagan, K. (2006) *Identifying Emotional and Psychological Abuse. A Guide for Childcare Professionals.* Maidenhead: Open University Press.

Olsen, R. and Clarke, C.L. (2003) *Parenting and Disability: Disabled Parents' Experiences of Raising Children.* Bristol: Policy Press.

Olsen, R. and Tyers, H. (2004) *Supporting Disabled Adults as Parents.* York: Joseph Rowntree Foundation.

Onyskiw, J.E. (2003) 'Domestic violence and children's adjustment: A review of research.' *Journal of Emotional Abuse 3*, 1, 11–45.

Oosterhoorn, R. and Kendrick, A. (2001) 'No sign of harm: issues for disabled children communicating about abuse.' *Child Abuse Review 10*, 4, 243–253.

O'Sullivan, T. (2011) *Decision Making in Social Work* (Second edition). Basingstoke: Macmillan.

Oxfam and Refugee Council (2002) *Poverty and Asylum in the UK.* London: Oxfam.

Owen, C. and Statham, J. (2009) *Disproportionality in child welfare: the prevalence of black and ethnic minority children within 'looked after' and 'children in need' populations and on child protection registers in England.* London: DCSF.

Parrott, L., Jacobs, G. and Roberts, D. (2008) *Stress and Resilience Factors in Parents with Mental Health Problems and Their Children.* SCIE Research Briefing No. 23. London: SCIE. Available at www.scie.org.uk/publications/briefings/briefing23, accessed on 23 July 2013.

Parton, N. (ed.) (1996) *Social Theory, Social Change and Social Work.* London: Routledge.

Parton, N. (2002) 'Postmodern and Constructionist Approaches to Social Work.' In R. Adams, L. Dominelli and M. Payne (eds) *Social Work, Themes, Issues and Critical Debates* (Second edition). Basingstoke: Palgrave.

Parton, N. and O'Byrne, P. (2000) *Constructive Social Work. Towards a New Practice.* Basingstoke: Palgrave Macmillan.

Piaget, J. (1969) *The Child's Conception of Time.* London: Routledge & Kegan Paul.

Piccinelli, M., Tessari, E., Bortolomasi, M., Piasere, O., Semenzin, M., Garzotto, N. and Tansella, M. (1997) 'Efficacy of the alcohol use disorders identification test as a screening tool for hazardous alcohol intake and related disorders in primary care: a validity study.' *British Medical Journal 14*, 420–424.

Pitcher, D. (1999) *When Grandparents Care.* Plymouth: Plymouth City Council Social Services.

Platt, D. (2006a) 'Threshold decisions. How social workers prioritize referrals of child concern.' *Child Abuse Review 15*, 1, 4–18.

Platt, D. (2006b) 'Investigation or initial assessment of child concerns. The impact of the refocusing initiative on social work practice.' *British Journal of Social Work 36*, 2, 267–281.

Platt, D. (2008) 'Care or control? The effects of investigations and initial assessments on the social worker-parent relationship.' *Journal of social work practice 22*, 3, 301–315.

Platt, L. (2007) *Poverty and Ethnicity in the UK.* Bristol: Policy Press.

Polansky, N.A., Chalmers, M.A., Williams, D.P. and Buttenwieser, E.W. (1981) *Damaged Parents: An Anatomy of Child Neglect.* Chicago, IL: University of Chicago Press.

Polnay, L. and Srivastava, O. (1997) 'Field trial of graded care profile (GCP) scale: a new measure of care.' *Archives of Disease in Childhood 76*, 4, 337–340.

Power, M. (2004) *The Risk Management of Everything: Rethinking the Politics of Uncertainty.* London: Demos.

Prochaska, J.O. and DiClemente, C.C. (1982) 'Transtheoretical therapy: Toward a more integrative model of change.' *Psychotherapy: Theory, Research and Practice 19*, 276–288.

Precey, G. (2003) 'Children and Risk of Illness Induction or Fabrication (Fabricated or Induced Illness).' In M. Calder and S. Hackett (eds) *Assessment in Child Care. Using and Developing Frameworks for Practice.* Lyme Regis: Russell House Publishing.

Print, B., Griffin, H., Beech, A.R., Quayle, J., Bradshaw, H., Henniker, J. and Morrison, T. (2007) *AIM2: An Initial Assessment Model for Young People Who Display Sexually Harmful Behaviour.* Manchester: AIM Project.

Pryor, J. and Rodgers, B. (2001) *Children in Changing Families: Life after Parental Separation.* Oxford: Blackwell.

Radford, L. and Hester, M. (2006) *Mothering Through Domestic Violence.* London: Jessica Kingsley Publishers.

Raistrick, D., Bradshaw, I., Tober, G., et al. (1994) 'Development of the Leeds Dependence Questionnaire (LDQ): a questionnaire to measure alcohol and opiate dependence in the context of a treatment evaluation package.' *Addiction 89*, 563–572.

Ratner, H., George, E. and Iveson, C. (2012) *Solutions Focused Brief Therapy. 100 Key Points and Techniques.* London: Routledge

Raynes, B. (2003) 'A Stepwise Process of Assessments.' In M.C. Calder and S. Hackett (eds) *Assessment in Child Care. Using and Developing Frameworks for Practice.* Lyme Regis: Russell House Publishing.

RCPCH (Royal College of Paediatrics and Child Health) (2013) *UK Growth Chart 2–18 years.* Available at www.rcpch.ac.uk, accessed on 6 November 2013.

Reder, P. and Duncan, S. (1999) *Lost Innocents. A Follow-up Study of Fatal Child Abuse.* London: Routledge.

Reder, P. and Duncan, S. (2003a) 'Understanding communication in child protection networks.' *Child Abuse Review 12*, 82–100.

Reder, P. and Duncan, S. (2003b) 'How Much Should Children's Views Count?' In P. Reder, S. Duncan and C. Lucey (eds) *Studies in the Assessment of Parenting.* London: Routledge.

Reder, P. and Duncan, S. (2003c) 'How Do Mental Health Problems Affect Parenting?' In P. Reder, S. Duncan and C. Lucey (eds) *Studies in the Assessment of Parenting.* London: Routledge.

Reder, P., Duncan, S. and Gray, M. (1993) *Beyond Blame: Child Abuse Tragedies Revisited.* London and New York: Routledge.

Reder, P., Duncan, S. and Lucey, C. (2003) 'What Principles Guide Parenting Assessments?' In P. Reder, S. Duncan and C. Lucey (eds) *Studies in the Assessment of Parenting.* London: Routledge.

Rees, S. (1978) *Social Work Face to Face.* London: Edward Arnold.

Repper, J. and Carter, T. (2011) 'A review of the literature on peer support in mental health services.' *Journal of Mental Health 20,* 4, 392–411.

Resolution Foundation (2012) *Who Gains from Growth? Living Standards to 2020.* Available at www.resolutionfoundation.org, accessed on 23 July 2013.

Richards, L. (2009) *Domestic Abuse, Stalking and 'Honour-based' Violence: Risk Identification, Assessment and Management Model: DASH.* Available at www.dashriskchecklist.co.uk, accessed on 6 November 2013.

Ricks, M.H. (1985) 'The Social Transition of Parental Behaviour: Attachment Across Generations.' In I. Bretherton and E. Waters (eds) *Growing Points of Attachment Theory and Research.* Chicago, IL: University of Chicago Press.

Ridge, T. (2009) *Living with Poverty. A Review of the Literature on Children's and Families' Experiences of Poverty.* London: Department for Work and Pensions.

Riebschleger, J. (2004) 'Good days and bad days: The experiences of children of a parent with a psychiatric disability.' *Psychiatric Rehabilitation Journal 28,* 1, 25–31.

Roberts, D., Bernard, M., Misca, G. and Head, E. (2008) *Experiences of Children and Young People Caring for a Parent with a Mental Health Problem.* SCIE Research Briefing No. 24. Available at www.scie.org.uk/publications/briefings/briefing24, accessed on 23 July 2013.

Robinson, C. and Williams, V. (2002) 'Carers of people with learning disabilities and their experience of the 1995 Carers' Act.' *British Journal of Social Work 32,* 2, 169–183.

Robinson, G. and Witney, L. (1999) 'Working systemically following abuse: exploring safe uncertainty.' *Child Abuse Review 8,* 264–274.

Robinson, L. (2007) *Cross-Cultural Child Development for Social Workers.* London: Palgrave Macmillan.

Rose, W. and Barnes, J. (2008) *Improving Safeguarding Practice: Study of Serious Case Reviews 2001–2003.* Department for Children, Schools and Families Research Report 022. London: DCSF. Available at http://dera.ioe.ac.uk/8613/1/dcsf-rr022.pdf, accessed on 23 July 2013.

Rosenberg, S.D., Drale, R.E., Wolford, G.L., Mueser, K.T., Oxman, T.E., Vidaver, R.M., et al. (1998) 'Dartmouth Assessment of Lifestyle Instrument (DALI): A substance use disorder screen for people with severe mental illness.' *American Journal of Psychiatry 155,* 232–238.

Rossi, E.L., and Ryan, M.O. (eds) (1998) *Creative Choices in Hypnosis. The Seminars, Workshops and Lectures of Milton H. Erickson. Volume IV.* London: Free Association Books.

Royal College of Psychiatrists (2004) *Being Seen and Heard: The Needs of Children of Parents with Mental Illness. (Video Resource)* London: Gaskell.

Rustin, M. (2005) 'Conceptual analysis of the critical moments in Victoria Climbié's life.' *Child and Family Social Work 10,* 11–19.

Rutter, M. (1999) 'Resilience concepts and findings: Implications for family therapy.' *Journal of Family Therapy 21,* 119–144.

Saint-Jacques, M.C., Drapeau, S., Lessard, G. and Beaudoin, A. (2006) 'Parent involvement practices in child protection: a matter of know how and attitude.' *Child and Adolescent Social Work Journal 23*, 2, 196–215.

Sanders, M.R. (2008) 'Triple P – Positive Parenting Programme as a public health approach to strengthening parenting.' *Journal of Family Psychology 22, 3,* 506–517.

Sanderson, H. and Taylor, M. (2008) *Celebrating Families. Simple, Practical Ways to Enhance Family Life.* Stockport: HSA Press.

Sardar, Z. (2008) *The Language of Equality. A Discussion Paper.* Manchester: Equality and Human Rights Commission.

Sawyer, C. (2006) 'The child is not a person: family law and other legal cultures.' *Journal of Social Welfare and Family Law 28*, 1, 1–14.

Scales, R., Miller, J. and Burden, R. (2003) 'Why wrestle when you can dance? Optimising outcomes with motivational interviewing.' *Journal of the American Pharmaceutical Association 43*, 5, 41–47.

Schizophrenia Commission (2012) *The Abandoned Illness.* London: Schizophrenia Commission.

Schofield, G., and Beek, M. (2006) *Attachment Handbook for Foster Care and Adoption.* London: BAAF.

Schofield, G. and Thoburn, J. (1996) *Child Protection: The Voice of the Child in Decision Making.* London: Institute for Public Policy Research.

Schoon, I. and Bartley, M. (2008) 'The role of human capability and resilience.' *The Psychologist 24*, 1, 24–27.

SCIE (Social Care Institute for Excellence) (2004) *Parenting Capacity and Substance Misuse.* Research Briefing No. 6. London: SCIE. Available at www.scie.org.uk/publications/briefings/briefing06, accessed on 23 July 2013.

SCIE (2005a) *The Health and Well-Being of Young Carers.* Research Briefing No. 11. London: SCIE. Available at www.scie.org.uk/publications/briefings/briefing11, accessed on 23 July 2013.

SCIE (2005b) *Helping Parents with a Physical or Sensory Impairment in Their Role as Parents.* Research Briefing No. 13. Available at www.scie.org.uk/publications/briefings/briefing13, accessed on 23 July 2013.

SCIE (2005c) *Helping Parents with Learning Disabilities in Their Role as Parents.* Research Briefing No. 14. Available at www.scie.org.uk/publications/briefings/briefing14, accessed on 23 July 2013.

SCIE (2008a) *Stress and Resilience Factors in Parents with Mental Health Problems and Their Children.* Research Briefing No. 23. Available at www.scie.org.uk/publications/briefings/briefing23, accessed on 23 July 2013.

SCIE (2008b) *Factors that Assist Early Identification of Children in Need in Integrated or Inter-Agency Settings.* Research Briefing No. 27. Available at www.scie.org.uk/publications/briefings/briefing27, accessed on 23 July 2013.

SCIE (2009) *Think Child, Think Parent, Think Family. A Guide to Parental Mental Health and Child Welfare.* London: SCIE. Available at www.scie.org.uk, accessed on 23 July 2013.

Scottish Executive (2002) *Growing Support: A Review of Services for Vulnerable Families with Very Young Children.* Edinburgh: Scottish Executive.

Scottish Executive (2003) *Getting Our Priorities Right – Policy and Practice Guidelines for Working with Children and Families Affected by Problem Drug Use.* Edinburgh: The Stationery Office.

Scottish Refugee Council (2006) *Poverty in Scotland.* Glasgow: Scottish Refugee Council.

Seebohm Report (1968) *Report of the Committee on Local Authority and Allied Personal Social Services.* Cmnd 3703. London: HMSO.

Shaw, M.C., Forbush, K.T., Schlinder, J. Rosenman, E. and Black, D. (2007) 'The effect of pathological gambling on families, marriages, and children.' *CNS Spectrum 12*, 8, 615–622.

Shelter (2004) *Toying with Their Future. The Hidden Cost of the Housing Crisis.* London: Shelter.

Shelter (2005) *Full House? How Overcrowded Housing Affects Families.* Shelter. Available at http://england.shelter.org.uk, accessed on 23 July 2013.

Sheridan, M.D. (1960) *The Developmental Progress of Infants and Young Children.* Windsor: NFER-Nelson.

Shipway, L. (2004) 'Domestic violence: The lifelong effects of early childhood adversity and toxic stress.' *Pediatrics 129*, 1, 232–246.

Shonkoff, J.P. and Garner, A.S. (2012) 'The lifelong effects of early childhood adversity and toxic stress.' *American Academy of Pediatrics 129*, 232–246.

Sinclair, R. and Bullock, R. (2002) *Learning from Past Experience – A Review of Serious Case Reviews.* London: Department of Health.

Skinner, H.A. (1982) 'The drug use screening test.' *Addictive Behaviours 7*, 363–371.

Slade, A. (2005) 'Parental reflective functioning: An introduction.' *Attachment and Human Development 7*, 3, 269–281.

Smale, G., and Tuson, G., with Biehal, N. and Marsh, P. (1993) *Empowerment, Assessment, Care Management and the Skilled Worker.* London: HMSO.

Smale, G., Tuson, G. and Stratham, D. (2001) *Social Work and Social Problems: Working Towards Social Inclusion and Social Change.* Basingstoke: Macmillan.

Snaith, R.P., Constantopolous, A.A., Jardine, M.Y. and McGuffin, P. (1978) 'A clinical scale for the self-assessment of irritability.' *British Journal of Psychiatry 132*, 164–171.

Social Exclusion Taskforce (2008) *Think Family: Improving the Life Chances of Families at Risk.* London: Cabinet Office. Available at http://tna.europarchive.org/20080521201536/http://www.cabinetoffice.gov.uk/social_exclusion_task_force/~/media/assets/www.cabinetoffice.gov.uk/social_exclusion_task_force/think_families/think_family_life_chances_report%20pdf.ashx, accessed on 23 July 2013.

Social Exclusion Unit (1998) *Bringing Britain Together: A National Strategy for Neighbourhood Renewal.* London: Social Exclusion Unit.

Social Work Task Force (2009) *Building a Safe, Confident Future. The Final Report of the Social Work Task Force.* Available at http://webarchive.nationalarchives.gov.uk/20130401151715/https://www.education.gov.uk/publications/eOrderingDownload/01114-2009DOM-EN.pdf, accessed on 23 July 2013.

Solomon, J. and George, C. (1999) 'The Measurement of Attachment Security in Infancy and Childhood.' In J. Cassidy and P.R. Shaver (eds) *Handbook of Attachment: Theory, Research and Clinical Applications.* New York: The Guilford Press.

Spratt, T. and Callan, J. (2004) 'Parents' views on social work intervention in child welfare cases.' *British Journal of Social Work 34*, 2, 199–224.

Stallard, P., Norman, P., Huline-Dickens, S. and Cribb, J. (2004) 'The effects of parental mental illness upon children: A descriptive study of the views of parents and children.' *Clinical Child Psychology and Psychiatry 9*, 1, 39–52.

Stanley, N. (2009) 'The Impact of Domestic Violence, Parental Mental Health Problems, Substance Misuse and Learning Disability on Parenting Capacity.' In J. Horwath (ed.) *The Child's World. The Comprehensive Guide to Assessing Children* (Second edition). London: Jessica Kingsley Publishers.

Stanley, N., Miller, P., Richardson Foster, H. and Thomson, G. (2009) *Children and Families Experiencing Domestic Violence: Police and Children's Social Services Responses.* London: NSPCC. Available at www.nspcc.org.uk/Inform/research/findings/children_experiencing_domestic_violence_summary_wdf68552.pdf, accessed on 23 July 2013.

Stein, M., Ward, H. and Courtney, M. (eds) (2011) Special Issue on 'Young People's Transitions from Care to Adulthood.' *Children and Youth Services Review 33*, 12, 2409–2540.

Straus, M.A., Hamby, S.L., Boney-McCoy, S. and Sugarman, D.B. (1996) 'The Revised Conflict Tactics Scales (CTS2): development and preliminary psychometric data.' *Journal of Family Issues 17*, 283–316.

Strickland, H. and Olsen, R. (2005) 'Children with Disabled Parents.' In CPAG (Child Poverty Action Group), *At Greatest Risk: The Children Most Likely to be Poor.* London: CPAG.

Stuart, M. and Baines, C. (2004) *Safeguards for Vulnerable Children.* York: Joseph Rowntree Foundation.

Sullivan, P.M. and Knutson, J.F. (2000) 'Maltreatment and disabilities: a population-based epidemiological study.' *Child Abuse and Neglect 24*, 10, 1257–1273.

Sunderland, M. (2006) *What Every Parent Needs to Know. The Remarkable Effects of Love, Nurture and Play on Your Child's Development.* London: Dorling Kindersley.

Tamasese, K. and Waldegrave, C. (1994) 'Culture and gender accountability in the "Just Therapy" approach.' *Journal of Feminist Family Therapy: An International Forum 5*, 2, 29–45.

Taylor, A. and Kroll, B. (2004) 'Working with parental substance misuse: dilemmas for practice.' *British Journal of Social Work 34*, 1115–1132.

Taylor, J. and Daniel, B. (2005) *Child Neglect. Practice Issues for Health and Social Care.* London: Jessica Kingsley Publishers.

Tertinger, D.A., Green, B.F. and Lutzker, J.R. (1984) 'Home safety: Development and validation of one component of an ecobehavioural treatment programme for abused and neglected children.' *Applied Behaviour Analysis 17*, 159–174.

Thomas, J. and Holland, S. (2010) 'Representing children's identities in core assessments.' *British Journal of Social Work 40*, 8, 2617–2633.

Thomas, N. (2002) *Children, Family and State. Decision Making and Child Participation.* Bristol: Policy Press.

Thomas, N. and O'Kane, C. (2000) 'Discovering what children think: connections between research and practice.' *British Journal of Social Work 30*, 6, 819–835.

Thompson, N. (2000) *Understanding Social Work. Preparing for Practice.* Basingstoke: Palgrave.

Thornton, D. (2002) 'Constructing and testing a framework for dynamic risk assessment.' *Sexual Abuse: A Journal of Research and Treatment 14*, 139–153.

Titterton, M. (2005) *Risk and Risk Taking in Health and Social Welfare.* London: Jessica Kingsley Publishers.

Totsuka, Y. (2008) '"Then Mum got taken into hospital": Young people's experience of parents' admission to psychiatric hospital.' *Feedback: Journal of the Family Therapy Association of Ireland 10*, 6, 8–12.

Trevithick, P. (2005) *Social Work Skills: A Practice Handbook* (Second edition). Maidenhead: Open University Press and McGraw-Hill Education.

TUC/UNISON (undated) *Diversity in Diction, Equality in Action.* London: TUC/UNISON.

Tunnard, J. (2002a) *Parental Drug Misuse – A Review of Impact and Intervention Studies.* Dartington: Research in Practice.

Tunnard, J. (2002b) *Parental Problem Drinking and Its Impact on Children.* Dartington: Research in Practice.

Tunnard, J. (2004) *Parental Mental Health Problems: Messages from Research, Policy and Practice.* Dartington: Research in Practice.

Turnbull, O. (2003) 'Emotion, False Beliefs and the Neurobiology of Intuition.' In J. Corrigall and H. Wilkinson (eds) *Revolutionary Connections. Psychology and Neuroscience.* London: Karnac.

Turnell, A. (2012) *The Signs of Safety Comprehensive Briefing Paper.* Resolutions Consultancy. Available at www.signsofsafety.net, accessed on 23 July 2013.

Turnell, A. and Edwards, S. (1999) *Signs of Safety: A Solution and Safety Oriented Approach to Child Protection.* New York: Norton.

Turnell, A. and Essex, S. (2006) *Working with Denied Child Abuse: The Resolutions Approach.* Maidenhead: Open University Press.

Unicef (n.d.) *A Summary of the United Nations Convention on the Rights of the Child.* London: Unicef UK. Available at http://childrenandyouthprogramme.info/pdfs/pdfs_uncrc/uncrc_summary_version.pdf, accessed on 23 July 2013.

Utting, D. (1995) *Family and Parenthood: Supporting Families, Preventing Breakdown.* York: Joseph Rowntree Foundation.

Vincent, C.A. (2004) 'Analysis of clinical incidents: a window on the system not a search for root causes.' *Quality and Safety in Health Care 13,* 4, 242–243.

Vrij, A. (2000) *Detecting Lies and Deceit: The Psychology of Lying and the Implications for Professional Practice.* Chichester: Wiley.

Vrij, A. (2004) 'Why professionals fail to catch liars and how they can improve.' *Legal and Criminological Psychology 9,* 2, 159–181.

Wagstaff, S. (2010) 'Depressed women talking about mothering.' *Context 108,* 3–5.

Walker, S. and Beckett, C. (2003) *Social Work Assessment and Intervention.* Lyme Regis: Russell House Publishing.

Wallace, C. and Davies, M. (2009) *Sharing Assessment in Health and Social Care. A Practical Handbook for Interprofessional Working.* London: Sage.

Ward, H. (ed.) (1995) *Looking after Children: Research into Practice: The Second Report of the Department of Health on Assessing Outcomes in Child Care.* London: HMSO.

Ward, H. and Rose, W. (2002) *Approaches to Needs Assessment in Children's Services.* London: Jessica Kingsley Publishers.

Ward, H. Brown, R., and Westlake, D. (2012) *Safeguarding Babies and Very Young Children from Abuse and Neglect.* London: Jessica Kingsley Publishers.

Wardale, L. (2007) *Keeping the Family in Mind Resource Pack.* Barkingside: Barnardo's. Available at www.barnardos.org.uk, accessed on 23 July 2013.

Warren, J. (2007) 'Young carers: conventional or exaggerated levels of involvement in domestic and caring tasks?' *Children and Society 21,* 2, 136–146.

Waterhouse, L. and McGhee, J. (2013) 'Practitioner-mother relationships and the processes that bind them.' *Child and Family Social Work,* advance publication on-line 30 April 2013.

Wates, M. (2002) *Supporting Disabled Adults in their Parenting Role.* York: Joseph Rowntree Foundation.

Watson, F., Burrows, H. and Player, C. (2002) *Integrating Theory and Practice in Social Work Education.* London: Jessica Kingsley Publishers.

Watson-Perczel, M., Lutzker, J., Greene, B.F. and McGimpsey, B.J. (1988) 'Assessment and modification of home cleanliness among families adjudicated for child neglect.' *Behaviour Modification 12,* 1, 57–81.

Weaver, T., Madden, P. and Charles, V. (2003) 'Co-morbidity of substance misuse and mental illness in community mental health and substance misuse services.' *British Journal of Psychiatry 183*, 304–313.

Webb, S. (2006) *Social Work in a Risk Society, Social and Political Perspectives.* Basingstoke: Palgrave Macmillan.

Webster, C.D., Douglas, K.S., Eaves, D. and Hart, S. (1997) *HCR-20: Assessing Risk for Violence (Version 2).* Burnaby, BC, Canada: Mental Health Law and Policy Institute.

Webster, J. (1992) 'Split in two: experiences of children of schizophrenic mothers.' *British Journal of Social Work 22*, 3, 309–329.

Weir, A. (2003) 'A Framework for Assessing parents with Mental Health Problems.' In M.C. Calder and S. Hackett (eds) *Assessment in Child Care. Using and Developing Frameworks for Practice.* Lyme Regis: Russell House Publishing.

Weir, A. (2004) 'Parenting and Mental Illness. Legal Frameworks and Issues – Some International Comparisons.' In M. Gopfert, J. Webster and M.V. Seeman (eds) *Parental Psychiatric Disorder: Distressed Parents and their Families* (Second Edition). London: Macmillan.

Wells, J. (1997) 'Priorities, "street level bureaucracy" and the community mental health team.' *Health and Social Care in the Community 5*, 5, 333–342.

Welsh Government (2000) *In Safe Hands. The Role of the Care and Social Services Inspectorate in Wales.* Available at www.nhswalesgovernance.com, accessed on 23 July 2013.

Westcott, H. and Davies, G. (1996) 'Sexually abused children and young people's perspectives on investigative interview.' *British Journal of Social Work 26*, 4, 451–474.

Westminster LSCB (Local Safeguarding Children's Board) (2006). *Serious Case Review. Executive Summary.* Available at www.westminster.gov.uk/workspace/assets/publications/EG-Executive-Summary-April-2012-1336483036.doc, accessed on 23 July 2013.

White, M. (1995) *Re-authoring Lives.* Adelaide: Dulwich Press.

White, S., Hall, C. and Peckover, S. (2008) 'The descriptive tyranny of the common assessment framework: technologies of categorization and professional practice in child welfare.' *British Journal of Social Work 39*, 1197–1217.

Whiting, B.B. and Whiting, J.W.M. (1975) *Children of Different Worlds. The Formation of Social Behaviour.* Cambridge, MA: Harvard University Press.

Williams, P. and Sullivan, H. (2010) 'Despite all we know about collaborative working, why do we still get it wrong?' *Journal of Integrated Care 18*, 4, 4–15.

Wilson, D. and Newton, C. (2011) *Keys to Inclusion.* Nottingham: Inclusive Solutions.

Wilson, S.M. and Ferch, S.R. (2005) 'Enhancing resilience in the workplace through the practice of caring relationships.' *Organisation Development Journal 23*, 4, 45–60.

Winter, K. (2009) 'Relationships matter: the problems and prospects for social workers' relationships with young children in care.' *Child and Family Social Work 14*, 450–460.

Wonnacott, J. (2012) *Mastering Social Work Supervision.* London: Jessica Kingsley Publishers.

Woodcock, J. (2003) 'The social work assessment of parenting: an exploration.' *British Journal of Social Work 33*, 87–106.

World Health Organization (2006) *Policy Basis.* Available at www.who.int/oral_health/policy/en, accessed on 23 July 2013.

Youth Justice Board (2006) *Asset Guidance.* London: Youth Justice Board.

Zeitlin, M. (1999) 'My Child is My Crown. Yoruba Parental Theories and Practices in Early Childhood.' In S. Harkness and C.M. Super (eds) *Parents' Cultural Belief Systems. Their Origins, Expressions and Consequences.* New York: The Guilford Press.

SUBJECT INDEX

AUTHOR INDEX